Genealogical Abstracts from The Autauga Citizen
1853
in Prattville
Autauga County, Alabama

Charlene Vinson

HERITAGE BOOKS
2008

HERITAGE BOOKS
AN IMPRINT OF HERITAGE BOOKS, INC.

Books, CDs, and more—Worldwide

For our listing of thousands of titles see our website
at
www.HeritageBooks.com

Published 2008 by
HERITAGE BOOKS, INC.
Publishing Division
100 Railroad Ave. #104
Westminster, Maryland 21157

Copyright © 2000 Charlene Vinson

Other books by the author:

Genealogical Abstracts from The Autauga Citizen *1854 in Prattville, Autauga County, Alabama*

Genealogical Abstracts from The Banner *1893 in Clanton, Chilton County, Alabama*

All rights reserved. No part of this book may be reproduced or transmitted in any form or by any means, electronic or mechanical, including photocopying, recording or by any information storage and retrieval system without written permission from the author, except for the inclusion of brief quotations in a review.

International Standard Book Numbers
Paperbound: 978-0-7884-1553-1
Clothbound: 978-0-7884-7489-7

Contents

Vol. 1, Thursday, February 3, 1853, No. 1 1
Vol. 1, Thursday, February 10, 1853, No. 2 7
Vol. 1, Thursday, February 17, 1853, No. 3 11
Vol. 1, Thursday, February 24, 1853, No. 4 17
Vol. 1, Thursday, March 3, 1853, No. 5 23
Vol. 1, Thursday, March 10, 1853, No. 6 27
Vol. 1, Thursday, March 17, 1853, No. 7 31
Vol. 1, Thursday, March 24, 1853, No. 8 35
Vol. 1, Thursday, March 31, No. 9 41
Vol. 1, Thursday, April 7, 1853, No. 10 45
Vol. 1, Thursday, April 14, 1853, No. 11 51
Vol. 1, Thursday, April 21, 1853, No. 12 55
Vol. 1, Thursday, April 28, 1853, No. 13 61
Vol. 1, Thursday, May 5, 1853, No. 14 65
Vol. 1, Thursday, May 12, 1853, No. 15 69
Vol. 1, Thursday, May 19, 1853, No. 16 79
Vol. 1, Thursday, May 26, 1853, No. 17 83
Vol. 1, Thursday, June 2, 1853, No. 18 87
Vol. 1, Thursday, June, 9, 1853, No. 19 91
Vol. 1, Thursday, June 16, 1853, No. 20 95
Vol. 1, Thursday, June 23, 1853, No. 21 101
Vol. 1, Thursday, June 30, 1853, No. 22 105
Vol. 1, Thursday, July 7, 1853, No. 23 109
Vol. 1, Thursday, July 14, 1853, No. 24 111
Vol. 1, Thursday, July 21, 1853, No. 25 115
Vol. 1, Thursday, July 28, 1853, No. 26 119
Vol. 1, Thursday, August 4, 1853, No. 27 123
Vol. 1, Thursday, August 11, 1853, No. 28 129
Vol. 1, Thursday, August 18, 1853, No. 29 133
Vol. 1, Thursday, August 25, 1853, No. 30 137
Vol. 1, Thursday, September 1, 1853, No. 31 141
Vol. 1, Thursday, September 8, 1853, No. 32 145
Vol. 1, Thursday, September 15, 1853, No. 33 147
Vol. 1, Thursday, September 22, 1853, No. 34 153
Vol. 1, Thursday, September 29, 1853, No. 35 157
Vol. 1, Thursday, October 6, 1853, No. 36 161
Vol. 1, Thursday, October 13, 1853, No. 37 163
Vol. 1, Thursday, October 20, 1853, No. 38 165
Vol. 1, Thursday, October 27, 1853, No. 39 169
Vol. 1, Thursday, November 3, 1853, No. 40 173
Vol. 1, Thursday, November 10, 1853, No. 41 175
Vol. 1, Thursday, November 17, 1853, No. 42 177
Vol. 1, Thursday, November 24, 1853, No. 43 181
Vol. 1, Thursday, December 1, 1853, No. 44 191
Vol. 1, Thursday, December 8, 1853, No. 45 197
Vol. 1, Thursday, December 15, 1853, Nov. 46 203
Vol. 1, Thursday, December 22, 1853, No. 47 205
Vol. 1, Thursday, December 29, 1853, No. 48 207
Index 209

Introduction

The stories in this book have been compiled from microfilmed copies of "The Autauga Citizen" newspaper which covers the year 1853. This newspaper was published weekly in Prattville, Autauga County, Alabama, and was edited by Messrs. Howell & Luckett. The first newspaper was issued February 3, 1853 and publication was ceased sometime around 1882. In 1866, Elmore County was established which included an area formed from the eastern section of Autauga County. In 1868, Chilton County was established and also included an area formed from the northern section of Autauga County. With the shifting of county lines after the publication of these newspapers, many genealogical researchers will find their Chilton and Elmore County ancestors in some of the articles. With inclusion of state and national information in these newspapers, the genealogical value of these publications increase again. Much care has been taken to correctly spell the names in these newspapers but you will find that the newspaper, at times, has used variations of the names, sometimes within the same story. This inconsistency has been maintained within the story and I have included the variations in the index. Articles cover a vast array of subjects including Probate Court Notices, Legislative reports, robberies, deaths and many more.

Dedicated to
My husband, Johnny
for being my best friend in life.

Vol. 1, Thursday, February 3, 1853, No. 1

EDITORIAL BREVITIES - Fire At Autaugaville-We have learned with regret the destruction, by fire, of a considerable amount of property at Autaugaville.-The stores of Messrs. Wilkinson & Howard and Pierce & Faulkner were consumed; also, several doctors' shops. It was doubtless the work of an incendiary. The loss to the parties will be chiefly the interruption to business, as we learn they were mostly insured.

A letter in the Boston Traveller, from Florence, says that the most popular dancer now in Italy is Miss Maywood, from Philadelphia.

The Cincinnati papers state that a fine picture of Gen. Pierce, hanging in the office of Maj. Avery, of that city, suddenly fell, and was broken in pieces, at the exact time that the general and his wife were made childless by the fearful accident at Andover - a coincidence which is invaluable to the lovers of the marvellous.

O.L. Anderson, who was arrested on a charge of robbing the mail between Coffeville and Linden, (Alabama) more than a year ago, at the recent Term of the Federal Court in Mobile, plead guilty, and was sentenced to the Penitentiary for five years.

We learn from the Tribune, that Jonathan Emanuel has resigned the post of Cashier of the Bank of Mobile, and that H.L. Higley has been elected by the Directory to fill his place.

On the 15th of January, Gen. Sam Houston was re-elected United States Senator by the Legislature of Texas, for six years from the fourth of March next.

The Nashville Whig says that Dr. Wren has established a division of the Lone Star in that city.

Oliver P. Baldwin, Esq., of Richmond, Vir., proposes to establish a new daily paper in that city.

Gen. Pierce, President elect, has, it is said, written a letter to Mr. Buchanan, soliciting his nomination of a member of the Cabinet from Pennsylvania, and stating that Mr. Marcy would be his preference for the New York representative in the Cabinet. It is also said that Mr. Buchanan has been offered the Premiership.

Col. W.R. King, Vice President elect, and family, arrived at Key West, Florida, on the 22nd ult, on the steamer Fulton. His health had slightly improved, and, if the climate proves beneficial, he will remain there for a time.

Slave Case In Ohio - On the 10th ult, a free negro man was brought before the county court of Ohio county, to answer the charge of abducting a negro woman, the property of W.H. Steele. The woman testified that the negro had persuaded her to run off from her master, planned the time and manner thereof, and had arranged for her reception in Ohio, and there to marry her. She said that she had never designed leaving her master until the free negro persuaded her to that course, and that she regretted her action in the matter. The free negro admitted he had arranged for her reception in Ohio, and had carried off her clothes. The court sentenced the prisoner to confinement in the penitentiary for two years.

Benjamin Franklin - George Bancroft, Esq., in a recent lecture before the New York Historical Society, pays an eloquent tribute to the philosopher: "Not the half of Franklin's merits," said Mr. Bancroft, "have been told. He was the true father of the American Union. It was he who went forth to lay the foundation of that great design at Albany; and in New York he lifted up his voice. Here among us he appeared as the apostle of the Union. It was he who suggested the Congress of 1774, and but for his wisdom, and the confidence that wisdom inspired, it is a matter of doubt whether that Congress would have taken effect. It was Franklin who suggested the bond of the Union which binds these States from Florida to Maine. Franklin was the greatest diplomatist of the eighteenth century. He never spoke a word too soon; he never spoke a word too late; he never spoke a word to much; he never failed to speak the right word at the right season."

There is already a troop of claimants for the honor of being "the first" to discover the principle of driving engines by calorie. - The Lynchburg Virginian ascribes the invention to a man by the name of Prouty, born and raised in the city of Richmond: "He learned the gunsmith business in the armory, removed to Augusta, Georgia, where he constructed and put into operation the very engine about which there is at present so much noise. His machine was publicly exhibited at the Bell Tavern, in Richmond, in 1832, at which date a patent was obtained, and an engine constructed in Augusta, which drove a pair of mill stones; but for want of capital the contrivance was temporarily made, and had to be abandoned."

Missing Expedition Heard From - The Panama Herald of the 24th ult. has the following: From a letter received in this city, we have been kindly furnished with the following interesting information relative to one of the expeditions sent in search of Sir John Franklin, for the safety of which considerable anxiety was beginning to be felt, as no intelligence of it has been received for a considerable time. "The friends of Capt. Collinson, of H.B.M. ship Enterprise, will be delighted to hear that he has been seen by some American whalers. This officer, it will be recollected, went in search of Sir John Franklin and his party, and was supposed to have been lost, as he had not been heard of for nearly two years."

The Madials - A large public meeting was held in Metropolitan Hall, New York city, to express sympathy for the Madial family and others, imprisoned in Tuscany for reading the Bible. Resolutions were offered by the Rev. Dr. Patten, and adopted, requesting the President of the United States to mediate in favor of the prisoners being allowed to emigrate to this country, declaring it to be the duty of our government to secure religious freedom for our citizens abroad &c. A committee was also appointed to raise funds for the sufferers.

Office Holders in New Mexico - There is a bold and brave public servant in the administration of national interests at present in New Mexico. There is something veritably proconsular in the following "rules", which have been issued in that remote territory, of which Mr. Wm. Carr Lane is at once Governor and Superintendent of Indian affairs. The utter inefficiency of the Indian Department seems to have annoyed him; and accordingly he thus sends forth his rescript:
1. Sinecures are abolished.
2. The public service is to be the great end and aim of all agents, interpreters, and other persons who may be employed in the department, and every possible exertion must be made to advance the public interest.
3. Private business must not interfere with the discharge of public duties.
4. The expenditures of agents must be confined to the narrowest possible limits, which may

be consistent with a proper discharge of public duty; and a careful discrimination must be made between the private and public expenditures of agents.
5. The residence of the agent must be within the limits of the tribe to which he is assigned, or as near thereto as practicable.
6. All orders from superiors must be promptly obeyed, or satisfactory reasons given for the failure to obey.
7. The expressions, "I can't," "I wouldn't,"or "I don't know ", are inadmissible phrases in reports to this superintendency.
8. All officers who may disregard or fail to observe these rules, will be deemed as "out of health," and will be relieved temporarily from duty; and should not satisfactory assurance be given that the "health" of the officer is lightly to mend, his unhappy case will be reported to Washington.
Wm. Carr Lane
There is warning as well as wit in these wholesome decrees of Governor Lane sentence and it cannot be denied that their enforcement elsewhere, in this Union, would be exceedingly efficacious. New Mexico appears to be sickly.

Benefit of Guano on Corn - Mr. Barnes of Winfield, Georgia, writes to the Plough, that he tried a small quantity of Peruvian guano this year, on corn, and not only got the money back expended for it, but seventy-five percent, advance on the cost. The crop was forty nine bushels per acre, on poor land. We think this will do pretty well for an experiment. Few speculations turn out better. Mr. Barnes intends to increase his purchase of guano considerably another year, all of which will be applied to the extension of his corn crop. The best way to apply guano to corn is to mix it half and half with Plaster of Paris or charcoal dust, spread broadcast at the rate of 200 to 400 lbs. per acre, and then plough in. If the land is ploughed over four inches deep, it will take the young corn roots some little time to reach the guano, in consequence of this, and in order to give it a good start, we would recommend when going below four inches, that only half of the guano be ploughed in, and the other half be dug in about an inch deep around the hills of the corn four to six inches from the stalks, the first time hoeing.

List of Letters - Remaining in the Post office at Prattville, for the quarter ending December 31, 1852:
John Averhart 1, Miss Adams or John G. Smedley 1, Malinda Britt 1, John Butler 1, Joseph Bowles 1, J.A. Boyless 1, Mary A. Burke 1, Wm. H. Cox 4, T.J. Camp 1, Miss Malinda Coker 1, Joshua English 1, George Floyd 1, Frederic Gates 1, Mrs. Mary C. Granvgist 1, William Holton 1, Joel Haney 1, Mr. Hubbard 1, Miss Nancy Jones 1, Robert Jones 1, Peter D. Luter 1, Matthew Luter 1, Elizabeth Luter 1, John McKibbon 1, George Mason 1, Mrs. Catherin May (formerly Davis) 1, William Nixon 1, Henry Nixon 1, James Orr 1, J.C. Odgen 1, J.H. Pulliam 2, Rev. E.O. Pitts 1, Edward H. Rencher 1, Eli Robinson 1, Joseph S. Reese 1, Joseph Roy 1, Martin M. Simms 1, Miss Harriet Shields 1, R.F. Srewder 1, Henry Sneads 2, H.M. Stringfellow 1, Charles H. Trask 1, Wm. H. Taylor 1, Bennett Wood 1, Wm. Wiley 1, David E. Williams 1, James C. Wolfe 1, Miss Martha Wiggins 1, Miss Martha Zentel 1
Persons calling for the above letters will please say they are advertised. S. Mims, P.M., Per Jas. Allen, Dep'y, Feb 3-nl-tf

The State of Alabama, Autauga County, Special Court of Probate - Jan. 24, 1853.
Ordered, that notice be given to the creditors of Aaron Ready, deceased, by publication in the Autauga Citizen, a newspaper published at Prattville, once a week for six successive

weeks, that the estate of the said Aaron Ready has this day been declared insolvent; and that the 22d day of March next has been appointed for the settlement of the accounts of Abram Martin, and Olivia M. Ready, administratrix. Witness - Henly Brown, Judge of Probate of said county. Henly Brown, Judge of Probate, Feb. 3, 1853, {pr. fee, $4}, nl-3t

The State of Alabama, Autauga County, Special Court of Probate - Jan.27, 1853,
This day came Edward Stoudemier and Lewis Houser, executors of the last will and testament of William R. Pickitt, deceased, and filed their account and vouchers for the settlement of the estate of said deceased; which was examined and ordered to be filed for the inspection of all concerned. It is therefore ordered, that notice be given for forty days, by publication for three successive weeks in the Autauga Citizen, notifying all persons interested to be and appear at a Court to be held on the 15th day of March next, to show cause why said account should not be stated and allowed. Henly Brown, Judge of Probate, Feb. 3, 1853, {pr. fee $4}, nl-3

The State of Alabama, Autauga County, Special Court of Probate - Jan.29, 1853,
This day came Henry Caver, guardian of Mary A.E. Caver, Sarah F. Caver, and Waid H. Caver, minors, and Samuel Caver, a lunatic, and filed his accounts and vouchers, for the final settlement of his said wards' estate, which was examined and ordered to be filed for the inspection of all concerned. It is therefore ordered, that notice be given for forty days, by publication in the Autauga Citizen, notifying all persons interested to be and appear at a Probate Court to be held on the 19th day of March next, to show cause why said account should not be stated and allowed. Henly Brown, Judge of Probate, Feb. 3-nl-lt-$5

Card - The unsigned begs to tender his thanks to his friends, and the public generally, for their past liberal support, and hopes, by prompt attention to the interests of his patrons, to give full satisfaction, and to merit a further extension of his business. C. Krout, Feb. 3, 1853-nl-lt

Government of The State of Alabama
Executive Department - Capital-City of Montgomery, (Montgomery Co.)
Henry W. Collier, Governor, $2,500
____ Garrett, Secretary of State, fees and $1,500
Joel Riggs, Comptroller, $2,000
William Graham, Treasurer, fees and $1,000
J.J. Mickle, Adjt and Ins. General, $200
Amand P. Pfister, Qr. Master General, $200
Brittan & De Wolf, State Printers.
Frank S. Lyon, Commissioner to place the State Bank in train for early liquidation.
Judiciary Department - **Supreme Court**
Edward S. Dargan, Chief Justice, $2,250
William F. Chilton, Associate Judge, $2,500
David G. Ligon, Associate Judge, $2,500
G. Goldthwaite, Associate Judge, $2,500
J.D. Phelan, Associate Judge, $2,500
M.A. Baldwin, Attorney General, fees and $425
Thomas P. May, Clerk, fees.
The Judges report.
Chancery Court.
Joseph W. Lesesna, Chancellor S. Div., $1,500

James R. Clarke, Chancellor M. Div., $1,500
Edw. Towns, Chancellor N. Div., $1,500
Circuit Court
Circuit 1, Judge Andrew Moore, Solicitor W.E. Clark
Circuit 2, Judge Ezkiel Pickens, Solicitor J.A. Stallworth
Circuit 3, Judge Geo. D. Shortridge, Solicitor W.S. Mudd
Circuit 4, Judge John Moore, Solicitor J.S. Kennedy
Circuit 5, Judge Thomas J. Walker, Solicitor W.O. Winston
Circuit 6, Judge Lyman Gibbons, Solicitor D.C. Anderson
Circuit 7, Judge _____ Huntington, Solicitor Daniel Coggin
Circuit 8, Judge J. Gill Shorter, Solicitor M.A. Baldwin
Circuit 9, Judge Robert Dougherty, Solicitor J.J. Hooper
Members of Congress
Senators - Benjamin Fitzpatrick, Jeremiah Clemens
Representatives:
First District, John Bragg, of Mobile
Second District, James Abercrombie, of Russell
Third District, S.W. Harris, of Coosa
Fourth District, Wm. R. Smith, of Coosa
Fifth District, Geo. H. Houston, of Athens
Sixth District, W.R.W. Cobb
Seventh District, Alexander White, of Talledega.
Judges of Probate:
For Autauga County, Henley Brown
For Shelby County, J.M. McClanahan
For Bibb County, J.W. Suttle
For Dallas County, T.G. Rainer
For Lowndes County, Edward H. Cook

Vol. 1, Thursday, February 10, 1853, No. 2

Editorial Brevities. - American Success. - Harrison Winans left Baltimore, a few years ago, a poor boy, but with an improved mind, acquired at a country school, with talent, ambition and enterprise. He worked in Europe at the head of machinists and engineers, and became a leading contractor on the great railroad between Moscow and St. Petersburg, 400 miles long. He made over $100,000. On his return to Paris he married an amiable and beautiful young lady, and will soon build a cage for her, in the shape of a villa and a park of three acres, beautifully ornamented, where rich and poor may feast their eyes on indigenous plants and rare exotics. He goes again to Russia to fill a contract with the Emperor, on public works, by which he will bring away $500,000 in gold for his labors.

A meeting of the citizens of this county was recently held at Autaugaville, at which resolutions were adopted recommending Col. Albert J. Pickett as a suitable person to run as a candidate for governor of the State.

President Fillmore, it is supposed, will make a visit to the South soon after the 4th of March; and we notice that a public meeting is suggested at Wilmington, N.C., to make arrangements to give him a suitable reception. He will be most cordially received by the masses of the whole South.

Commodore Stockton, it is said, will, on his return to the U.S. Senate, now detained by sickness in his family, propose to increase the navy, by the addition of ten steam vessels, two of them to be twelve or fourteen hundred tons burden, and to be constructed with side wheels, for express service; and the others of the largest dimensions of steam frigates, and with stern propellers.

Advices have been received at Boston from Buenos Ayres to the 23rd of December, which state that political affairs are very much disturbed. Urquiza has deposed the Governor of Santa Fe and appointed Gen. Galan as his successor. A large force had been sent from Buenos Ayres to Rio de Janeiro to stir up an invasion against Urquiza.

Marble in Utah. - Mr. J.D. Manlove gives the St. Louis Intelligencer a description of a mountain of marble, which he says exists in the Great Salt Lake valley. He says the marble is of almost every colored and shade, in slabs of very large area, and from an inch in thickness to blocks of an immense size. Mr. Manlove judges the marble to be of the best quality, and that it is inexhaustible.

Hon. Edward Everett has been elected United States Senator by the Legislature of his State. His term commences 4th March next.

Hon. W.L. Marcy and son arrived at Savannah, Georgia, from Florida, on Tuesday of last week.

The Anti-Slavery Convention is in session in Boston, and Parker Pillsbury, Wendell Philips and Garrison are making queer speeches again. The latter thinks the church is friendly to slavery, and that it is a question whether Christianity will not give place to something better. The burthen of their speeches was denunciation of the church, bible societies, and foreign missions, with a great many hard hits in the course of their remarks.

The "Alabama" Afloat. - The Montgomery and New Orleans packet Alabama, says the Advertiser which has been lying on our wharf for a month past, was set afloat on Sunday last. Capt. Roberts had made all necessary arrangements to launch her, when the heavy rains of last week came on, and the river rising very rapidly on Saturday night and Sunday morning, she was soon surrounded by the water, and was easily got off. The boat, we believe, was not damaged by any of her parts by her long airing on the wharf, and was, in a few hours, ready for freight.

A native African, called Uncle More, resides in Wilmington, N.C., eighty-three years of age, for forty-five years a slave. His time is chiefly occupied in reading the Scriptures in Arabic. He writes the language with remarkable accuracy and beauty of penmanship, and his original version of the sacred text, is said to be highly instructive.

Santa Anna. - This personage, it appears, is invited to Mexico again by the authorities, who have appointed a committee to wait upon him and request his return. Overtures, it is said, will also be made to Gen. Adrian Woll, to take command of the Eastern Division of the Mexican Army. Something is going on that will make a noise before long.

A millionaire of Baltimore, Miss Rachel Calvin, the largest real estate holder in that city, died on the morning of the 24th ultimo, at an advanced age. She had been deranged for some years, and her property, which was entailed by a most singular will from her progenitors, who also died deranged, has long been in the hands of commissioners appointed by the orphans' court, and will doubtless cause considerable litigation.

NEWS BY TELEGRAPH. - France. - Napoleon was to have been married to Madame Montigo on the 30th ult.. The dowry demanded for the bride was five million francs. Twenty line of battle sheds, eighteen frigates and twenty smaller vessels are being built in the French navy yards.

Committed to the Jail of Autauga county, Ala., as a Runaway Slave, by Henly Brown, Judge of Probate, February 1st, 1853, a negro boy, who calls his name Nathan Davis, and says that he belongs to Thuston Lumpkin, of Madison Co., Ala. also says that he was sent to Messrs. Lavon & Foster, negro traders, in Montgomery, last fall, by Mr. Mosley, and that he ran away from Messrs. Lavon & Foster, at Montgomery. Said boy is about 5 feet 9 or ten inches high; black complexion; slim face; full about the mouth; will weigh between 150 and 160 pounds; some 22 or 23 years of age; very quick spoken. The owner is required to come forward, prove property, pay charges, and take him away, or he will be dealt with as the law directs in such cases. James A. Lawler, Shff. of Autauga Co., Feb. 10-n2-tf

Committed to the Jail of Autauga county, Ala., as a Runaway Slave, by Henly Brown, Judge of Probate, February 5th, 1853, a negro man who calls his name Jacob, and says that he belongs to Charles Meriwether, of Montgomery county, Ala.. Said boy is about 5 feet 7 or 8 inches high; dark copper color; about 30 or 35 years of age; rather slow spoken. The owner is required to come forward, prove property, pay charges, and take him away, or he will be dealt with as the law directs in such cases. James A. Lawler, Sh'ff of Autauga Co., Feb. 10-n2-tf

Administrator's Notice. - Letters of Administration on the estate of Eugenia E. Knox, deceased, having been granted to the unsigned, on the 17th day of January, 1853, by the Honorable Henly Brown, Judge of Probate in and for Autauga county, all persons having claims against said deceased, are hereby notified to present them, properly authenticated, within the time prescribed by law, or they will be barred. Wm. H. Northington, Administrator, Feb.10-n2-6t

The State of Alabama, Autauga County, Special Court of Probate, Feb. 3, 1853.
This day came Hugh Jones, one of the administrators of the estate of William Kemp, deceased, and filed his statement, setting forth that said estate is insolvent, and that the second day of April next has been appointed and set apart for the propose of hearing and determining the same, at the Probate Court Room, in the county aforesaid. It is therefore ordered, that notice be given to the creditors of said estate, by publishing this order once a week, for six successive weeks, in the Autauga Citizen, to appear at the time and place above stated, to show cause why said estate should not be declared insolvent. Witness - Henly Brown, Judge of Probate of said county, at office, this 3d day of February, 1853. Henly Brown, Judge of Probate, Feb.10-n2-5t{$7}

Vol. 1, Thursday, February 17, 1853, No. 3

The Autauga Citizen. - We have received the first number of a newspaper bearing the above title by Messrs Howell & Luckett. It presents the proprietors to the public in a very favorable light, and gives assurance that under their management, the Autauga Citizen will be a useful and interesting paper. It affords, too, as we take it, a correct map of the flourishing town of Prattville, which will make a most favorable impression upon readers at a distance. Advertisements of manufactories, stores, &c., crowd its ample pages, showing it to be quite a town. We wish the Citizen every success, and will be glad at any time to extend the freedom of the city to it. - *Mobile Tribune.*

American Cotton Planter. - We have received the second number of this monthly - issued at Montgomery, by Dr. Cloud. It is got up in excellent style, and filled with articles of permanent value to culturists. Forming an opinion from the number received, Dr. Cloud will make a valuable periodical, alike creditable to himself and useful to planters and others. We wish him all success in his noble undertaking; and although he did not put his hand to the plough for pecuniary profit, we hope the liberal tillers of the soil of Alabama will not let him lose money. Our people can sustain a publication of this kind, and it is their duty to do it. We hope that within the year Dr. Cloud will be able to announce that he has five thousand subscribers at least.

The French Empress. According to the latest information received from France, Napoleon has come to the conclusion to get himself a wife, and has addressed a long and able document to his officers of State, in which he informs them formally of his intention to marry Mm'lle Eugenia Montigo. He says he conforms to the wish of the nation in marrying, but in the selection of a partner he casts away old political tradition, royal alliances, and besides it was humiliating to go begging for a wife of royal blood. For seventy years past foreign princesses had ascended the French throne only to be unhappy, with the exception of Josephine, and she was not of a royal family. He sneers at Austria for jumping at an alliance with Napoleon the First, and sarcastically alludes to the long chase of the sons of Louis Phillippe after wives. He instances the circumstances of Louis Phillippe taking for a wife the Duchess of Orleans, a princess of the third rank, and for himself he says he does not want any monarch's alliance. He admits that he is a Parvenu, but Parvenu elected by a great nation, and therefore determined to select a wife to please himself. Being more free, therefore, he will not be the less strong. He says the lady is a Catholic, and endowed with every virtue, and he will soon at Notre Dame present her to the people and the army. This address has caused great sensation. The Bourse had fell, but soon recovered.

Is Slavery A Sin? - The New York Day Book says the Rev. Dr. Spring of that city recently declared that, if by praying for the abolition of slavery he could accomplish it, he would not dare to make that prayer. In discussing the subject, the Day Book makes the following sensible remarks: "The Bible teaches us what is and what is not lawful in the eyes of God, and is no longer a sealed book, but open to all, and each individual can judge for himself weather slavery is or is not a sin. We go to a lawyer to learn what is law, and the decision of eminent judges upon questions of law, are received, not only with deference and respect, but are regarded as binding upon parties who, disagreeing, appeal to them for their decision. The lawyer and judges examine their books, they look into the matter and tell us plainly that the law is, and we abide by their declaration. Is it not quite as reasonable then to appeal to eminent divines upon questions in dispute as to what is gospel. One man says slavery is a sin, another says it is not a sin; neither party is as well acquainted or as familiar with the

Bible as he ought to be, and they therefore appeal to men who have made it their study all their lives, and have become eminent for their wisdom in things pertaining thereto. These men told over again that the Bible does not condemn slavery as a sin, and that it plainly does not make it obligatory on the master to manumit his slave. This is almost the universal opinion of the eminent clergy in the Northern States. Why, then, should the newspaper and the lait continue to admit that slavery is an evil? The Supreme Court of the United States, the Constitution, the Bible and the clergy have all passed judgment upon it; and all admit the moral and the legal right of man to property in the services of man."

A young gentleman, a short time since, was about making an excursion for fish, and on one of the thoroughfares of the lake met and made the acquaintance of a lady named Mary Pike, with whom he became very much pleased, and from whom he could not part without some pangs of sadness. He expressed a hope that he might hear from her occasionally. To which she replied, that if he was not successful in taking fish at the lakes, she had no objections to his dropping a line to her.

EDITORIAL BREVITIES. - Quite an excitement, says the *Picayune*, was caused by the publication of a rather fanciful statement of a difficulty which occurred not long since, between Lola Montez, her maid and some police officers. We have learned the following facts in relation to the occurrence from good authority. Before leaving New York, Lola Montez made an agreement with Catharine Nugent, her maid, to travel South with her, and return to New York, Lola paying certain wages and all the expenses. After arriving in this city the maid found several friends, and wished to leave her employment and reside with them. To this Lola assented, and offered to pay the wages due, but refused to pay any sum for expense back to New York. Catharine employed a lawyer, who persuaded her that she ought not to settle in the manner offered, but to bring a suit of assault and battery for injuries received at diverse times. The affadavit was made, the warrant issued, and on Tuesday evening the police officers went to execute it. There are different versions of the scene that ensued, but all agree that the interview between the parties was far from civil or amicable. The officers were rude, and Lola indignant. Finally, after much trouble, Capt. Forno was sent for, when this tempest in a tea-pot was settled by the maid, Charlotte, receiving her wages, withdrawing the suit, the officers retiring, and everybody seemingly satisfied with the amicable adjustment of the matter.

We learn from the New York *Times* that the foreign department of the Crystal Palace is being actively attended to. Letters from agents in Europe and Asia communicate daily the fact of contributions of a most interesting nature being got in readiness by various nations for the exhibition. The Sulton of Turkey has expressed his intention of devoting a war steamer to the purpose of conveying the contributions to this country. He has also issued a firman, ordering all the merchants of Constantinople to prepare samples of their wares, which he promises shall be conveyed hither free of expense. The German sculptor, Kip, whose splendid statue of the Amazon attracted such notice in the English exposition, has determined on sending some of his works, and several other eminent sculptors have consulted him as to the best mode of contribution also. It is probable that among other works of art, we shall receive from Germany some very fine plaster casts of antique and modern statues. Baron Marochetti, who has just completed his colossal statue of Washington, has entered into communication with the committee of the Crystal Palace, as to what site has been determined on for his great work.

Mexico. - The St. Yach has arrived at New Orleans with highly important news from the Rio

Grande. Matamoras pronounced in favor of the revolution on the 28th ult. The military and citizens rose *en masse,* when a battle ensued, in which the insurgents were successful. Gen Avalos, on the 1st, resigned his command to Col. Basare, who will retain the post until the arrival of Col. Cruz from Camargo. He has also retired to the American side of the Rio Grande. The State of Tamaulipas has also declared in favor of the revolution. Dates from the City of Mexico to the 15th of January state that the new President, Cevelos, had been invested by Congress with extraordinary powers, which were before denied to President Arista. Cevelos immediately released a large number of prisoners, imprisoned by Arista for political offences.

Appointments By The President. - *By and with the advice and consent of the Senate.* - John L. Barnard, to be Register of the Land Office at Lebanon, Ala., vice Sampson Clayton, resigned. Obediah W. Ward to be the Receiver of Public Moneys at Lebanon, Ala., vice Peter J. Walker, resigned. Nimrod E. Benson to be Receiver of Public Moneys at Montgomery, Ala., his term of service having expired.

Several important bills have been reported in the Pennsylvania Legislature within the last few days - one to prevent colored persons from acquiring a residence in that State; and another to prevent fugitives from labor in other States, and slaves manumitted by their masters from settling in Pennsylvania. We observe also, that the Ohio Legislature has before it a bill prohibiting free colored persons from settling or holding property in that State.

Baltimore, Feb. 11. - The U.S. Senate was engaged on Friday in debating the claims of the creditors of Texas. The Hon. Samuel Houston, of Texas, addressed the Senate and denounced strongly the conduct of the speculators in Texas bonds.

Mrs. Stowe, the writer of that most delectable book, Uncle Tom's Cabin, has received the further sum of $10,000, which makes $20,000 she has received in nine months' sales of the book.

In consequence of the late domestic affliction of the President elect, it has been determined at Washington, not to give the balls which have been customary on the occasion of the inauguration of a new President. General Pierce has envinced his desire to pass through the country on his way to the capital, without any public receptions or demonstrations.

The *Picayune* learns from a gentleman, just from Havana, that the Captain General had sent a special messenger to Key West inviting Mr. King, Vice President elect, in case he visited Havana, to take up his quarters in the Captain General's palace. The Captain General also requested the American Consul, Judge Sharkey, to give him immediate notice the moment Mr. King should arrive in the harbor of Havana.

The Maury Intelligencer says, Mr. John Kennedy, who resides some eight miles north of Columbia, has 18 children living - all fully grown - 74 grand-children, and 51 great grand children! There has not been a single death in the family since the year 1806.

One of the papers of the 'spirit rappers,' in pretending to be informed of the affairs of the dead, states that Napoleon and Wellington are quarreling about the affair of Waterloo. This should teach people to get through with their fighting and quarreling before leaving this world.

In New York, on the 2d inst., John Comegys, a native of Alabama, committed suicide at the boarding hose of Mrs. Perry, 119 Beekman street, by blowing his brains out with a pistol. No cause is assigned for the commission of the act.

The New York Times calls Billy Bowlegs, Mr. Cruikshanks. This is carrying politeness some considerable distance, although it may be said, not quite so far as Billy carried his deception of the government.

The Hon. Mr. Dixon, Senator from Kentucky, has been in bad health for some time in Washington, and by the advice of his physicians, has gone to Havana - leaving Washington on the 2d inst.

The Power of Gold. - Mr. Meagher, the Irish exile-patriot, in a lecture on Australia, recently delivered in New York, thus apostrophises "filthy lucre." It is as truthful as it is eloquent, and affords food for much reflection: "Gold, which has caused many a brain to ache, has blistered many a hand, broken many a heart, has wounded many a soaring soul, and clinging to it, has brought it to the dust; gold which has bought the integrity of the statesmen, and led his wisdom captive; gold, which has silenced the tongue of the orator, and bought the flatteries of the poet; gold, for which, in the gay saloons of fashion, many a fair and noble girl has plighted the vow which has consigned her life to bitterness, and locked upon her radiant neck the snake that swells her veins with venom; gold which has stolen into the councils of the struggling nation, has bred dissentions among her chiefs, has broken the seal of her sacred secrets, has forced the gates of her strongest citadels, has bought the evidence which hurried her apostles to the scaffold, has bought the votes which made over her inheritances to others and her glory to a strange people. - gold, which has led the traitor to the garden, and with a kiss betrayed the Redeemer of the world, - gold, which in so many shapes has stepped with stealthy tread or rioted among men - chich has been the fever, the madness, the despair - has been in torns and quick succession, the spy, the swindler, the perjurer, the assassin - the foe of innocence, the blight of beauty, the bane of genius; gold has become a fountain of life and joy and freedom - the serpent has been transformed into a blossomed wand. - Lucifer has become the morning star. To you, the citizens of America, it must be pleasing indeed, to behold a new republic rising up to share with you the labors and glories of a future, before which the conceit of the old world shall be humbled, and in the light which humanity shall grow strong."

Kossuth, *alias* John Smith, it is said, is about to return to this country.

For Constable - James L. Alexander would inform the citizens of Prattville Beat, that he is a candidate for the office of Constable. Election, first Monday in March. Feb. 17 - n3-3t

The State of Alabama, Autauga County, *Special Court of Probate* **- Feb. 10, 1853.**
This day came Alexander McKeithen, administrator of Catherine Cotton, deceased, and filed his account and vouchers for the annual settlement of the estate of said deceased, which was examined and ordered to be filed for the inspection of all concerned, and that the second day of April next be appointed for said settlement. It is therefore ordered, that notice be given for forty days, by publication for three successive weeks in the Autauga Citizen, notifying all persons interested to be and appear at a Court to be held on the 2d day of April next, to show cause why said account should not be stated and allowed. Henly Brown, Judge of Probate, Feb. 17-n3-3t-$4

The State of Alabama, Autauga County, *Special Court of Probate* **- Feb. 15, 1853.**
Ordered, that notice be given to the creditors of Green Hampton, deceased, by publication in the Autauga Citizen, a newspaper published at Prattville, in said county, once a week for six successive weeks, that the estate of the said Green Hampton, deceased, has this day been declared insolvent; and that the 15th day of April next has been appointed for the settlement of the accounts of William H. Northington, administrator of the estate of said deceased. Witness - Henly Brown, Judge of Probate of said county. Feb. 17-n3-6t Henly Brown, Judge of Probate

Administrator's Sale. - By virtue of authority vested in me by a decree of the Honorable the Judge of Probate of Autauga county, I will sell to the highest bidder, *On Monday, the 21st day of March next,* during the legal hours of sale, in the town of Kingston, in front of the court house door of said county, *Seven Valuable and likely Negroes*, consisting of one woman and four children; a girl about 17 years old; and a man about 50 years old; belonging to the estate of Eugenia E. Knox, deceased. One negro will be sold for cash, and the remainder on a credit until the 1st day of January, 1954. Notes, with at least two approved securities, will be required of those who purchase on a credit. Wm. H. Northington, Adm'r of Eugenia E. Knox, deceased. Feb. 17, 1853, n3-5t

Committed To the Jail of Autauga county, Ala., as a Runaway Slave, by Henly Brown, Judge of Probate, February 5th, 1853, a negro man who calls his name Jacob, and says that he belongs to Charles Meriwether, of Montgomery county, Ala. Said boy is about 5 feet 7 or 8 inches high; dark copper color; about 30 or 35 years of age; rather slow spoken. The owner is required to come forward, prove property, pay charges, and take him away, or he will be dealt with as the law directs in such cases. James A. Lawler, Sh'ff of Autauga, Feb. 10-n2-tf

New York Worlds' Fair. To the citizens of Alabama, Louisiana, Mississippi, Texas, Arkansas and Tennessee:
1. The Board of Directors of the New York Crystal Palace having appointed a Committee for the Southwestern States, resident at New Orleans, consisting of James Robb, Lucious Duncan, E. LaSere, W.E. Gasquet, W.N. Mercer, H.R.W. Hill, A.F. Axson, Maunsel White, S.D.B. DeBow, A.M. Holbrook, A. Walker, C.J. Leeds, Newton Richards, the undersigned, upon the part of said committee, would present the following address:
2. The Fair will be opened on the 2nd day of May, 1853 for the exhibition of the industry of all nations, in the splendid structure on Reservoir Square, New York, embracing an area of 173,000 square feet, or four acres. - The building has been made a bonded warehouse by Government, and already assurances are given of an extensive representation of foreign industry.
3. The object of the exhibition cannot be subserved without an equal representation of all the great industrial interests of our own confederation, whether in raw materials, manufactured products, or in the fine arts. The Fair will be opened to the cereal products of the Northern and Western states, the cotton, sugar and rice of the South; the hemp, tobacco, and other miscellaneous productions of the West; the mineral productions of all these regions. It is extremely desirable that all these great interests should be represented as well as the manufacturing, in order that the New and the Old World should be contrasted together, and the two regions mutually instruct and be instructed.
4. Applications for admission of objects of exhibition must present their nature and purpose, with the number of square feet required, whether of wall, floor or counter. The machinery will be exhibited in motion, the motive power to be furnished by the Association, and appli-

cants must state also the amount of the power required. Paintings in frames will be received. Where ores are exhibited, they should be accompanied by the rocks in which they are found, and also, if possible, by plans and sections of the measures in which they lie, and models and drawings of processes or manufacture.

5. Prizes for excellence in the different departments will be awarded under the direction of capable and eminent persons.

6. Applications from any of the States named in this address may be made at any time before the first of March, 1853, and must be directed to the Chairman of the Committee at New Orleans, complying with all the requisitions in section four above. The applicant must describe with precision - state the time the product will be ready for shipment, the port from which he desires to ship, and must also provide for the expenses incurred upon it in the way of freight, drayage, &c., until delivered into the custody of the New York Board.

7. The committee at New Orleans will decide upon all such applications, and upon receipt of their favorable judgment, the party will be supplied with a certificate to be forwarded to New York at the time of shipment. They desire to be informed by the first of March of the quantity of space which will be required from their division, in order to report to the central committee.

8. Citizens of the Southwest, you are invited and earnestly solicited to be represented in the first great American fair. We have products in all abundance in every department of industry and ingenuity, if we will but send them, sufficient to delight and instruct every observer. We were comparatively unrepresented at the London Fair, but every consideration of patriotism should induce us to co-operate in this one upon our own soil. We are a part of the nation that must obtain the glory of success or the shame of discomfiture and defeat. Let us unite with our fellow-citizens of the North in this great enterprise, and rely upon their co-operation in any movement we may make hereafter for similar exhibitions in our immediate regions.

Thus shall we obliterate local feelings, prejudices and antipathies - strengthen the bonds of amity and concord - realize, indeed, that we are one people, with one hope and one inheritance, one faith and one destiny.

Lucius C. Duncan, Ch'n}
J.D.B. DeBow   }
E. LaSere   } Com.
A.F. Axon   }
New Orleans, Jan. 13, 1853

Vol. 1, Thursday, February 24, 1853, No. 4

Men of Our Time. - O.W. Holmes, the gentleman that "never dares to write as funny as he can," is (?) three years of age. Wm. Ho(?) is fifty-seven, he published verses at the age of thirteen. Humboldt is eighty-three. Leigh Hunt is sixty-eight. Fitz-Green Hallock fifty-seven. Washington Irving, son of an eminent New York merchant, is sixty-nine years of age, in his nineteenth year he began to contribute to his brother's paper, the Morning Chronicle. Douglas Jerrold, forty-seven years of age, is the son of the manager of the Sh(?) (?), the sea was his first love, and for a short (?) he served as midshipman on board of a (?) of war. G.P.R. James is about fifty years old, it was Washington Irving who first recommended him to a career of authorship. Sheridan Knowles, sixty-eight years old, is the son of a famous Irish character, who was cousin to Richard Brinsley Sheridan. Mr. Knowles wrote his first play in his twenty-first year, his plays are thirteen in number. He now enjoys a government pension of L200 a year. Lamartine is sixty-two, his father was a Major in the French Cavalry under Louis XVI. Abbot Lawrence is in his sixtieth year. Henry W. Longfellow, forty-five years of age, is the son of Hon. Stephen Longfellow. Portland, Maine, is the birth place of the poet, he was appointed Professor of Cambridge, in his twentieth year. Macauley, the son of a wealthy African merchant, is fifty-two years of age, his essay on Milton was written in his twenty-sixth year, for the Edinburgh Review. Macready is fifty-nine; his father was a theatrical manager. Herman Mellville is the son of an importing merchant of this city, he is thirty-three years of age; his grandfather was one of the Boston tea-party; he began his wanderings in his eighteenth year; a sailor before the mast; he is author of seven popular works. Metternich is seventy-nine. Ik Marvel is thirty years of age, is a native of Norwich, Connecticut, a graduate of Yale, and resident of New York. J.K. Paulding, whose collective works fill seventy-five volumes, is seventy-three years of age; he is a native of Dutchess county, in this State. Prentice is a Yankee, born at Preston, Ct., forty-eight years old. He has been editor of the Louisville Journal since 1831. Prescott, the historian, is in his fifty-sixth year. Powers, the sculptor, is fifty-seven; his parents were plain country people who cultivate a "small farm" in Vermont. Seward is fifty years old. Talford fifty-seven. Tennyson, son of a clergyman, is forty-two. Th(?)ay, born at Calcutta, is forty-one. Tienor, sixty-one. H.T. Tuckerman, thirty-nine. Victoria is thirty-three years of age, "she has", says the author, "a large and rapidly increasing family, which seems the distinguishing mark of the Hanoverian dynasty." - *Home Journal*

The Ball. - We had the pleasure of attending on last Friday evening, the Examination Ball, given by Mr. Temple to his patrons and scholars, and must say, in justice to him, the permance of his pupils on the "light fantastic toe" exceeded the expectations of every one present. Although the night was dark, wet and gloomy, yet, there was a goodly number in attendance, and all, we believe, seemed to enjoy the dance - at least, we judged so, from the fact "that night stole away, and the dawn caught them there." The youth and beauty of Prattville (of course we mean the fairer sex,) were well represented - "and when Music arose with its voluptuous swell, Soft eyes looked love to eyes that spoke again, And all went merry as a marriage bell." Miss I. P—e, "floating, sylph-like, upon a sea of air," seemed the perfection of grace and beauty - her countenance, ever and anon, lighting up with sweet smiles, and winning, by her gentleness and modesty, the mute admiration of all around her. The graceful form of Miss H. F—y moved through "the mazes of the giddy dance" like that of a fairy. Indeed is she "Fair as the first that fell of woman-kind," and admirably "Formed for all the witching arts of love." Our cousin, E—n, if not the belled amongst the younger portion of the company, was assuredly one of them, and bids fair, when "deeper in her teens," to be in "face and form and graceful gait," all that could be desired. Cousin M—t, a younger sister of the preceeding "a rose bud scarcely blown," was noticed for her gracefulness. A sweet child is Miss B—, "A rose with all its sweetest leaves unfolded," was deservedly praised for the manner in which she executed the Sailor's Hornpipe. The elegant and queen-like Miss R—e, "With cheeks before whose bloom the rose Its blushing treasure-house might close," was much admired for her case and dignity of manner. Miss K—e, of Montgomery, as lovely a daisy was e'er from prairie culled, was admired for her modesty and easy gracefulness. A pensive smile played upon her lips, and "The mild expression spoke a mind in duty firm, composed, resigned," that must have excited the "soft and silent" admiration of every heart. There were others present, and among them married ladies, equally lovely and fascinating, who contributed largely, by their graceful and dignified deportment, to the pleasures of the evening. Indeed, the youth and beauty assembled on Friday night would compare with the "fairest of the fair" - and, if we are not mistaken, many an old bachelor went home struggling to free himself from love's dominion. As for ourself, we certainly should have left our h-h-h-h-a-t, had we not been a m-a-r-r-i-e-d-m-a-n!

Murder. We learn from the Selma *Enterprise* that Mr. George T. Sharp was shot near (?)ville, in that county, on the 14th inst., by a man named Noles, while attempting to arrest the latter under a warrant for the infamous crime of incest. Noles immediately fled, and though hotly pursued, made his escape. A reward of $500 is offered for his arrest, and parties are now out in pursuit of him. It is to be hoped they may speedily succeed in arresting and bringing him to justice.

Editorial Brevities. - The folks "way up to Maine," seem to approve of one of the "down South" nigger customs - their mode of marrying. The following appears under the hymenial head of a Bangor paper: "We, the undersigned, have pledged ourselves to each other for life, or as long as we can live in harmony, and now sustain the conjugal relations. This we do without conforming to the laws and customs of this nation in regard to marriage, believing it to be an affair exclusively our own, and that no others, whether friends, church or State, have aught to do or say in the matter. We deem it necessary to give this notice that our friends and the public may know of our union, that we may not be exposed to slander. Benj. F. Shaw, H.N. Howard

The death of the Australian traveller Leighardt has been ascertained. He was killed by the natives after having penetrated 1200 miles into the interior of that continent.

Gov. Blake has returned to Washington from Florida. It is understood that he anticipates no serious difficulties with the Indians.

Great Yield of Wheat. - Mr. James R. Garrison, of the county of Accomac, Virginia, raised the present year, from one bushel of wheat, seeded *broadcast*, on one acre and one peck of good clean wheat, which is equal to eleventh of an acre of land, 60 bushels and one fifty-five bushels to the acre. This is hard to beat.

The Washington *Republic* states that Mr. Fuller, recently shot by Schaumburg, is much better, and his physician thinks he will recover.

Col. Joseph Pickens, youngest son of Gen. Andrew Pickens, of Revolutionary memory in South Carolina, died at Eutaw, Ala., on the 4th inst.

Texas Pioneers .- It is stated, that of the three hundred illustrious families of pioneers and patriots, first introduced into the province of Texas, by Stephen F. Austin, only 19 heads of families are now remaining.

The mother of the Empress of France, it is stated, is nearly related to Bishop Fitzpatric, of Boston.

A letter from Havana to the Charleston Courier, says that the Vice President elect, the Hon. W.R. King, arrived at Havana on the 6th inst. Great attention is paid him, we understand, by the authorities. On the arrival of the Fulton with him on board, the British man-of-war Vestal sent a boat to her to know if Mr. King would accept a salute. This, however, Mr. King declined. Mr. King is staying at an American boarding house.

The Old Folly. - A Paris letter of the 20th January, mentions that the necessary papers for taking out a patent for an invention said to realize "perpetual motion," was to come by the next steamer to Washington. A locomotive, one-fifth the size of railroad engines, has, says the inventor, been working continually since June. Cyrus W. Murray, of Page county, Va., it is also said, has discovered what will produce perpetual motion, a model of which he intends to exhibit at the New York World's Fair.

Congressional . - In the Senate, on the 15th, the Deficiency bill was considered till two o'clock, when it was laid aside, and the resolutions for the Committee on Foreign Relations, on the subject of the right of way across Tehuantepee, were taken up, and debated by Messrs. Hale and Brooke.

On the 16th, in the Senate, after further debate on the Deficiency bill, it was passed. The resolutions on the subject of Tehuantepec were debated by Mr. Brooke.

Presents to Gen. Pierce. - The Boston friends of Gen. Pierce, not content with presenting him with a splendid carriage and a fine pair of horses, have ordered a beautiful inauguration suit for him, which was finished on the 10th inst. It consists of six garments, as follows:
1. A fine black dress coat, made from the same cloth which took the premium at the late World's Fair in London. Coat superbly lined with satin dechene, sleeve linings also of satin.
2. Undress waistcoat of plain black silk, back made of satin dechene, and lined throughout with white satin.
3. Full-dress vest of plain white silk, back and linings of white satin. On the satin lining of the right side are thirty-one stars, representing the thirty-one States of the Union, forming a circle, wrought in silver. Within this circle of stars, is the Anchor of Hope, worked in gold. Outside of all is an endless circle. - Translation of these emblems: "In the Union of the States is our only hope. - God watches over the Republic - eternal be its duration!" On the opposite white satin lining is wrought a chaplet of bay leaves, tied at the bottom with a golden knot, outside of which is another golden circle.
4. Pants of plain black doeskin, of the finest material that could be procured.
5. Undress pants of plain black, very fine, silk and wool mixture.
6. Overcoat of plain black, superbly lined, and made in the form of a surtout.
The embroidery is executed by a lady of Boston. It is intended that the suit shall be the finest specimen ever manufactured in America.

Important From Mexico, New Orleans, Feb. 21. - Mr. Sloo, of this city, has obtained a grant from the Mexican Congress to the Techuantepec route for fifty years, on favorable terms. Cavellos has resigned the Presidency. Uraga and two other generals have succeeded him.

We copy the following from the Journal, in reference to the deficit in the Mobile Post Office: "The examination in reference to the deficit in the Mobile Post Office, is still in progress, without, sofar, throwing any light on the cause by which the deficiency was occasioned. Mr. Sands, it appears, was the first clerk, and had the exclusive management and control of the cash, strong-box, disbursements, &c., and yet it does not appear that any one knows what has become of the money. He managed the whole matter, and insists that he has not been robbed; but what has become of the great deficiency of the twenty thousand dollars, he has no knowledge. This is somewhat strange. Some one got the "ready" which belongs to Uncle Sam, and the old gentleman is, as usual, the sufferer. A singular mystery hangs over the whole matter; but one thing is evident, and that is somewhat important, the money is gone to the Tomb of Capulets. One of the witnesses suggests that the fire at the Mansion House, several years since, in which the Post Office was burned, may account for some of this difficulty and irregularity in accounts. A fire is at times a very convenient cover for delinquencies. The burning of the Treasury Department at Washington, years since, wiped out many questionable records in pension matters. So, also, the burning of the general Post Office, made a general clearing of old scores. Nothing like a fire for those matters - it, like charity, covers a multitude of sins."

England And The Slave Trade in Cuba. - The English press boldly charge the Spanish Government with conniving at the slave trade, and a very forcible article upon the subject published in the London Times, contains the following significant declaration: "Better that the 'Lone Star' of America should revolutionize Cuba; that the authority of the Court of Madrid should be expelled from its most valuable remaining colony than that it should be allowed to renew in all the ancient abominations the outrages on Africa. And this, it is to be hoped, Lord John Russell and his forthcoming successor, the Earl of Claredon, will plainly tell the Court of Madrid. The British nation and Government can take no interest in the retension of Cuba by Spain whilst Spain refused to do which recent experience has demonstrated she can easily do suppress and terminate the slave trade in that Island. It is useless longer to argue or to remonstrate, it is now indispensable to substitute a determination that cannot be disregarded."

Lime Water For Hens. - During the last season, Mr. Joseph Wilcox, of this town, having occasion to administer lime water to a sick horse, inadvertently left a pail of the preparation in his barn, which remained there for some months, serving as a favorite drink for his hens. He soon afterwards found that the laying of his hens was apparently increased to a considerable extent. Being convinced of the importance of the (to him) new discovery, he has, during the present season, kept his hens constantly supplied with lime water, placed in troughs within their convenient access, and the result was an increase in eggs of nearly fourfold as compared with previous experience. He is willing to share the benefits of the experiment with his neighbors, if they wish to try it; and hence this publication. The newness of the discovery (though it may not now be new to all,) is claimed only as applicable to the mode of imparting the lime in this case - its use in another form for the same purpose having been previously understood by many. - *Wayne Sentinel.*

Whose Cotton? - Found, on the plantation of Mrs. Matilda Pope, one bale of Cotton, marked II.C.A, No. 18. The owner is requested to come forward, prove property, pay all charges, and take it away. Apply to Mr. J.S. Potter, at the plantation of Mrs. Pope, six miles below Washington. Feb. 24-n4-6t

List of Letters - Remaining in the Post Office at Robinson's Springs, Feb. 28, 1853,
Whitworth, Thomas D.
Phillips, Amanda C.
Boniface, Mrs. Delpha
Atkinson, Miss Ann M.
Johnson, Joseph A.
Feb 27-nt-5t Malachi Spigener, P.M.

Take Notice. - The undersigned having disposed of his interest in the Prattville Drug Store, and being compelled by business matters to leave Prattville, has left all notes and accounts in the hands of W.H. Northington, Esq., and if not settled by the second Saturday in March, will go into the mill, as I have large drafts to take up, and must depend upon the promptness of my friends to help me out. So, look out! *A word to the wise is sufficient.* W.C. Fowler.
Prattville, Feb. 24, 1853, n4-tf

The State of Alabama, Autauga County, Special Court of Probate - Feb. 17, 1853
This day came John T. Livingston, administrator of Rachel R. Livingston, deceased, and filed his accounts and vouchers for the annual settlement of the estate of said deceased, which was examined and ordered to be filed for the inspection of all concerned. It is therefore ordered, that notice be given for forty days, by publication for three successive weeks in the Autauga Citizen, notifying all persons interested to be and appear at a Court to be held on the 19th day of April next, to show cause why said account should not be stated and allowed.
Henly Brown, Judge of Probate,
Feb. 27, 1853 (pr. fee, $4) nf-3t

The State of Alabama, Autauga County, Special Court of Probate - Feb. 17, 1853
This day came John T. Livingston, guardian of Henry J. Livingston, a minor, and filed his accounts and vouchers for the annual settlement of his said wards' estate, which was examined and ordered to be filed for the inspection of all concerned. It is therefore ordered, that notice be given for forty days, by publication for three successive weeks in the Autauga Citizen, notifying all persons interested to be and appear at a Probate Court to be held on the 19th day of April next, to show cause why said account should not be stated and allowed.
Henly Brown, Judge of Probate
Feb. 24-nt-3t-$4

The State of Alabama, Autauga County, Special Court of Probate - Feb. 22, 1853
This day came Lewis Stoudenmier, executor of the last will and testament of Luke Hoffman, deceased, and filed his account and vouchers for the final settlement of the estate of said deceased; which was examined and ordered to be filed for the inspection of all concerned. It is therefore ordered, that notice be given for forty days, by publication for three successive weeks in the Autauga Citizen, a newspaper published in Prattville, Ala., notifying all persons interested to be and appear at a Probate Court to be held on the 2d day of May next, (1853,) to show cause, if any, why said account should not be stated and allowed.
Henly Brown, Judge of Probate
Feb. 27-n4-3t [$4]

The Soil of the South, For 1853. - A monthly journal, devoted to Agriculture, Horticulture, and the General planting interests of the South. James M. Chambers, Agricultural Editor;

Chas. A. Peabody, Horticultural Editor.
Published at Columbus, Ga., on the first of each month, on the following terms:
One copy, one year, in advance, $1
Six copies, one year in advance, $5
25 copies, one year, in advance, $20
100 copies, one year, in advance, $75
All subscriptions must commence with the volume.
Characteristics. Both the editors of this journal are engaged in the cultivation of the soil of the South. In the Agricultural Department, our list of contributors embraces many of the most successful agriculturists of the South; and each number, for 1853, will contain a contribution from one of the most distinguished scientific agriculturists in the United States. In the Horticultural Department, Mr. Charles A. Peabody, who has attained unrivalled excellence, has secured the co-operation of Iverson L. Aaris, J. Van Buren and Dr. Camak, distinguished horticulturists of Georgia, who have pledged themselves to contribute regularly to our columns...

Vol. 1, Thursday, March 3, 1853, No. 5

V.B. Palmer, the American Newspaper Agent, is the only authorized agent for this paper in the cities of Boston, New York and Philadelphia, and is duly empowered to take advertisements and subscriptions at the rates required by us. His receipts will be regarded as payments. - His offices are - Boston, Scollay's Building; New York, Tribune Buildings; Philadelphia, N.W. corner Third and Chestnut streets.

Benton A feet. - All the world and the "rest of mankind" are, doubtless, aware that Col. Thomas Hart Benton - "Old Bullion", - of Missouri, has written, and is about to publish, a book - the title of which, if we mistake not, is to be, "My Own Life and Times." Gov. Foote, of Mississippi, following the example of the redoubtable Missourian, has announced that he, too, has written a similar book, in which, he says, Col. Benton will "figure conspicuously;" whereupon the famous Colonel flings this brick about "a feet" into Foote: "His (F.'s) name will not be in *my* book; I put no name in it which is not worthy of history - of which something good cannot be said." That, we take it, is *per se* right good.

New Advertisements. - The attention of the public is called to the new advertisements in today's paper, among which will be found Mr. George Coe's. Having fitted up his shop, and provided himself with a good workman, he is prepared to do work in the neatest and most substantial manner. We have seen much of Mr. Coe's work, and do not hesitate to say that it will compare with any other of the same kind made in the State. Those wishing anything in his line will do well to give him a call, as we feel confident he will spare not pains to please those who may favor him with their patronage. We omitted to call the attention of our readers to the new advertisements in our last week's paper. Those wishing anything in the Carriage line will do well to pay Mr. Benj. M. Baker, of Montgomery, a visit, and examine his fine and large assortment of Carriages, Buggies, Rockaways, &c. C. Pomeroy & Co., of the same place have just received a fine assortment of Spring style hats, to which they invite the attention of those in need of good beavers. C.R. Hansford, Montgomery, invites the attention of the public to his large collection of books and stationary. Call and see him, when you go to Montgomery, should you wish anything in his line. There are others worthy of notice, which our readers will find, by perusing the advertising columns.

The Washington *Union* regrets to learn that, in consequence of the effort and exposure resulting from the delivery of his recent speech in the Senate, while in a debilitated state of health, the Hon. Mr. Clemens, of Alabama, has been for a few days past prevented by indisposition from resuming his seat and his duties in that body.

Editorial Brevities. - Information has been received at the Department of State at Washington, from the U.S. Consul at Matanzas, J.M. Rodney, Esq., of the destruction by fire, on the 28th and 29th of January, during a severe gale of wind, of the whole business part of the town of Cardensas, on the island of Cuba.

Gov. Johnson, of Virginia, in a message to the Legislature, recommends to a favorable consideration, the New York World's Fair, and suggests that some measure be taken to arouse the citizens of the State to take an interest in its success.

Secretary Everett, in answer to an inquiry respecting Mr. Wm. Fitzpatrick, grandfather of the Countess Montijo, Empress of France, officially confirms the statement, already named in the newspapers - namely, that he was appointed Consul of the United States for Malaga, by President Adams, January 18, 1800. He retired from the office on the 26th day of June, 1818, his successor being Mr. G.G. Barrell.

Two slaves, who ran off from the estate of the late William Tefft, of Parkersburg, Va., about two years ago, and went to Ohio, have recently voluntarily returned to slavery, on the ground that they were suffering from want of food, and were unable to procure work.

Liberal Bequests. - Mrs. Dorothea Abrahams, aged 73 died at Savannah on Sunday two weeks ago. She left $1000 towards building a free Episcopal church at Savannah; $1000 to the Savannah Hebrew Benevolent Society, and after some legacies to friends, the remainder of her estate, valued at $15,000 to $20,000, is to be expended on a building for the Widow's Society, to be used as a home for indigent widows and single women.

Murder. - We learn, says the Alabama *Democrat*, that on last Tuesday, Mr. W.S. Irby, who was overseeing the plantation of the estate of Doctor Aquilla D. Hutton, deceased, whipped a negro man belonging to the plantation, so severely, that he died under the lash. He was immediately arrested and held to bail in a bond of $5,000 for his appearance at the next term of our Circuit Court. Such outrageous cruelty should meet the condign punishment it so richly merits.

A new bank has been established at Knoxville, Tenn., under the name of the "Bank of Knoxville." It is based upon State stocks. W.M. Churchwell is President, and Samuel Morrow, Cashier.

Horace Mann, in his lecture on Woman, says: "I see but one reason why woman should not preach the Gospel, and that reason is, that it is ten thousand times better to go about practising the gospel than even to preach it."

Traveling in Minnesota. - The way in which the legislators of Minnesota travel, we learn by the news from the Territory, Mr. Kittson, of the Council, and Messrs. Gingaris and Rolette, of the House, (the members from Pemblina,) left their homes with four dogs, and were twenty days in performing the journey to St. Paul, which is good traveling considering the depth of snow in that part of the Territory. They made the journey to Crow Wing, on snow shoes, walking ahead of the trains to harden the track for the cogs. The snow in the Pembina region is from three to five feet deep on a level.

Died in Pike county, Ala., on Sunday the 20th Dec. last, Wm. Wicker. The deceased was aged 106 years. He served as a soldier in the revolutionary war. He was in the battle of Eutaw Springs, and was engaged in several skirmishes with the British and Tories under General Marion, of South Carolina. - *Spirit of the South*

Attention, Battallion! The 2d Battallion of the 47th Regiment A.M. will assemble at Pineflat Muster Ground, on the 19th March, armed and equipped as the law directs, for a battallion muster or drill, by 10 o'clock a.m. The commissioned and non-commissioned officers will assemble on the 18th inst., in order for inspection and drill. James S. Bullard, Maj. 2d Bat., 47th Rgt., March 3-n5-3t

Executors' Sale. - Will be held at Prattville, on Saturday, the 26th day of March, instant, a likely Negro man, named Henry, belonging to the estate of Thornton Rice, deceased, on a credit until the first day of January, 1854. Luther S. Rice, Surviving Executor.

Executors' Notice. - Letters, testamentary upon the estate of Henry DeBardelaben, deceased, having been granted to the undersigned by the honorable Henly Brown, Judge of Probate, in and for Autauga county, on the 26th day of February, 1853, all persons holding claims against said deceased are hereby notified to present them properly authenticated within the time prescribed by law, or they will be barred. F.S. DeBardelaben, John A. Houser, Executors

Vol. 1, Thursday, March 10, 1853, No. 6

See New Advertisements. - By referring to our advertising columns you will find many new advertisements in today's paper, for all of which we bespeak an attentive perusal by every one of our readers. The majority of them, you will perceive, are from Montgomery.

Mr. N.H. Frear, at the Dexter House, is prepared to take Daguerreotype likenesses in a superior manner, and solicits the patronage of the people of Autauga. By the way, we visited his gallery, and there found some of the best likenesses we have ever seen. If any of our friends hereabouts wish a life-like picture, go to Frear's and let him take it.

Mr. B.C. Owens, the well known proprietor of the best Livery Stable in Montgomery, solicit a continuance of the liberal patronage heretofore extended to him by the citizens of this county.

R.R. Jones & Co., Druggists, invite the attention of our readers to their fresh drugs, medicines, &c.

The card of E.S. Rogers, proprietor of the Hall, will be found. He keeps an excellent table, and uses every exertion to render his guests comfortable.

Wm. H. Taylor, proprietor of the Madison House, solicits a share of the patronage of this county. He endeavors, by his agreeable manners and gentlemanly deportment, to make all feel themselves at home. His table is well supplied with the best the market affords.

Wash. Tilley, proprietor of the Exchange Hotel, invites the patronage of the public. This house is well known as being one of the best in the South.

Lewis Owen & Co. invite the attention of purchasers to their large and splendid stock of Watches, Clocks, &c. Those wishing anything in the jewelry line will find it to their interest to pay them a visit.

L.H. Dickerson keeps on hand a large lot of Pianos, Furniture, Metallic Coffins, &c., to which he invites the attention of the people of Autauga.

Geo. Cowles is now offering for sale a large and extensive stock of Fancy Dry Goods, &c., to which the attention of the ladies, particularly, is called.

James Fountain, Carriage Manufacturer, keeps on hand a large number of Carriages, Buggies, Rockaways, &c., all of which are offered low.

Gilmer, Taylor & Co. offer rare inducements in their line. They keep constantly on hand a large and well selected stock of Groceries, of every description. Persons wishing to purchase will do well to give them a call.

W.A. Grant, also, keeps on hand a large and extensive stock of Groceries, which he offers for the lowest cash price. Families and country dealers will find it to their advantage to give him a trial.

The New Government. - The "great agony" is over. Gen. Pierce has been installed into the national chair of State, and it will now be seen whom he has selected for his constitutional aids and advisers. The little agony is to come yet, and it will require some time - a trying time, too, it will doubtless be to the new President - to get over it. There are lots of spoils to be divided - but scarcely enough for all who think they are entitled, by virtue of "services rendered," to a share. We wish, however, that all may get a bite - not excepting ourselves - we do that.

Here is the President's Cabinet:
Wm. L. Marcy, of New York, Sec'y of State.
Jas. Guthrie, of Kentucky, Sc'y of Treasury.
R. McClelland, of Michigan, Sec'y Interior.
Jeff. Davis, of Miss., Secretary of War.
J.C. Dobbin, of N.C., Sec'y of Navy.

Jas. Campbell, of Pa., Postmaster General.
Caleb Cushing, of Mass., Attorney General.
All these gentlemen, with one or two exceptions, are well known in the political world. Taking everything into consideration, we think Mr. Pierce has supplied himself with an active and efficient cabinet, who will prove themselves equal to any emergency, and loyal to their country...

A Strange Murder. - A man named William Fisher shot Robert Kirkland in his own house in this county on last Saturday morning, as we are informed, under the following circumstances. Fisher it seems had been addressing a lady who resided with Kirkland, but Kirkland was opposed to his marrying her, and told him he should not if he could prevent it. On Friday evening F. asked leave of K. to send off for some whiskey, and sent for half a gallon. Next morning he was endeavoring to get a bottle to put some of his whiskey in, when Kirkland told him he had drank enough, that he should not have any more. Fisher looked at him sternly and asked, "do you say so?" Kirkland replied "yes, I do." Fisher instantly pulled out his pistol and said - "Dang you, I'll shoot you," and fired at his breast. Kirkland cried out as he fell, "Oh Lord, Bill, you have killed me," and died in a few moments. The ball penetrated about 3 inches below the left nipple. Col. McKnight, deputy sheriff, hearing of this fatal deed, promptly and very properly arrested Fisher without a warrant, and he was regularly committed to jail to answer the offense. - *Florence Gazette.*

Editorial Brevities. - Jethro Cotton. - Twenty-two bales of Jethro Cotton, from the plantation of Wilds Robb, Esq., of Morgan county, were sold in the Augusta market, on the 21st Feb., for 16 cents per lb.

The Dauphin Romance. - The New York Tribune states that Mr. Putman has received from the prince de Joinville a reply to the romantic account of his interview with the Rev. Eleazer Williams, lately published in Putman's Monthly. The nature of the reply is not known. It is said, however, that the Prince meets (which mean, we suppose, denies) every point of the Rev. Eleazer Williams's narrative with which he was concerned, and gives his own account of what passed between them.

A singular discovery is mentioned by a Cuba correspondent of the Raleigh Standard. Dr. Tinsley, an English practitioner of long experience in Cuba, and a graduate of Paris, has discovered, in the course of his practice in cases of small pox, that vaccine virus, after having once passed through a negro's system, becomes useless as a preventive to the white race.

The Governor of Arkansas has made a requisition upon the government of Texas, for Col. A.E. Thornton, a respectable citizen of Galveston, charged with forgery, alleged to have been committed eight years ago.

The New York Commercial Advertiser learns from a credible source that Madame Goldsmith (formerly Jenny Lind) has signified her determination to pay another professional visit to this country. She will sing at various places in Germany during the present year, and the following season will appear in opera at London. Afterwards she will come to the United States and give opera in all the principal cities, remaining here probably two or three years.

The New York Herald says that ex-President Van Buren is about to make a tour through

Europe, in company with his son Martin Van Buren, Jr., for the benefit of whose health, it is said, the journey is undertaken. It adds that it believes it is the first time that any person who had held the distinguished position of President of the American Union has ever visited Europe, and the event is, therefore singular, and worthy of remark.

(Correspondence of the Autauga Citizen.), Selma, Feb. 1853.
Gentlemen - At your request I promised to write you from this place. I am not sure that I should do so now - choosing, rather, to refer you to an article in the last issue of the Selma Enterprise, which gives, in a more interesting form that I could present, the position and prospects of Selma...The schools are in a flourishing condition. The names of one hundred and twenty-five pupils have been entered at the Masonic Institute (now entirely female,) of which the Rev. O. Rockwell, a gentleman of fine attainments and reputation, is President...Cahaba, Feb. 27, 1853. Having failed to mail the above in time for your paper of the present week, I will, in the way of a postscript, add a few words from this place, which must suffice for the letter mentioned above. I came down yesterday on the favorite steamer Fashion - whereof Capt. Jesse J. Cox is commander, and Mr. W.E. Drummond clerk. Capt. Jesse, being from Old Autauga, and well known to everybody there, and to the traveling community generally, it would be superfluous for me to attempt to add any thing to the well merited encomiums of which he is daily the recipient. "It does us proud" to see the many flattering paragraphs in the papers respecting his eminent fitness - his watchfulness for the comfort and safety of his passengers - his care and excellent management on all occasions - his fine dinners and agreeable manners, - and, in fact, every element which constitutes a skillful commander and perfect gentleman - put down to his credit. Nor is this all - the *ladies* sometimes say more; but lest I may stand in danger of receiving a challenge, I won't say it. At home, we all know his worth, and it is with pleasure that we see him so well appreciated by others. Mr. Drummond is in every respect his counterpart. Those travelling with him cannot help admiring his attention to passengers, and his pleasant and gentlemanly bearing to all. Those who may have occasion to travel on the river will not regret it if they fall into such hands...

The Caloric Shop Ericsson. - This magnificent ship has made a trial trip most satisfactorily, and is now lying in the vicinity of Washington, where she will be visited and inspected by members of Congress, and the officers of the Government. The Washington *Republic*, of the 23d, gives the following account of this test trip: "This ship arrived at Alexandria on Monday afternoon, from the mouth of the Potomac, where she had lain at anchor for twenty-seven hours, during the late snow storm and thick weather. Capt. Lowber weighed anchor at half-past nine o'clock last Wednesday morning at Sandy Hook, and in persuance of instructions, stood to the east in the face of a strong gale and heavy sea. He kept his course for eight miles, when the wind shifted to the northwest. He then stood in shore again in the face of the gale. During these two gales, the ships stood the test nobly, and though she pitched her bowsprit under water, with her lee guard immersed, her engines performed with the utmost regularity, the wheels making six turns and a half a minute, with entire uniformity. Not the slightest motion was perceptible in the frame work and bracing of the engines. After the ship and engines were thus fully tested, Captain Lowber shaped his course for the Chesapeake, and in going up the bay encountered a heavy snow storm.. On approaching the mouth of the Potomac the weather became so thick that the pilot declined to go further, and the ship came to anchor at ten o'clock Saturday morning. The engines had then been in operation for seventy three hours without being stopped a moment or requiring the slightest adjustment, only one fireman having been on duty at a time during the whole trip. The consumption of fuel was under five tons during the twenty-four hours: Capt. Sands, of the navy, who was on board to witness the performance, is delighted with the result, and says that he would willingly go to Australia in her. Thus the great principle of the new motor is now a demonstrated reality." Five tons of coal per day to propel a ship of 2200 tons! This looks impossible, but it is a fixed, a demonstrated fact, and one which is destined to exercise an overshadowing influence over the marine interests of the Western waters. All boat-builders should prepare for the Ericcson motor. Heated air will now completely supersede the more costly steam, and as firemen will be almost entirely unnecessary, and as fuel won't cost one dollar where it now costs five, the process of freight and passage must inevitably come down materially. Add to these the fact that danger from explosions will be obviated, and the value of the invention may be somewhat appreciated.

There was a terrible and melancholy homicide committed in the lower part of this District a few days since. Col. T.E. Ware and his father-in-law, Capt. Jones, had a dispute about some trivial affair, when Capt. Jones becoming exasperated, struck Col. Ware, whereupon he drew a revolver, and shot him three times, causing instant death. The Colonel gave himself up immediately, and left the morning after in charge of the Sheriff, for Newberry, to appear before Judge O'Neal to give bail. *Charleston Mercury.*

The State of Alabama, Autauga County, Special Court of Probate, March 5, 1853
This day came James Ramsey, Guardian of Alcey F. Pollard, a minor, and filed his account and vouchers for the annual settlement of his said ward's estate, which was examined and ordered to be filed for the inspection of all concerned. It is therefore ordered, that notice be given for forty days, by publication for three successive weeks in the Autauga Citizen, notifying all persons interested to be and appear at a Court to be held on the 26th day of April next, to show cause why said account should not be stated and allowed. Henly Brown, Judge of Probate

Dissolution. - The copartnership hereto existing between E.A. Cowles and Geo. Cowles was dissolved on the 1st inst., by mutual consent. All persons indebted to them are most respectfully, but earnestly, requested to make immediate payment, as their business *must be closed.*

Vol. 1, Thursday, March 17, 1853, No. 7

The Last Night. - We would advise all who have not yet visited Prof. Mac Evoys Exhibition, to do so tonight, which is the last. Independent of the beauty of the painting, there are other attractions - the "performance of the young Minstrels - the exquisite singing of Madam Warren - the Irish Dwarf - and lastly, the distribution of numerous costly jewels. Our time will not permit us to speak as we could desire of these little minstrels - they are interesting and talented, and deserve all the encomiums bestowed upon them by the press wherever they have performed.

Southern Ladies' Book. - We have on our table the March number of this magazine. It is published at New Orleans, and is edited with much ability by L. Virginia French (formerly Smith,) and its mechanical execution is unexceptionable. We are much pleased with the article on "Going North," and, had we the first part, would transfer it to our columns. - We take pleasure in directing the attention of those who desire a thoroughly Southern work to this magazine.

Tornado at Columbus. - In the Columbus (Ga.) Sentinel and Times we have an account of a destructive Tornado, which passed over that city on Thursday night last. In addition to the particulars furnished by the Times, we learn from other sources, that its effects on plantations and settlements in Russell Co., was still more destructive.

Hail Storm. - At about a quarter after two o'clock yesterday, a terrible hail storm swept over our city, and during the space of ten minutes, did immense damage. Almost every house in the city was injured. The warehouses of Mr. Rankin, Guby, Daniel & Co., and H.S. Smith & Co., were all partially blown down and unroofed. Six or eight stores about Rankin's corner had their front walls entirely prostrated. Many private residences were partially unroofed. Almost every chimney in the city is down, and our shade trees cumber the streets with their fallen trunks and broken branches. Taylor & Co.'s Gin Factory was unroofed and incalculable injury done to a large number of Gins already finished, and to the tools and machinery used in the manufacture. It is reported that the bridge in Gicard was blown down, and a wagon, driver and team precipitated into the depths below. No lives were lost in our city. It is useless to grieve over unavoidable calamities. Industry and energy will repair it, and we are happy to see that even before the storm had abated, many of our energetic citizens were busily engaged in removing the wreck and repairing the damage it had caused. The damage is immense, but in the confusion consequent upon so great a calamity, it is impossible to estimate it. *Columbus Times*

Adjournment of Congress. - Both houses of Congress adjourned *sine die* at noon, on the 4th ins. - thus terminating the Thirty second Congress. The last business transacted was the passage of the Civil and Diplomatic Appropriation Bill. This bill, amongst other things, increases the salaries of the Vice President and Heads of the Departments to eight thousand dollars per annum - heretofore six thousand; appropriates one hundred thousand dollars towards furnishing Washington with a better supply of water; and creates the office of Assistant Secretary of State, with a salary of three thousand dollars per annum. All the general appropriation bills were passed; and, in addition to other measures of importance, the organization of Territorial Government of Washington. Immediately after the adjournment, the special session was formed. An account of its proceedings is as follows: On Friday, at five minutes past 12, m. the Senate of the United States, in pursuance of the call the President of the United States, convened in their Chamber, and were called to order by the Hon. Lewis Cass. After a prayer by the Rev. C.M. Butler - Mr. Badger submitted a resolution, that the oath of office prescribed by the Constitution be administered to the new members by the Hon. Lewis Cass, of Michigan, the oldest member of the body; which was agreed to. Mr. Cass then administered the oath of office to the new Senators. On motion of Mr. Shields, it was unanimously resolved that the Hon. David R. Atchison, of Missouri, be continued as President *pro tempore* of the Senate. Mr. Atchison, on assuming the Chair, said; Senators, permit me to return you my sincere thanks for the honor you have again conferred upon me. I take it as an evidence of your personal regard and consideration, and also of your confidence in my integrity and impartiality. The Senate then remained in session for some time, awaiting the arrival of the President elect. The Diplomatic Corps then arrived in their full costume and uniform, and were assigned seats on the sofas, on the north side of the Chamber. The Judges of the Supreme Court were assigned places on the left of the Presiding Officer. The members of the late House of Representatives filled the east and south lobbies. Maj. Gen. Scott was present. The circular gallery was, at an early hour, filled exclusively with ladies. Shortly after one o'clock, the President elect entered, resting on the arm of Senator Bright, and was followed by the President of the United States, leaning on the arm of Senator Pratt. The Hon. W.L. Marcy, Judge Campbell, Hon. Messrs. Dobbin and Guthrie, entered in company with the Executive. The Senate received the President standing. Immediately after, the procession was formed in the order prescribed in the programme of the committee of the Senate, and proceeded to the eastern portico of the capitol, where the oath of office was administered to the President elect, by the Chief Justice of the United States. On the conclusion of the President's inaugural address, the Senate returned to their Chamber, and then adjourned.

Editorial Brevities
Mammoth English Ships. - The largest mercantile ship in the world, the screw steamer *Himalaya*, of 3,600 tons measurement, built for the Penisular and Oriental Steam Navigation Co., is nearly ready for launching at London. She will be propelled by machinery of 700 horse power. The largest man of war in the world, has just been put in commission by Captain Henry Byam Martin, son of the admiral of the fleet. She bears the name of the *Duke of Wellington*, and carries 131 guns. - She has engines of 780 horse power, screw machinery, and she will have a crew of 1100 men.

It is stated by the New York Mirror, that instructions have been received from Louis Napoleon, to contract for the immediate construction in New York of a fleet of war steamers.

The Firing at the Black Warrior. - Capt. Shufeldt, of the steamer *Black Warrior*, in a letter published in the New York papers, considered the Spanish man-of-war was justified, under the circumstances, in the firing into his vessel. He was not aware the brig was a vessel of war, or he would have hoisted his flag before she fired; and as the *Black Warrior* was going very fast at the time, she would have been beyond the reach of the Spanish vessel in a few minutes, had the latter not immediately fired a gun in order to let him know she was a nation vessel. The second gun was fired before the order of Captain S. to hoist his flag could be executed.

Another Webster and Parkman Tragedy. - A letter in the Lynchburg (Va.) Express, from the Kanawha Salires, states that a man named Stoghin went to the house of a neighbor to pay him several hundred dollars he owed him. As he was not seen afterwards, his friends instituted inquires for him and finally searched the house where he had gone, without success, until one of them commenced scraping the ashes of a large fireplace, and, to his surprise, found several hundred teeth and a cheek-bone; also, pieces of flesh supposed to be that of the missing man, which had run into a crevice in the fire place, partly roasted. The occupant of the house was immediately arrested.

Diabolical Murder. - On last Saturday evening some thirteen negroes were committed to jail by N.P. Booker, Esq., a Justice of the Peace at Uniontown, in this county. Ten or more of these negroes are charged with the murder of an old man by the name of John Rickard. Mr. Rickard had for many years followed the business of ditching, and was, during the time of his murder, engaged in his vocation. It seems that he had been missing from the neighborhood, some eight miles North-East of Uniontown, in this county, where he resided, and was operating with several of his own, and some five or six hired negroes. It had been reported by the negroes that he had gone to New Orleans, after the lapse of five or six weeks the neighbors began to suspect something was wrong, commenced a search, and investigation of the cause of his absence. One discovery led to another, until the old man was found buried some few feet below the surface, under the dirt thrown out of the ditch they were at work on. We are informed that the whole transaction has been confessed, and fully explained by the negroes themselves, who were in one way or another engaged in this most horrible transaction and unpardonable deed. There is said to have been nor reasonable apparent inducement or pretence of apology for the act; but we say as little as possible, considering the state of the feeling, and that the law has charge of the accused. - *Marion Commonwealth*

England's Humanity. - It is generally known that the savages were employed by the king of England, George III, and paid at so much per scalp of man, woman and child during our revolutionary war. A few items from this terrible trade in human flesh may perhaps interest some of our readers, and show them how this paternal king strove to crush out the noble spirit of independence of our early heroes. Here is a list of a number of packages that were sent by one James Boyed from a Captain Crawford to the British governor of Canada, Col. Heidleman. These packages of scalps were found among the baggage of the English army after the defeat of Burgoyne, cured and dried, with Indian marks upon them. The letter accompanying them reads thus:
"Package 1. Containing forty-three scalps of congress soldiers killed in different skirmishes, stretched on black hoops four inches in diameter.
Pack. 2. Containing ninety-eight scalps of farmers killed in their houses, on red hoops, with a figure of a hoe painted on each to denote their occupation.
Pack. 3. Containing ninety-seven farmers' scalps, on green hoops, to show that they were killed in the fields.
Pack. 4. Containing one hundred and two farmers' scalps, eighteen of them marked with yellow flames to signify that they were burnt alive.
Pack. 5. Containing eighty-eight scalps of women; hair long and braided, to show that they were mothers.
Pack. 6. Containing one hundred and ninety three scalps of various ages, on small green hoops."
Such was the stuff of which English royalists were made in the days 'which tried men's souls.' - *Boston Post*

A full attendance of the members of Autauga Lodge No. 17 I.O.O.F. is requested at their next regular meeting, Friday, 18th inst. T.D. Ormsby, Sec'y

Vol. 1, Thursday, March 24, 1853, No. 8

A correspondent of the Alabama Journal suggests the name of our worthy fellow-citizen, Daniel Pratt, as a suitable candidate to represent this and Montgomery county in the Senate of the State Legislature. We give below the concluding paragraph of his communication: "I am a Montgomery man myself, yet, I am very free to confess that Autauga has within her limits a number of as good and true whigs as ever rallied under our time honored standard, from whom a selection might be made every way worthy the confidence of the people. Among them, I take the liberty of mentioning in this connection the name of Mr. Daniel Pratt - than whom none is more worthy. I am aware that Mr. Pratt is no aspirant for office, but then his moral worth and practical usefulness most eminently suggest him as a suitable candidate to represent this Senatorial District in the State Legislature - and I am sure that though he does not aspire to any office within the gift of the people, that he will not decline should he be called by them into their service. Montgomery."

The Texan Ranger, Ben McCulloch, is in Washington, and, as we see by the N.Y. Sun, has had a small scrimmage: The telegraph will have told you of an affray at the National Hotel today between Major McCulloch, of the Texan Rangers, and a hot and wrong-headed Mexican. The Major, by way of premise, is a quiet, unobtrusive man, who respects right for its own sake, "slow to anger", but capable of maintaining his own cause in any emergency. The Mexican had previously determined upon a quarrel, and when "his man" was pointed out, he accosted him in a rude manner. But in words the Major rather tripped him up, and got the advantage, and so to end the matter he deliberately told the imperturbable Texan that he wanted a fight with him, and then tapped him gently in the face. Scarcely was the provocation given ere the assailant received a deserved and sufficient punishment, and the Major went about his business as coolly as though nothing had happened. The incident has made quite a lion of him.

Editorial Brevities.
A Singular Man. - Reese F. Price, a resident of Cincinnati, a gentlemanly and philanthropic individual, has made a proposition to the legislature of Ohio for a dissolution of his partnership with the State. He considers the notions of the commonwealth antagonistical to those entertained by himself, and does not desire fellowship with it. He proposes to pay his proportion of the State debt, which he estimated at $500, and he absolved for all allegiance.

Senator Benjamin. - At the extra session of the Senate, a petition was presented to that body, signed by twenty members of the Louisiana Legislature, against Hon. J.P. Benjamin, the newly elected Senator from that State, being allowed to take his seat, on the ground of his being a naturalized citizen of the United States. No notice, however, was taken of it.

Arthur Spring, charged with the murder of Mrs. Lynch and her sister, Mrs. Shaw, in Philadelphia, it is said, has been fully committed. The testimony against him was of a positive character.

A Woman in Breeches. - The Lynn Bay State says that Miss Lucy Stone lectured in that city recently on "Woman's Rights." Miss Stone has the credit of practicing what she preaches, and lays direct claim to the breeches. She appears in a handsome suit of broadcloth, sack, pants, and good thick boots, and lacks the beaver to make her a good looking man.

Peter G. Washington, of Washington, has been appointed Assistant Secretary of the Treasury, vice Hodge. The democracy of the District are said to be much incensed at the appointment of Mr. W., as they had excluded him from their club-rooms.

The Savannah Republican states that a naturalized citizen of Georgia, Mr. C. Schmidt, has been arrested in Bremen on the requisition of a Hanoverian magistrate for military service due that kingdom. He was released on the interposition of Mr. King, the American Consul at Bremen.

The Wetumpka State Guard is authorized to state that Col. Howell Ross does not, under any circumstances, wish his name to go before the people as a candidate for Governor.

Vice-President King. - We learn from Cuba, says the Charleston Courier, that the oath of office was not administered to the Vice-President on the 4th inst. Mr. Rodney, the U.S. Vice Consul at Matansas, visited him on the 3d inst. for that purpose; but Mr. King considered the ceremony an unnecessary one, fearing, as he said, that he should never be able to reach Washington to assume the duties of his office - if he should, (which we sincerely hope may be the case,) the oath of office could be administered to him on his arrival at Washington. The friends who accompany the Vice President are encouraged to hope that the salubrity of his present location may yet restore him to health.

The proposition of Mr. Henry O'Reilly for a line of telegraph from St. Louis to San Francisco, before the last Congress, is for the Government to establish a chain of stockades from St. Louis to the Pacific, twenty miles apart, and protected by U.S. Dragoons. - They will convey the U.S. mail and protect emigrant trains. A line of telegraph is to be constructed on this route by Mr. O'Reilly, without any compensation from the Government, either in land or money. The project can be completed, it is averred, in twelve months.

It is stated that the contract to supply the U.S. Navy with tobacco for four years, has been awarded to Robert A. Mayo of Richmond Virginia.

Mr. Meager arrived at Washington on the 27th ult. He spent the evening with General Pierce. He visited both houses of Congress the next day, and was paid marked attention by distinguished senators and representatives. He was accompanied during the day, as special aid, by Captain Key, of the Washington Montgomery Guards, and several friends. He was received every where with enthusiasm. He proposed remaining in Washington till after the inauguration; then go to Richmond, and thence southward to New Orleans.

The bride-cake at the marriage of Napoleon III and Madame de Montijo was made in London, by Messrs. Pursells. It weighed 620 pounds without its ornaments.

A fatal encounter occurred at Lawrenceburg, Tenn., on the 22d ult., between Mr. D.F. Wilson, of Maury county, and John Field, of Lawrenceburg. The difficulty originated in consequence of a levy upon a small boy, the property of Field, but which he insisted was not a slave. Field commenced the attack, firing three times before Wilson drew his pistol. There were in all ten shots - three striking Wilson without serious injury; two balls took effect on Field - one in the arm and one in the left breast. Field's frontal bone was fractured by a blow from Wilson. Field died about an hour afterwards. The arms used were six barrelled revolvers. Wilson was arrested and an investigation had, but it appearing from the evidence that he acted in self-defense, he was discharged.

The Hon. John W. Otey, Judge of the Probate Court of Madison county, died in Huntsville on Monday the 28th ult., from a disease of the heart.

John Mitchell, the Irish patriot, has written a letter, which has been published in the Irish papers, substantially saying that he does not thank the persons who have petitioned Queen Victoria for his pardon.

J.C. Morrison, of Tazewell county, arrived safely in Oregon. Their teams gave out 500 miles this side of their destination. They left their oxen and those who had families, and started down Lewis river on the beds of their wagons; and out of twenty young men so embarked, only four ever got ashore alive, so rapid was the stream and so full of rocks. The four having escaped, started through an uninhabited country with but little provision and few clothes. They arrived at the settlement at last, after passing through trials and dangers beyond the power of tongue or pen to describe.

Legislative Fun. - The other day in the Senate, Rev. R. Cuyler, by permission, presented the petition of the ladies of Mercer county in favor of the Maine Law. In his appeal to the Senators, he said: Many of you are husbands - all of you are *fathers*! Now several of these gentlemen are bachelors, and the reverend gentleman's remarks created a smile on the faces of the outsiders, some of whom wrote the words above quoted on slips of paper, and circulated them among the Senators who were living lives of single blessedness. - *N.J. Eagle*

Returned to Slavery. - The Wheeling Times states that Lewis, a colored man belonging to H.M. Jamison, Esq., of that city, who had ran away a short time ago, voluntarily returned, recently, perfectly disgusted with the condition of the "free niggers" in Pittsburgh, Pa., where he had been stopping.

A Terrible Picture of Suffering. - In a letter to the Galena Advertiser, written from Oregon, the sufferings of an emigrant party are briefly given, which make up a sad picture of Western adventure: Zeb Davis, Esq., has resigned the office of Timber Agent for North Alabama, and Nathaniel Davis, Esq., who was the bearer of the Electoral vote of Alabama to Washington, has been appointed by President Fillmore as his successor. So says a letter writer to the Tuscumbia Enquirer.

A Novel Enterprise. - The vast travel through Broadway, New York and the great length of that thoroughfare, have produced much inconvenience, and many schemes have been proposed for its relief. We have before us a drawing which represents the plan devised by P. O'Neil, of South Brooklyn. It proposes to erect two rows of iron pillars the whole length of the street to support a double track railroad eighteen feet above the pavement, with a promenade each side of it on a level with the second story permitting communications to be made with ranges of stores in that story. The distance of the rows of supporting pillars from each other is forty feet, and the pillars are twelve and a half feet apart, each pillar forming a conductor for surface water to the sewer underneath the pavement. It is proposed to lay the track of the railroad on plant over cast iron flagging, and to floor the promenade and intervening spaces with glass protected by perforated cast iron. Opposite the middle of each block a double flight of steps lead to the road and promenade above; and it is proposed to attach the street lamps and telegraph posts to the supporting pillars at convenient distances. The whole plan is original, and we see no reason to believe it impracticable. - *Washington Union.*

Affecting Incident - A Master's Life Saved By His Slave. - On Sunday last Mr. G. McCann, while crossing the Mississippi river alone in a canoe, from Battle Island to his plantation, whither he had been on a visit to his friend and neighbor on the island, Ben Hardin, Esq., was upset in the middle of the river, he clung to the canoe until he had floated opposite to the wood yard on his farm, when his cries attracted the attention of one of his negro men, the boy immediately put off in a skiff, to the rescue of his master. Before the negro arrived, Mr. McCann had become exhausted, and sunk. The faithful negro succeeded, however, at the imminent peril of his own life, in reaching his master, which he did by seizing him by the hair, and took him in the skiff. Mr. McCann was in an insensible state, and life was nearly extinct. By the assiduous attention of the servant, and the application of such restoratives as were at hand, he was brought to consciousness. On Wednesday, when John Simonds passed his plantation, he was slowly recovering. This is another fact to illustrate the truth of history, touching the social and moral condition of the master and the slave. - *St. Louis Republican*

Hiram Powers. - This greatest of the American sculptors writes home from Italy, under date of the 12th of January, a private letter from which the following interesting extract is taken: You invite me to come home, on a visit at least; and I am fully sensible of the priority and great kindness of all you say, and I thank you most heartily for it. But the truth is, I cannot, and I will tell you why. My engagements forbid it, at least for the present; besides I should have to discharge my workmen - eight fine fellows, some of whom have been with me for fourteen years. In short, I should have to break up my establishment for the time being, and it would be difficult to reunite it as I now have it. My workmen would engage elsewhere, and everything would fall back. It would take me a long while to make up for lost time, and it would cost me some three or four thousand dollars, and all for what? You intimate that I should get some valuable commissions, and I think it probable that I might; but I do not want then so much now as I did. I have plenty to do; but perhaps my orders do not pay so well as government orders would. But this consideration will never induce me to seek an order from our government. I never have done this while here, and shall never go home for such a purpose. If I am overlooked or forgotten by the members of Congress, it is the best proof I have of their disregard and my services are not required. I have left nothing undone that I could do, short of personal importunity, to win the favorable regard of our government. I have modeled a statue, to which I have given the name of our country "America, " and I have sent daguerreotypes of it home to be seen by our leading men; and some of these men - my gratitude is unbounded to them - have petitioned to Congress, for several years past, to give me an order for this, as I intended it, national work. I can meet and stand up against opposition, but I bow and turn away from indifference. A handsome commission from Congress might justify my breaking off here for a season, in order to gratify the burning desire, which my wife shares with me to go home and see once the numerous relatives and friends we have in America. We never see the sun go down, spreading his glorious mantle over our western home, without a sigh, nor do I see rising in the east, without fresh resolves to follow him in his course as soon as possible. This may give you some idea how I feel, and how much we long to leave this forever. I know not how many have told me that I should receive a hearty welcome if I would go home, even a visit. This, of course, is most gratifying to hear; it shows that I am not forgotten. But this would not justify my going. I came abroad to learn my art, and I have lived here for more than fifteen years during which time a large family has grown up around me. We have seven children, the three eldest nearly grown. Our eldest boy has been sent home to finish his education by learning to be an American. You have asked for a catalog of my works. It will not be busts, but a few statues - those of Greek Slave, Eve, Calhoun, the Fisher Boy, California, La Penserosa and Washington. The three last are not yet finished. I have executed five of the Greek slave. Three of the Fisher Boy, one of Eve and one of Calhoun, and the others are engaged. Washington is for the state of Louisiana. The order was given, I am proud to say, by a unanimous vote of the Legislature. I hope you will understand me rightly in all that I have said above. I do not complain of anything, for I know how the world goes, as the saying is, and I try to take it calmly and patiently, holding out my net, like a fisherman, to salmon, shad, or pilchards, as they may come; if salmon, why then we can eat salmon; if pilchards, why then we can eat them, and bless God that we have dinner at all. Sincerely your friend, H. Powers

A Nut for Historical Societies. - A few days since was handed to us, by two worthy and reliable citizens, Mr. Gray and Mr. McCray, of Clay hill, in this county, a singular curiosity. A negro had cut down a large red-oak for the purpose of splitting it into rails. It was a large tree, some three feet diameter, making (so says our informants) 140 rails to the cut. He had split all except the heart piece, when, upon wrenching it open, he discovered, in the center of the heart, something black, which he took to be a worm. He called the attention of Mr. Gray to it, who, upon an examination, found it to be a lock (or rather two locks) of hair. Before it was disturbed, it's position is thus said to have been. The lock of jet black hair, and evidently from its finance fineness, the hair of a European female was wound round in a beautiful little curl of the size of a half-dollar, and in its center the sandy lock was placed. The female's hair was smooth at one end as if clipped with scissors. - The other appeared to be pulled from the head by hand, the roots were apparent. Now for your surmises, ye Historians, ye Picketts, Jacksons, DeBows, &c. From the texture, fineness, &c, expels every thought of its being the hair of an Indian. From the difference of the two locks, they are unmistakably male and female. The red-oak, considering its size, and the fineness of its green grain, (for an oak with course grain would never have produced so many rails,) must have been three or four hundred years old. Was there any white people here then, though Mr. Pickett says, in his " History of Alabama ", that De Soto entered the present bounds of this state in 1540, which was three hundred and thirteen years ago. But it appears that De Soto entered up the Coosa river, came down on the west side of it, crossed over to Tallassee on the Tallapoosa, down it, down the Alabama to Mobile, and from thence into Mississippi, and never came into the State again. - So he was never this low down. But Mr. Pickett also says that De Soto left Maldinado in charge of his ships at Pensacola Bay, and that he became tired of waiting for De Soto's return home and sailed along the coast, hoping to the expedition, blazing trees, &c. Now, let us conjecture: might not Maldinado having dispatched couriers in different directions, by land, to meet the expedition, and might not one of them, taking the intermediate direction between De Soto's course when he left and the one he expected to return, have straggled off, and pursued by the Indians, reached thus far? But what of the female hair? Ah! We explained that. The poor fellow was from the land of chivalry. Don Quixot's stamping ground. Before leaving Hispanola he secured a lock of his Dulcina's hair, which never left his (?). Pursued by savages, starving for the want of food, and from fatigue he laid down beneath a shady little grove to die. His slumbers are disturbed. His Dulcina appears to am in his dreams, beseeching him never to part from her gift. He awaits, searches for his treasure, finds it, and bedews it with his (?), snatching a handful from his own head, he curls hers around his own, and, splitting a little oak bush, placed it between the fork, closes it, and lays him down; and thus (?) sickening, withering, he sank to (?) no more. The oak would heal if it was summertime. Is this romantic? Then give us some more reliable information. But until they do this, we must be allowed to indulge our bachelor thoughts. *Troy Palladium*

We obtain from the New Orleans Picayune the following sequel to a case recently tried in the U.S. Supreme Court. General Chambers is certainly acting the part of a man of honor: Gen. Thomas J. Chambers, of Texas, lately gained in the U.S. Supreme Court a suit brought against him by several American citizens, for money paid him for lands sold by him during the Texas revolutionary war, he covenanting to give title to the purchasers whenever they called on him. This purchase money was expended in equipping soldiers for the revolutionary army. Gen. Chambers was lately in San Antonio, and the Ledger says he expressed his determination to comply with all contracts of the above nature, according to their original spirit and intent. When this suit was instituted the titles of most if not all off these lands, as well as to all his landed estates in Texas, were assailed and in dispute. He was compelled to defend these titles in the state tribunals, or forever lose the power to execute these contracts and save his property, and at the same time defend his suit on purely legal grounds to avoid a degree which would still further have embarrassed these same titles. He has now secured his own titles, and as an evidence of his intent to the matter, while in San Antonio, he conveyed 2,500 acres of the finest lands on the Brazos to a gentleman of Kentucky, under precisely such a contract as the Supreme Court of the United States pronounced void.

The State of Alabama, Autauga County, Special Court of Probate, March 14, 1853.
This day came A. Andrews, guardian of Robert (?) and John D. Perry, minors, and filed his accounts and vouchers for the annual settlement of said wards' estate which was examined and ordered to be filed for the inspection of all concerned. It is therefore ordered, that notice be given for forty-five days, by publication for three successive weeks in the Autauga Citizen, notifying all persons interested to be and appear at a court to be held the 9th of May next, to show cause why said account should not be stated and allowed. Henly Brown, Judge of Probate

Vol. 1, Thursday, March 31, No. 9

President Pierce has nominated John (?), of La., as Minister to Central America, and Joseph Law for collector of Pensacola. The following additional appointments have also been confirmed:

Postmasters
John Bowen, San Antonio, Texas
R.S. Cheny, Jackson, Michigan
Wm. D. Marrset, Tuscaloosa, Ala.
A. Galt, Norfolk, Virginia
T.B. Bigger, Richmond, Va.
J. Carter, Concord, N.H.
T.W. Ashby, Alexandria, Va.
G.(?) Katalaugh, Huntsville, Ala.
T.L Toulmin, Mobile, Alabama

Editorial Brevities.
Joseph Nela accused of murdering George T. Sharpe, at Burnsville, in this State, on the 14 ult., was arrested a few days since, at the residence of his brother, in Dooly county, Ga., by Mr. McCaine and Mr. A.B. King, of Dallas county. A reward of five hundred dollars was offered for his apprehension. Besides the murder, the offender is charged with the commission of the most revolting crime known to the criminal calendar.

The mayor, high sheriff, and the leading magistrates, consuls, merchants and citizens of Cork, Ireland, have forwarded a memorial to President Pierce, praying him not to remove Mr. Mitchell, the U.S. Consul at that port, from his office.

In the Senate of the United States, a pension was granted to Betsy Norton, a widow of ninety odd years, "to continue for life, unless she marry again." Wasn't it outrageous in the Senate fixing such a restriction as that on the young lady's desires!

A telegraphic dispatch from Baltimore to the Charleston Courier, says that Mr. Fillmore is not expected to start for the South until the 1st of April, in consequence of the continued indisposition of Mrs. Fillmore, and perhaps he will not come at all.

Another dispatch of the same date, says, that in the U.S. Senate, on Monday, the 21st, Mr. Everett made a speech, showing that the affairs of Central America were progressing towards an amicable settlement, and that England had already abandoned the Mosquito Protestorate.

A Comet was discovered at Harvard Observatory, on the evening of the 8th inst., by C.W. Tuttle. It is situated about five degrees south of the bright star Regel.

The English say that the Messrs. Stirling Associated in working a caloric engine, as early as 1828. Mr. Le Moine, a Frenchman, claims the merit of having invented the wire-gauze part of the new motor.

Wm. Echols, Jr., Esq., has received the appointment from Governor Collier of Probate Judge of Madison county, in place of the late Capt. J.W. Otey, and has entered upon the discharge of the duties of the office.

John Boston, Esq. has been appointed Collector of Savannah.

Chevalier Wikoff has been liberated from prison at Genoa, where he was confined on a charge of attempting to force a young and wealthy English lady to marry him. He has since made his appearance in Paris. His adventures and trials have made quite a hero of him. It is rumored that the Chevalier has written a history of his courtship, in the course of which he makes all sorts of revelations.

John H. Campbell has been confirmed as a Judge of the Supreme Court of the United States, and Dudley Mann as Assistant Secretary of State.

Mr. DeBow discharged one hundred of the Census clerks on Monday.

At the late meeting of the Maryland State Agricultural Society, Messrs. C.B. Calvert, President, John Merryman, Jr., Vice-president for Baltimore county, and C.P. Holcomb, Vice-president for Delaware, were appointed a delegation to represent the State of Maryland in the Convention of Southern Planters, to be held in Montgomery on the first Monday in May.

We learn that the celebrated Irish patriot, Thos. F. Meagher, arrived in Montgomery on his way to New Orleans. He is one who has won a deserve reputation everywhere, as an unostentatious but able and true man and honest patriot, and a most eloquent advocate for the wrongs of his countrymen.

Joseph Mallet, a Frenchman, died in Providence, R.I., of hydrophobia, week before last. He was bitten on Sunday and died on the succeeding Wednesday, in all the horrors of mania.

Resolutions have been introduced into the Massachusetts Legislature, expressing "deep regret and abhorrence at the conduct of the Grand Duke of Tuscany, in cruelly imprisoning Francesco and Rosa Madiai for reading the scriptures." The resolution was referred to a joint special committee.

It is said that a son of Senator Soule will be appointed Secretary of Legation at Paris.

Lynch Law on the Bigbee. - We heard of a somewhat curious and prompt application of the jurisdiction of Judge Lynch to one of the passengers - ' a crab' - on the Bigbee river last week. It seems that on the passage up the river, a gentleman from the interior, well-known in the state, was lite in his birth chewing the end of some pleasant memories of the Theater, Eutaw House, and George Williams Oyster Saloon, when suddenly some one entered his room, and commenced about his person, running his hand over and under his body, and finally inserting it under his head. He gentleman said nothing until he had rummaged pretty well around his head and pillow, when thinking it time to act he reached out his hand and seized the fellow by the wrist. The rascal struggled violently, but it was of no use; he was in the grasp of a powerful man, standing six feet two inches in his stockings, and soon with the aid of a watchman, he was tied and locked up in a state-room until morning. When morning came the affair was made known to the passengers, and a jury at once empanelled and sworn, and a judge selected on the spot for his trial. The gentleman who caught him appeared in his defense, but he was not so successful in his defense as in his apprehension. The jury found him guilty and sentenced him to be taken ashore at the first woodyard and whipped by two "buck " negroes until the negroes were satisfied. The sentence was carried out before they reached Demopolis, and the negroes laid on the blows in good earnest, much to the satisfaction of the bystanders, and it would seem, to the satisfaction of the culprit himself, for he preferred this to the penitentiary. - *Evening News*

The Columbus Argus says Mr. W. Dodds, of Carrol county, offers to bet from $100 to $1000, that he has a negro man and woman that can pick more cotton in one day, than any other two field hands in the United States. The race may take place any time between this and next Christmas. Full particulars can be obtained from the editor of the Carrolton Democrat, by those who are disposed to sport on Mr. Dodd's proposition.

The State of Alabama, Autauga County, Special Court of Probate, March 21, 1853
This day came Robert J. Glenn, guardian of William R. Bugg, a minor, and filed his accounts and vouchers for the final settlement of his said guardianship, which was examined and ordered to be filed for the inspection of all concerned. It is therefore ordered, that notice be given for forty days, by publication for three successive weeks in the Autauga Citizen, notifying all persons interested to be and appear at a Court to be held on the third day of May next, to show cause why said account should not be stated and allowed. Henly Brown, Judge of Probate

The State of Alabama, Autauga County, Special Court of Probate - March 21, 1853
This day came Joel Zeigler, executor of William Zeigler, deceased, and filed his account and vouchers for the annual settlement of said estate; which was examined and ordered to be filed for the inspection of all concerned. It is therefore ordered, that notice be given for forty days, by publication for three successive weeks in the Autauga Citizen, notifying all persons interested to be and appear at a Probate Court to be held on the third day of May next, to show cause why said account should not be stated and allowed.
Henly Brown, Judge of Probate

The State of Alabama, Autauga County, Special Court of Probate - March 16, 1853
This day came Ann L. McNeil, formerly Ann L. Whetstone, administratrix of Wm. A. Whetstone, deceased, and filed her account and vouchers for the final settlement of the said estate; which were examined and ordered to be filed for the inspection of all concerned. It is therefore ordered by the court, that the 29th day of April next (1853) be set for a hearing of said account, and that notice be given for forty days notice, by publication for three successive weeks in the Autauga Citizen, notifying all persons interested to be and appear at a Probate Corut, on said day, to show cause why said account should not be stated and allowed.
Henly Brown, Judge of Probate

Vol. 1, Thursday, April 7, 1853, No. 10

The Louisville Ky., Courier, of the 19th ult., says: " Capt. Frank Johnson, of the Sam Dale, of Alabama river, has contracted for a caloric engine, to be used in California. "

Steamboat Explosion. - We have received an Extra of the Galveston News, sent us by a friend, which gives the details of an awful steamboat explosion, which occurred on the 23d ult.. It appears that the steamboat Farmer, Captain E. Webb, while on her way from Houston to Galveston, exploded her boilers, when within about eight miles of the latter city. She was racing at the time with the steamer Neptune, and after having run close with the last named steamer for some sixty or seventy miles, she all at once passed her with the speed of lightning, and after getting the distance of one hundred and fifty or two hundred yards ahead of the Neptune, her boilers exploded with a tremendous shock, all three boilers exploding at the same instant, shivering the boat, with the exception of the ladies cabin, into atoms. One of the engines was blown to the distance of sixty or seventy yards from the boat. Of sixty-five persons on board, about forty were killed, and several are missing. Among the latter is the Captain and second Clerk, with whom we were acquainted, besides several others who chanced to be on the ill-fated boat.

Spiritual Rapping. - We have heard and read much about the Spiritual Rappers, but must confess we never put much faith in such things, nor do we now, although none have, as yet, discovered the secret of the modus operandi, or enlightened us as to how these rappings are produced. There is something very strange about the whole affair, and almost persuades one to have faith and believe, when such men as Gov. Talmadge, General Thompson, Judge Edmonds, and others, are so deeply impressed with the exhibitions. But we shall await further developments before we can consent to become one of the disciples of Mrs. Fox, or any other medium. The following is an extract of a Washington letter from Mr. Perry to the Southern (S.C) Patriot. Mr. Perry is considered a worthy gentleman, and has considerable eminence before the public. He is now one of the counsel of Dr. Gardiner, whose trial is proceeding at Washington. If he had no claim to respect, one might be disposed to laugh at the curious statements of this extract. He says: Last night I went, in company with General Thompson and Mr. Colcock, to Gov. Talmadge's room, to see and hear the wonders of spiritual rappings, writing mediums, and speaking mediums. Mr. Atchison, President of the Senate, Mr. Jennifer, former Minister to Austria, and Gov. Hamilton, were there also for the same purpose. Gov. Talmadge has been a Senator from New York, and Governor of Wisconsin. He is a gentleman of high character, great acquirements and talents. He was intimate with Mr. Calhoun whilst in the Senate. He is a good looking gentleman, with a large head, full face, stout person, and about the ordinary height. He was distinguish for good practical hard sense and great labor and investigation. So much for the Governor's character. Now for his narrative and experience in the occult sciences and spirit rappings. I will give it as he gave it to me and the other gentleman above named. Remember who they were listening to these astounding revelations. The President of the U.S. Senate, and ex-Governor of South Carolina, an ex-Minister to Mexico, a member of Congress and my humble self. The narrator was no old woman, or juggler or mountebank, but a Governor and Senator. Gov. Talmadge said he had heard of these spiritual rappings, and laughed at them as everybody else did for a great while. One day he saw it stated in the New York Herald that Judge Edmonds was a believer, and assisting in experiments. This startled him. - He knew Judge Edmonds to be one of the purest, best and most able men he had ever been associated with. If such a man could be imposed on, he desired to see the impostor. Consequently he went to Mrs. Fish's, in New York. There were four or five persons in the room. He knew none of them, and none of them knew him. Whilst seated at the table, a spirit rapped and said, "My old friend, I wish to communicate with you - I am J.C. Calhoun!" The company said, " is there any one amongst us who knew Mr. Calhoun?" Gov. Talmadge replied he did. The spirit was then asked if the message was to him, and the response was, " Yes. " Gov. Talmadge then asked Mr. Calhoun if he still believe in nullification an secession. He said, " Yes. " (Here Governor Hamilton remarked to us in an under tone, "I am glad Calhoun sticks to his principles in the world of spirits. ") " But," said Mr. Calhoun, "my notions of public policy have undergone some change." From this Gov. Talmadge became a constant visitor to Mrs. Fish, and has a volume of manuscripts which he read to us, containing communications of the most extraordinary character from Calhoun, Webster, and others. These manuscripts the Governor intends publishing. Next, the Governor informed us of his going to a speaking medium - a woman - ignorant and uneducated; who possessed the power of withdrawing her own spirit from her body, and permitting her clay tenement to be occupied by Calhoun, Webster, Gov. Talmadges' mother, uncle and others. The first communication he received from this source, was from his mother. She spoke fifteen or twenty minutes, and her communication was taken down in shorthand by Judge Edmonds, and this also was read to us. In the same way, and through the same medium of this old woman, Mr. Calhoun addressed Gov. Talmadge, and Judge Edmonds took down his speech, which was also read to us. Mr. Calhoun commenced by saying "This is a novel position for me to occupy." (the body of an old woman) and I thought so, too. Whilst speaking, this lady had all the manner and gesture of Mr. Calhoun, with his philosophical condensation of thought. My impression was that the language was entirely too figurative. Hamilton remarked, that he was now speaking from the world of spirits, which might very naturally affect his style, and imbue with imagery, &c. Lastly, Gov. Talmadge told us of the writing medium - a young man who holds a pen in his hand in any sort of way, and the spirit of Calhoun, or some other spirit, will guide the pen and make it write, with the rapidity of lightning, the most eloquent and profound discourses. These discourses were read to us, and the handwriting shown to us. Gov. Talmadge also informed us that he said on one occasion he wished some physical sign given him of the presence of Mr. Calhoun; whereupon the spirit told him to get on the table, and it should rise up. He did so, and the table rose up and jolted him about pretty severely. He was then told to put paper and pencil under the table, and Mr. Calhoun wrote on the paper, "I am with you." His writing was shown to us, and both Gen. Hamilton and Thompson said they would swear to the handwriting. I would say it looked exactly like Mr. Calhoun's writing, but I should not like to swear it was written by Calhoun.

Samuel R. Potter, of Wilmington, N.C., has lost, in the course of a few weeks, ten valuable slaves at Point Peter, by a disease resembling pneumonia. They were taken sick in succession, and died after a brief illness. The negroes were hearty and healthy up to the contracting of the disease which hurried them off. Near Weldon, Mrs. A. Powel, her son-in-law, Mr. Walker, and a Mr. Walker, all residing in the same house, died within two days of each other, of the same illness.

Texas Correspondence. - Washington, Texas, March 18, 1853
Messrs Howell & Luckett: I have been requested by several friends to write back when I arrived in Texas, and it being tedious to write to each one separately, I propose addressing them through the columns of your valuable paper. I arrived at Washington on the 26th of December, being forty-six days from the time I left Autauga county. I have had but little time, as yet, to see the country. The lands on the Brazos river are very rich and productive. I learn at the cotton crop of last year averaged, on upland, 2000 pounds per acre, and river lands from one to two bales, and everything else in proportion. But it is unnecessary to

mention anything else, as cotton is the great item. Land sells very high in this county - in fact, there is very little sold for less than five to fifteen dollars per acre - that is, when it is improved - unimproved sells from three to sixteen dollars per acre. But it is said to be higher in this section than in any other part of the State. This is an old settled county, and the lands are owned, principally, by old feathers settlers, who have become, if I may so speak, wedded to Washington county, and who do not care to sell out, unless they can get a good price. Thus it is that land is rated so high - and moreover, it is increasing in value every year, and if the rapid tide of emigration continues, it will not be many years before the whole State will become densely populated, which will, as a natural consequence, make land as dear as it is in the older States. But at present there is plenty of good land, which can be bought at from fifty cents to $2,00 per acre. With regard to society I find as could here as I have any where. There are plenty of schools, and churches of all denominations - therefore, a man need not think, if he emigrates to Texas, that he will get into an entire wilderness. But I do not pretend to say it is the case over the whole State - for, I doubt not, there are many places where it is as dark as the ace of spades. I have found quite a number of Alabamians in this State. I was told, on my way here, by a man who kept a bridge, and also a record of all the emigrants' names, that there were more from Alabama this season than all the other States together. I would advise emigrants, by all means, to come by land. It is by far the cheapest and safest route. I have tried it, and can speak advisedly. My expenses, during the journey, amounted, in the aggregate, to $1,14, while other families, no larger than mine, who came by water, have paid out five times that amount. Besides, those coming by land will have their wagons and teams when they get here, which, by the way, cannot be procured on very reasonable terms in this country. Those who contemplate emigrating next fall, should begin to prepare in time to start by the first of October. You should be supplied with good wagons and teams, for it is not worth while to store with an old wagon and broken down horses, for they will not hold out - neither is it necessary to bring much furniture, &c. as it is better to sell out at a reduced price, before leaving home, than to be troubled with it. You should, by all means, have good oxen along. No one knows, but those who have tried them, how they can travel. By feeding them well on corn, and driving them a little faster every day, you may finally get them to walking as fast as horses, and should you get stuck in the mud, your oxen will be sure to pull you out. A few words to Mechanics - nearly every branch of mechanism is profitable. There is a great demand for work, but few workmen, consequently, mechanics' wages are twice as high as they are in Alabama. A good Tinner, I think, could do well in this country, as there is plenty of milk and butter, and, of course, there is a great demand for tin ware. In short, Tinners, Blacksmiths, Carpenters, Millwrights and Wheelwrights can make their fortunes here in a little less than no time. Provisions are tolerably cheap. There was an abundant corn crop made last year, in consequence of which, corn is cheaper than it has never been known before, and is now selling at 25 cents per bushel. Pork is worth 5 cents per pound. In consequence of the short crop of corn year before last, hogs have begun very scarce, therefore, pork is higher than it has ever been known before. But I am confident it will not sell for more than 3 cents next winter. Adieu for the present, Yours &c, Thos. A. Wilson

A notorious pickpocket named Bob Sutton, sixty years old, at present confined in the Auburn, New York, State prison, where he was sentenced for five years, for robbery, received a letter from England, a few days since, stating that by the death of a relative in England, he is heir to property valued at over ninety thousand dollars.

Editorial Brevities. - The long mooted question whether stealing an umbrella is larceny, is about to be tested in the Court of General Sessions, in New York, the grand jury having found a bill of indictment against Henry Bell, charging him with having taken away, with felonious intent, a cotton umbrella valued at 87 cents, the property of Wm. Wood, against the "peace and dignity" of the State of New York. The final decision in this case will no doubt be looked for with interest by every owner of a "cotton umbrella".

We are authorized, says the Union, to announce the story of the altercation between the Postmaster General and Senator Hunter, published in the New York Tribune a few days since, to be a sheer fabrication from beginning to end. Those who know the courtesy and dignity of Mr. Hunter's character will need no assurance that he is incapable of uttering the low language attributed to him by the irresponsible correspondent of the Tribune. The scandalous story is an utter falsehood.

The Vice-president. - A telegraphic dispatch from Baltimore to the Charleston Courier, dated March 29, says that advices from Havana state that Mr. King proposes to sail for Mobile on the 1st of April, as he has a horror of dieing in a foreign land, and entertains hope of his recovery.

The Whigs of Mississippi talk of running Col. Joseph B. Cobb, of Lowndes county, for Governor of that State.

Col. Meyer Jacobs, Surveyor of the Port of Charleston, S.C., and John I. Martin, Esq., of South Carolina, Secretary of Legation at Peru. Brown, Collector at Philadelphia, and Miller, Postmaster of that city. Joseph Sierri, Collector at Pensacola, William Gillespie, Receiver at Jackson, Mississippi, and Samuel D. Davis, United States Attorney for Texas.

Died: At his residence, in this county, March 26th, 1853, Mr. Joel Floyd, in the 71st year of his age. Mr. Floyd was an old resident of this county, an was much respected and beloved by all who knew him. His death has cast a gloom over the community in which he lived, and has left a family and many friends and acquaintances to mourn his irreparable loss. He was a strict and pious member of the Methodist church, having embraced religion many years ago, and died trusting in Him who rules our destinies. Peace be to his ashes.

List of Letters. Remaining in the post office at Prattville for the quarter ending March 31, 1853:
Mrs. Baynton, Flemming Bates, James Brittum, Joseph Bowles, Mrs. Stephen Brown, Ira Britt, F.T. Camp, Miss Jane Copread, Gillum Carpenter, J.S. Dickerson, Ben Duran, Caroline Heath, Mrs. Adelia J. Johnson, Mike Leonard, Thos. P. Morgan, Thos. L. Picket, Easter Pike, William Reynolds, James Runadel, J.S. Reese, Mrs. Smith, George M. Smith, C.P. Shasler, Richard Skugs, H.S. Smith, John Thomas, Jemima Thacker, William Thomas, Penina Vick, L. Walker, Margaret L. Wilkins, William Willis, Aaron Williams, J.M. Willson, John A. Whetstone, Geo P. Willcox. Persons calling for the above letters will please say they are advertised. S. Mims, P.M. per Jas. Allen, Dep'y.

Father Gavand, the Italian orator, made a speech on religious matters in the Tabernacle, New York, on Wednesday evening the 30th ult., to a crowded house. Some of the papers allege that his remarks were very intemperate, and calculated to create discord. He declares himself crusader for the freedom of Italy, and an enemy of Austria and the Pope.

Jack Stevens, the fugitive robber of the Portsmouth (Va) Bank was re-arrested at Philadelphia on Saturday, the 20th ult.. Before he was taken he shot officer Markie through the hand with a revolver.

The State of Alabama, Autauga County, Special Court of Probate - March 17, 1853
This day came John K. Terry, late sheriff and ex officio administrator with the will annexed of Jeremiah Smith, deceased, and filed his account and vouchers for the final settlement of his administration of the said estate of said deceased; which was examined and ordered to be filed for the inspection of all concerned. It is therefore ordered, that notice be given for forty days, by publication for three successive weeks in the Autauga Citizen, notifying all persons interested to be and appear at a Probate Court to be held on the 3d day of May next (1853), to show cause, if any, why said account should not be stated and allowed.
Henly Brown, Judge of Probate

Vol. 1, Thursday, April 14, 1853, No. 11

Convicts Escaped. - Much excitement was created in our quiet town on yesterday, by the presence of some seven or eight convicts in our neighborhood, who made their escape from the penitentiary on Monday night last. We learn they had stolen some clothes and provisions from a plantation below here, and, doubtless, will again try their hands at the same game, if not soon apprehended. It is to be hoped the rascals may be caught before committing any more of their felonious acts. Just as we are going to press, we learn that one of the convicts was arrested, near town, by our townsman, Mr. E.S. Morgan, and is now in chains, under a strong guard, and will, doubtless, soon be in his old quarters.

A friend has kindly furnished us with the results of the elections held in this place, for the purpose of electing two Justices of the Peace. An election took place on the first Saturday in last month, when the vote stood: For John C. Reid 95, For L. Spigener 85, For J.T. DeJarnette 76. The gentlemen elected, however, having neglected to file their official bonds within the time prescribed by the New Code, another election was held on the 9th inst., which resulted as follows; For John C. Reid 96, For L. Spigener 85, For J.T. DeJarnette 76. John C. Reid, Esq., and Col. L. Spigener, it will be perceived, are the two successful candidates - both of whom, we doubt not, will give general satisfaction.

The election for Judges of the Supreme Court of Louisiana took place, throughout the State, on Monday the 4th. Sufficient returns have been received to indicate the choice of the following persons: Chief Justice, Thomas Slidell; Associate Justices, A.M. Buchanan, Miles Taylor, C. Vorrhies and W. Dunbar. The election turned, to a great extent, on political preferences, and the successful candidates are all Democrats.

Mr. Marcy, Secretary of State, has decided to demand an explanation from the British government, in relation to the recent Honduras affair, and the Secretary of the Navy has been instructed to report what effective forces he has at his disposal for active operations.

Editorial Brevities.
A beautiful badge of solid gold has been manufactured at Boston, which is to be presented to Gen. Pierce. It has on it the deal and devices of the Cincinnati Society.

Mr. James Campbell, Postmaster General, is a son-in-law of Mr. Chapron, a highly respectable planter, residing near Arcola, in Marengo county, in this state, and is conservative and orthodox upon all the great questions that have agitated the country. Instead of being thirty, he is now about forty-two years of age.

The Herald, published at Montevallo, Shelby county, says Capt. Stewart George is now busily engaged, six miles from that place, near the Railroad, in getting our spars for the French Government.

The Senate have confirmed Ex-Senator Sturgeon as Treasurer of the Mint at Philadelphia, and Edmund Wright as Collector at Edenton, N.C.

Santa Anna Elected President. - Advices have been received at New Orleans from Mexico to the 10th ult, from which we learn that Gen. Santa Anna has been elected President of that Republic.

Tragic Occurrence. - We learn that F. Kapp, of Demopolis, Ala., jumped overboard a few weeks since, while on one of the lake boats, running from Mobile to New Orleans, and was drowned. His life was an eventful one. He came from Haggerstown, Maryland, about 1841, to Demopolis, where he settled, without means. The Whigs of the place finding him a practical printer, and an intelligent man, bought him a printing press, and he commenced the publication of the Marengo Patriot there, which he published until 1850, amassing with it a fortune of 15 or $16,000. His wife, a very intelligent lady, much beloved by all who knew her, and to whom he was much devoted, became insane, in 1849, we believe, and while on her way to her relatives in Maryland, in the charge of her brother, she jumped overboard from one of the Mobile and New Orleans boats, and was drowned. After this event, Kapp appeared to live for no purpose. He became dissipated, married a dissolute woman, and squandered the property he had labored so earnestly to amass, and now ends his tragic life near the spot his wife was lost, and they both now rest in a watery grave. He leaves two sons, both printers. Columbus Argus

A Model Cock Fight. - John Leonard, an Engineer on one of our Lake Steamers, was great on a cock-fight. He kept a well-trained rooster, and fought him at every port between Buffalo and Chicago. Hearing of a crack bird of the pit at Windsor, John went with a half dozen friends, to see it and rejoice with them over the anticipated sudden demise of John Crapau's celebrated game stock; the birds were let loose, and at the first blow of the little Frenchman's bantam, John's bird was numbered with the things that had been - he was dead. Greatly mortified and astonished was John, he left the field crest-fallen, amid the laughter of his compeers. "Egad," said the engineer, " I'll try him again." On his first trip to Buffalo, John bought a full grown eagle, cut his feathers into shape, twisted up his tail rooster-fashion, fastened a cock's comb on his crown, and otherwise metamorphosing him into a game-cock, brought him up to this city, again rallied his friends, put his bird into a bag, and over they went for another fight. Parlezvous brought out his bird again, certain of success, and placed him ready for action. The engineer took him out of the bag - they slowly approached each other - the bantam stooping and picking, as he advanced to the assault, while the engineer's walked boldly on, with his head erect, beak open, and an eye of fire that never blanches in the midday sun; the bird of Jove seized the gallant bantam, and with beak and claws, tore him to pieces, and ate him up, to the utter astonishment of the crowd. The little Frenchman danced all sorts of figures and cried out - "Sacre ventre blew, me nevaire see one roostaire like dat, he eat him up mon bon chicken. Vat one crooket nose your sacre dam Yakee roostaire's got; I fight no more wid de Yanke recostaire." Ever more since that, John has been considered the Santa Anna of the cock-pit in the west. - Detroit Free Press.

Administrators' Notice. Letters of Administration having been granted to the undersigned on the estate of John S. Robinson, deceased, on the 3d day of March, by the Hon. Henly Brown, Judge of Probate of Autauga county. All persons having claims against said estate will present them within the time prescribed by law, or they will be barred. Raymond Robinson.

Administrators' Sale. Will be sold on Thursday, the 19th day of May next under an order of sale from the Probate Court, at the late residence of John S. Robinson, deceased, all the perishable property belonging to the estate on said deceased, consisting of horses, mules, cattle, hogs, sheep, goats, corn and house and kitchen furniture. Raymond Robinson

Notice. Will be sold on Tuesday, the 24th day of May next, at my residence, under an order of the Probate Court, the perishable property, and house and kitchen furniture, belonging to the estate of Margaret A. Drummond, deceased. Raymond Robinson

Vol. 1, Thursday, April 21, 1853, No. 12

A report has gone abroad, to the effect, that there are several cases of Small Pox now in Prattville, brought here by persons from Columbus. It is strange, indeed, how such reports can be manufactured out of nothing and from no other motive, we believe, but to create a little excitement. We are authorized, by Dr. Samuel P. Smith, to state that there is not one single case of Small Pox in Prattville or its neighborhood, nor has there been, or likely to be. Therefore, those of our country friends wishing to visit our town need not be apprehensive of any danger, as we can assure them there is not a case of the disease in the place.

At the term of the Circuit Court of this county, which adjourned last Saturday, Mr. —— Carroll was convicted of murder in the second degree, in shooting his overseer, whose name we do not just now remember, and sentenced to the penitentiary for the term of ten years. It was thought by many that, from the circumstances connected with the killing, Mr. Carroll would be acquitted. He was ably defended by Mr. Yancey and Mr. Harris, but their eloquent appeals were made in vain. Mr. C. is quite an old man, on account of which, doubtless, his friends will endeavor to procure the intercession of the Governor in his behalf.

Death of Vice President King. - We learn, from a telegraphic dispatch to the Alabama Journal, dated Cahaba, April 19, that the Hon. William R. King died at his residence, six miles from that place, on Tuesday evening last, at six o'clock. His burial took place on yesterday morning at eleven o'clock. He came up from Mobile on the Cuba two days previous, and arrived in season to "die among his kindred." The universal estimation, says the Journal, in which Col. King was held in his civic qualities, as an upright gentleman, and true patriot, makes his decease a national, as well as State loss, though the event has long been deemed inevitable by his friends. Col. King was a veteran politician, and a gentleman of the old school of Statesman, and has been continuously in the service of the Republic in various capacities. From his early youth, all these duties, in all the various grades and relations, he discharged uniformly, creditably to himself, and faithfully to the country. During all this long service, there has been no blot on his political reputation or personal honor; he has passed through the fierce and dark storms of a political half century, without even the "smell of fire on his garments," and has gone to his rest without a soil or reproach on his memory. We can speak this freely, for though always opposed to him in party sentiment, we could not avoid a just respect for the purity and patriotism of the man. Though not, perhaps, brilliant, he was better - sensible, honest, never running into utraism, but in the contests between the State and federal government, so necessary to the preservation of the constitution, the rights of the States and the Republic. Col. King was born in 1786, in North Carolina, and educated at the University of that State. He studied and practised law, and in 1806, at the age of 20 years, was elected to the Legislature from the county of Sampson, in that State. He was re-elected the next canvass, and elected by that body Solicitor. In 1810, he was elected member of Congress from the Wilmington District, and did good service during the "war session." In 1819, he resigned his seat, having been appointed Secretary of Legation to Wm. Pinckney, Minister Plenipotentiary to the Courts of Naples and St. Petersburg. After remaining and traveling in Europe two years, he returned to North Carolina, and removed to the new territory of Alabama, Dallas county, in 1818. He was, in a few months after his arrival, elected as a member of the Convention "to establish a State government," and was by that body appointed a member of the committee which drafted the State Constitution. While traveling in Georgia, from N. Carolina, where he had gone for the purpose of removing his property to Alabama, he received notice of his appointment as one of the Senators of the State, and repaired to Washington. He was again elected in 1823, '28, '34, and '40, as

Senator. In 1844, Col. King was appointed Minister to France, the duties of which office were performed creditably. He resigned and returned in '46 and '48 was defeated by Dixon H. Lewis for a seat in the Senate, but in a few months afterwards was appointed to the seat vacated by the resignation of A.P Bagby. At the next session of the Legislature was elected for the full term. During his long continuance in the Senate, Col. King was often elected presiding officer, and was ex-officio Vice-President of the United States, which position he held at the time of his election. The history of this long and honorable career in the public service, was compiled from various documents before us, which can be relied on as authentic.

Sentenced to the Penitentiary. - At the term of the Circuit Court of Tuscaloosa county, closed last week, Jacob Jackson, indicted for the murder of Philander Fletcher, was found guilty of manslaughter, and sentenced to ten years' imprisonment. Robert Russell, recently of St. Clair county, for slave stealing, was sentenced for a like term. John Sceitz of Mobile, for assault with intent to murder his mother-in-law, was sentenced for two years.

Whig Meeting at Kingston. - At a meeting of the Whigs of Autauga County held at Kingston on Wednesday the 13th day of April, 1853, Dr. J.D. Moodie was called to the chair, and Wm. N. Thompson, Jr. requested to act as Secretary. The object of the meeting having been explained by the chairman, and on motion of Gen. E. Shackelford, it was ordered that the chairman appoint three committees of five persons each - the first to attend the Convention to be holden at Montgomery for the nomination of Governor. The second to attend a Convention for the nomination of a member to Congress from this district, and the third to attend the Convention to nominate a candidate for the State Senate. Whereupon, the Chairman appointed on the first committee, Jesse R. Jones, Esq., John C. Reid, Esq., Gen. Edmund Shackelford, Caleb Moncreif and Daniel N. Smith. On the second committee, Thos. Smith, Sr., W.G.M. Golson, Jacob Murph, Henry S. McNeil and Wm. Caver. On the third committee, Jacob H. Golson, John Lamar, Dr. Samuel P. Smith, Arthur P. Love and James S. Bullard. On motion of J.C. Reid, Esq., it was carried that if a vacancy occur in any of the committees a majority of the same have power to fill it. On motion of Gen. Shackelford, the Chairman and Secretary were added to the first committee. On motion of Daniel N. Smith, that the proceedings of this meeting to be published in the Autauga Citizen, and that the Whig papers in the district be requested to copy. On motion of Dr. S.P. Smith, the meeting adjourned.

Democratic Meeting. - At a large and highly respectable meeting of the Democratic party of Autauga County, held on Thursday the 12th inst., at Kingston, on motion of Wm. H. Northington, Esq., Leonidas B. Howard, Esq., was called to the Chair, and Col. Joseph B. Wilkinson requested to act as Secretary. Gen. C.M. Jackson explained the object of the meeting, after which Malcom Smith, Esq., introduced the following resolutions, which were unanimously adopted:
Resolved, That we cordially approve of the proposition to hold a Democratic Convention in the city of Montgomery, on the first Monday, in May next, for the nomination of a candidate for Governor, and that this meeting appoint fifteen Delegates to the same.
Resolved, That whilst expressing our preference for the Hon. Albert J. Pickett as the Democratic standard bearer in the approaching gubernatorial contest, we distinctly disclaim any intention to dictate to our friends in other counties, but, on the contrary, declare our readiness to use all necessary efforts to procure harmony in the Democratic party - its success being dependent upon concert of action.
Resolved, That should the Convention in its wisdom select some individual other than the

first choice of a majority of this meeting, we will give a cordial support to the nominee - provided, always, that he be true to the South and the general principles of the Democratic party.

Resolved, That our delegates be instructed to co-operate with our friends from other portions of the States, in any legitimate plan having for its object the success of our principles, and the consequent triumph of our party, and to support any Democrat of known integrity, who will concentrate the greatest strength and procure most harmony and unanimity of sentiment in his behalf.

The following gentlemen were appointed Delegates: Gen. C.M. Jackson, Major A.S. Elmore, Hon. Wm. Graham; Malcom Smith; Joseph H. Hall; Jas. J. Barber; Thomas Nelson,; Lewis M. Whetstone; Dr. T.A. Davis; Dr. Joseph P. DeJarnette; Hon. Henly Brown; John Steele; Theodore Nunn; Major Benjamin Davis.

Maj. A.S. Elmore introduced the following resolutions which were adopted.

Resolved, That we cordially approve the course pursued by our late representative in Congress, the Hon. Sampson W. Harris, and that we respectfully recommend him to the Democracy of the District for re-election.

Resolved, That whilst we do not perceive the necessity for a Convention, if our party friends in other counties desire it, we will cheerfully agree to holding the same, at such time as may be generally indicated, and that we will be represented therein - it being expressly understood that our delegates be authorized to pursue such a course as, in their estimation, the good of the party may demand.

Resolved, that we would prefer that said Convention should meet, if at all, in Selma.

Resolved, That the Chairman appoint fifteen delegates to said Convention. William H. Northington, Esq.; Joseph S. Reese; Sydney McWhorter, Esq.; Maj. A.S. Elmore; Joseph Sandford; D.C. Jones; Dr. A.R. Hutchinson; Jas. T. DeJarnette, Sen. N.M. Howard; H.J. Stoudemier; A.W. McNeil; H.D. Holmes; L.B. Parker, and William Motley were appointed under the last resolution.

George L.F. Mason, Esq. offered the following preamble and resolutions, which were adopted. Whereas, it is desirable that the Democratic party of this Senatorial District should meet in Convention for the nomination of a candidate for State Senator:

Be it therefore Resolved, That this meeting recommend the holding of a Convention for the purpose indicated at the city of Montgomery, on the first Monday in June next, and that our party friends in Montgomery county be requested to co-operate with us.

Resolved, That fifteen delegates be appointed by the Chairman of this meeting to represent Autauga county in said Convention. - Whereupon the following gentlemen were appointed: G.L.F. Mason, Esq.; A.C. Baker; Evans Pressly; John Carpenter; Col. L. Spigener; James T. DeJarnette, Jr.; James J. Barber; D.C. Jones; Thomas Nelson; Joseph Sanford; J.M. Gordon; James A. Lawler; John R. Mcbryde; John Pool; Wm. Nunn; James Benford; Wm. T. Hale; Dr. John Wood; T.J. Motley and Jno P DeJarnete, Esq.

On motion of Gen. C.M. Jackson, the Chairman and Secretary of the meeting were added to the respective delegations.

It was further Resolved, That the proceedings of this meeting be published in the Autauga Citizen, and that the Democratic papers throughout the State be requested to copy that portion relation to the nomination of a candidate for Governor, and that papers in the District publish the other proceedings. The meeting then adjourned. Leonidas B. Howard, Ch'n. Joseph B. Wilkinson, Sec'y.

Editorial Brevities.

Gov. Collier has appointed The Rev. Benjamin Lloyd to fill the vacancy in the Board of Inspectors of the Penitentiary, caused by the resignation of John Hardy.

It is stated, in knowing circles, that the Hon. P. Soule, Minister to Spain, has been vested with unrestricted powers to negotiate with Spain for the purchase of Cuba.

Mr. Sanford, editor of the Mobile Register, has been appointed Collector at Mobile. - Thomas Walsh, Postmaster at Montgomery.

C.M. Clay. - Cassius M. Clay, Esq., has published a communication in the Cincinnati Enquirer in which he is said to be severely up on ex-Secretary Corwin, for some remarks alleged to have been made by him, at a party in Washington, not very complimentary to the abolitionists.

There was a re-union of about one hundred original friends of Henry Clay on Tuesday evening, the 12th inst., at the Irving House, in New York city, where they partook of a dinner. The flags were displayed throughout the city in honor of the day.

The Washington papers of the 6th inst., notices the presentation, with appropriate ceremonies, of the block of Marble from the Free Swiss Confederation, to the Washington Monument. The address for the Swiss Confederation was made by Mr. L'Muller, and responded to by Walter Lenox, Esq.

Parker Perry, charged with the murder of his wife, was found guilty at Raleigh, N.C., on Monday, the 11th inst.

A sort of a general fracas took place at Vienna, in this county, on the 2d inst.; says the Huntsville Advocate, during which a man named Lafayette Robertson was killed by Simon N. Turner, and another - Noah Hanna - dangerously stabbed. Turner was bound over to court in the sum of $3,000.

John R. Tucker, whig, was re-elected Mayor on Monday, the 11th inst., of Trenton, N.J. There was very little excitement, and a small vote.

Mr. Pulszky, Kossuth's private secretary, has been in Washington for the last few days past. The telegraph reports that he has been dining with the President, and having private interviews with the Secretary of State.

Fletcher Webster's House, at Marshfield, Mass., was struck by lightning on the 5th inst. The interior was somewhat shattered, but the wife of Mr. W., who was in the house at the time, escaped uninjured.

Mr. Rives, the United States Minister in France, has tendered his resignation to General Pierce.

Married - In Galesville, N.Y., March 17th, 1853, by Rev. J.P. Mason, Hart Philips to Mrs. Lucinda L.M. Patterson, all of Galesville.

Notice. Letters of Administration was this day granted to the undersigned by the Honorable Judge of Probate in and for the State of Alabama and the county of Autauga, on the estate of Robert L. Scott, deceased. All persons having demands against the said estate will present them within the time prescribed by law, or they will be barred. Albert Elmore.

The State of Alabama, Autauga County, Special Court of Probate, April 2, 1853
Ordered, that notice be given to the creditors of Wm. Kemp, deceased, by publication in the Autauga Citizen, a newspaper published at Prattville, once a week for six successive weeks, that the estate of the said Wm. Kemp has this day been declared insolvent; and that the 28th day of May next has been appointed for the settlement of the accounts of Hugh Jones and Gabriel Ray, administrators. Witness - Henly Brown, Judge of Probate of said county. Henly Brown Judge of Probate

The State of Alabama, Autauga County, Special Court of Probate, April 11, 1853
This day came J.B. Wilkinson, guardian of E.A. Taylor, a minor, and filed his accounts and vouchers for the annual settlement of his said guardianship, which was examined and ordered to be filed for the inspection of all concerned. It is therefore ordered, that notice be given for forty days, by publication for three successive weeks in the Autauga Citizen, notifying all persons interested to be and appear at a Court to be held on the 6th day of June next, to show cause why said account should not be stated and allowed and said settlement be made. Henly Brown, Judge of Probate

The State of Alabama, Autauga County, Special Court of Probate, April 16, 1853
This day came A.C. Taylor, guardian of John F. Taylor, a minor, and filed his account and vouchers for the annual settlement of said ward's estate, which was examined and ordered to be filed for the inspection of all concerned. It is therefore ordered, that notice be given for forty days, by publication for three successive weeks in the Autauga Citizen, notifying all persons interested to be and appear at a Probate Court to be held on the 6th day of June next, to show cause why said account should not be stated and allowed. Henly Brown, Judge of Probate

Administrators' Notice. Letters of Administration having been granted to the undersigned on the estate of John S. Robinson, deceased, on the 3d day of March, by the Hon. Henly Brown, Judge of Probate of Autauga county. All persons having claims against said estate will present them within the time prescribed by law, or they will be barred. Raymond Robinson

Administrator's Sale. Will be sold on Thursday, the 19th day of May next, under an order of sale from Probate Court, at the late residence of John S. Robinson, deceased, all the perishable property belonging to the estate of said deceased, consisting of horses, mules, cattle, hogs, sheep, goats, corn and house and kitchen furniture. Raymond Robinson

Vol. 1, Thursday, April 28, 1853, No. 13

The Washington Monument. - Stirring appeals are now being made to the American people, in behalf of the Washington National monument, which is now in process of erection in memory of the "Father of his Country", George Washington. It is painful to contemplate the reluctance which has been manifested by the people of a great nation, in contributing to the erection of a monument in honor of the memory of one who shared in the toils and hardships of warfare, and surmounted difficulties and obstacles unknown in the annuls of a nation's history, for the achievement of our liberty. Is it possible the American people can forget, so soon, the services rendered country in its darkest days! - is it even probable we shall permit the name of Washington, who rescued us from the tyrants yoke, to sink into oblivion? We answer no, as every native born American should do, in whose bosom lies hidden one spark of patriotism. But it cannot be concealed that the American people have reluctantly, and with the greatest indifference, contributed to the erection of the monument - which fact, in the history of our republic, cannot fail to reflect last discredit on the gratitude and patriotism of its citizens, and prove to the world that republics are too apt to be forgetful of what is due to themselves, and to the memory of those, who, under Providence, have made them great, prosperous and happy. In Norway, a sufficient amount was voluntarily contributed, in two days, for the erection of a monument in honor of Charles the Twelfth, while in the republic of the United States, brought into existence by the valor, perseverance, energy and patriotism of Washington - in a nation which now contains a population of nearly twenty-five millions of souls, enjoying all the benefits of freedom and independence, and prosperity no where else to be found, has, after the most unceasing efforts for seventeen years, contributed only one-fifth of the amount required to complete a monument worthy of the men in whose honor it is now being erected. We think it the duty of all, both poor and rich, old and young, to contribute as much as will be in accordance with their means. Poor, indeed, must be the man who cannot spare, from his appointed daily earnings, one dollar for the completion of this noble undertaking - and parsimonious is he who refuses to do it. Every citizen in the United States should be proud of having it in their power to show the world the respect and admiration entertained by them for the "Father of his Country," by generously assisting, in the way of contributions, for the elevation of a suitable monument in honor of his memory - and they certainly should avail themselves of this opportunity. We feel confident there are many in Autauga county who will be glad to contribute as much as their means will permit, and also use their influence with others, which they should do, and demonstrate to other portions of the State the heart-felt gratitude entertained by the people of old Autauga for the defender of our glorious country - the immortal Washington. Messrs Wm. O. Ornsby, Amos Smith and Thos. W. Hutchinson, citizens of Prattville, have been appointed by the Secretary of the Washington National Monument, a committee for the collection of funds, to aid in the erection of the monument above mentioned. Those wishing to contribute can forward the money to the address of either of the above named gentlemen, at this place. Come, reader, do not delay one moment, but enclose two or three dollars, or as much as you can spare, and send it along. You may, perhaps, never have another such chance. You may rest assured so small amount will not break you - but if it should, trust to a kind Providence for more, and you will surely be provided for. We shall now ascertain if those who call themselves patriots, are patriots indeed!

Autauga Circuit Court, Spring Term, 1853. - The Grand Jurors sworn and charged to inquire for the body of Autauga County, in closing the labors of the present term, respectfully report to be Honorable Circuit Court, that, in pursuance of the Statute, they have examined the present jail of the county, and find the same in a very unsafe and dilapidated condition, and no inmate therein. The Jury has been informed that there is a new brick jail for said county now under course of erection. The Jury has also examined the offices and official bonds of the county officers, and find the bonds all to be good and sufficient, and the several offices appear to be kept in good order. The office of the County Treasurer the Jury has not been able to examine, as the same is kept, as the Jury are informed, some twenty-two miles from the Court House. - The jury would respectfully suggest the propriety of the said office being located at or near the court house of the county. The Jury would also present, that from the abundant evidence before them, some of the retail groceries, (or doggeries, as they are sometimes called) are a fruitful source of evil, a terror to the community where they are located, and calculated to demoralize the young men and youth of our county, to destroy the peace of society, to cause much mischief among our slaves - and are, therefore, a public nuisance. Yet the Jury take real pleasure in being able to report that they find the morale of the county generally in a very sound state. In taking leave of the Court, the Jury would return their thanks to his Honor Judge Cook for the very full and able manner in which he would express their gratification at the dignified course he has pursued while presiding at our Court. The body has every confidence in his fitness and qualifications for the office he now fills. Nor would the Jury omit to return their thanks to their most worthy Solicitor, Henry C. Lea. His attention, ability and courtesy has been marked and eminent. We request that the above report be published in the Autauga Citizen, and other papers of the State. Signed - A.C. Baker, Foreman; E.J. Zeigler, W.P. Williams, Alex Sample, Jas. M. Bradford, Boling Hall, John N. Golson, Jacob A. Murph, J.M. Gorgon, Murdock McQueen, John Steele, Peyton B. Smith, John M. Griffis, Jacob Griffis, Raymond Robinson.

Col. A.J. Pickett has refused to assent to be placed before the democratic state convention for the nomination for Governor. In his letter to the Montgomery Advertiser, communicating this fact, he says: For the last nine months, I have been engaged in the reparation of a literary work of considerable magnitude, embracing the history of the country from the river of Savannah to the river of the Rio Grande. As I progress with that work, I am, day by day, more convinced that I ought not to relinquish it. - For its successful completion, it is necessary that I should go to Europe. It is important that I should remain some time in Madrid, Rome and Paris. It is my intention to visit Europe in the early part of the ensuing year as a private American citizen, on my own means, relying upon what address I can command to be permitted to explore the colonial records which relate to this country. Alabama has much of her history locked up in the archives of France, Italy and Spain. While abroad, it shall all be embraced in the great work to which I have referred. When I return to Alabama, and after I shall have accomplished all for her that I can, if then my fellow countrymen choose to honor me with a distinguished position, it will be accepted. If on the other hand, they should determine that I am to remain in private life, I shall bow with respect to their decision.

Sheriff's Sale. - Will be sold for cash at the Court House door, in the town of Kingston, on the first Monday of June next, within the legal hours of sale, the following Real Estate, to wit: The south-west fourth of south-west fourth and south-east fourth of south-west fourth of section 33, township 19, range 16; and the north-east fourth of north-east fourth of section 5, township 18, range 16. Levied on as the property of John N. Cook, to satisfy two executions in my office from the Circuit Court of Autauga county, both in favor of James M. Cook and Cader Rogers, administrators, &c., and against John N. Cook, et. al. James A. Lawler, Shff, Autauga County

Gov. Seymour, to whom it is reported that a mission to Mexico has been tendered, is a gentleman of the highest character, and noblest impulses. He was educated at Partridge's Military Academy, at Middleton, Connecticut; appointed a Major in the Regiment of which

Ransom was Colonel, became Colonel when Ransom was killed at Churubusco; and on the conclusion of the war, was elected Governor of Connecticut. He is about forty-five years old, handsome, accomplished and gallant; and just the man to encounter Santa Anna.

Notice. Will be sold on Tuesday, the 24th day of May next, at my residence, under an order of the Probate Court, the perishables property, and house and kitchen furniture, belonging to the estate of Margaret A. Drummond, deceased. Raymond Robinson

Vol. 1, Thursday, May 5, 1853, No. 14

Democratic Convention. - The Montgomery Advertiser, Extra, of Tuesday evening, furnished the following proceedings of the Convention which was held in that city for nominating a candidate for Governor: The Convention commenced balloting for a candidate for Governor this morning - Col. J.A. Winston, Judge T.A. Walker, Hon. S.W. Harris, and Col. J.L. Cottrell, having been placed in nomination by their respective friends. The friends of Maj. Harris from Coosa desired to withdraw his name, as it was the wish of that gentleman, often privately and publicly expressed, that he should not be placed in nomination. After several ballotings, the name of Col. Cottrell was withdrawn, and on the call for the eighth ballot, the names of both Judge Walker and Maj. Harris were withdrawn by the gentlemen who had placed them in nomination, when Col. John A. Winston was nominated by acclamation.

Last Moments of the Vice President. - Mr. F.E. Beck - a kinsman of the Vice President, and who was present at his death - furnished the Southern Republic a brief account of his last moments. "He was quiet and resigned to the fate which he had seen for some time awaited him. Shortly before six o'clock on Monday evening, while a few friends were sitting around his bed-side, the only ones that he would allow in his sick room, he suddenly remarked that he was dying. The watchers arose to their feet, under some excitement, when the Colonel said - 'Be still - make no noise - let me die quietly.' He refused to have the balance of his household notified of his dying condition. His physician came in and examined him. The Colonel said to him - 'Doctor, I am dying. It seems as though I shall never get through with it. - I am dying very hard. Take the pillows from under my head.' The pillows were accordingly taken from under his head; but affording no relief, the Doctor turned him from his back on his side, when he died in a moment."

Southern Planters' Convention. - We copy, from the Journal, the following proceedings of the Southern Planter's Convention, which met in Montgomery on Monday last:
The First Day's Proceedings. The Delegates assembled in the Capital, when the Convention was organized by Dr. W.C. Daniel of Georgia, in the Chair. Dr. Daniel addressed the Convention. On motion of Dr. Cloud, Dr. Lucas, of Montgomery, was appointed Secretary. On a motion of Dr. Powell, of Macon county, a committee of five was appointed by the Chair to nominate officers for the permanent organization of the association. On motion of Judge Bibb, a committee of fourteen was appointed by the Chair to prepare business for the association. On motion of Col. Young, of Mississippi, the delegates were requested to come forward and register their names by States. On motion, the meeting adjourned to meet at 4 o'clock in Estelle Hall.
4 o'clock p.m. The meeting met pursuant to adjournment, then the committee of five reported by their chairman, Dr. Powell, the following officers: Hon. G.R. Gilmer, of Georgia, President. Colonel Vick, of Miss.; Col. Young, of Miss.; George W. Anderson and Dr. W.C. Daniel, Vice President. Dr. Lucas and Dr. Cloud, Secretaries. On taking the Chair, Gov. Gilmer addressed the association. The association was then addressed by Prof. Toumey, of Tuscaloosa. The association then adjourned to 11 o'clock Tuesday.
Second Day's Proceedings. It met again at the hour appointed, and the committee of thirteen reported a constitution and business for the association. After which, the association was addressed by Col. Cobb, of Mississippi, when the association adjourned to 4 o'clock, at which time Mr. Nelson will address the association.

Through Willard (?) Farwell, Esq., of the San Francisco Whig and Advertiser, and bearer of dispatches from the United States Legation at Mexico, we learn that an express arrived in the city of Mexico on the 8th of April, bringing the news of the occupation of the Mescada Valley, in Chichuahua by the Governor of New Mexico. The announcement caused very considerable excitement, and a general determination was expressed to drive the American forces from the disputed territory at the point of a bayonet. An armed force was ordered to proceed at once to the scene of action, to reinforce the Governor of Chichuahua, and to assist in expelling General Lane and his troops. A delegation of the proper authorities waited upon Judge Conkling, on the 9th instant, and entered their protest in the name of the government against the proceedings.

Arrival of the Steamship Texas. - Sixty-six hours from the Vera Cruz - Loss of the Albatross. - The steamship Texas, Captain Lawless arrived from Vera Cruz yesterday, making the run from Vera Cruz to this city in sixty-six hours - the quickest time on record. The passage of the Texas from New Orleans to Vera Cruz was made in seventy hours. On Monday evening at four o'clock, a dispatch arrived at Vera Cruz, to the agent, Mr. Markoe, advising him that the steamship Albatross had gone ashore the preceeding night on the Cabeza, a reef ten miles from the shore, and about twenty-six miles from the city; that six of the passengers succeeded in reaching the shore, and were in great distress from the impossibility of getting away. At daylight on Thursday morning, Captain Lawless, of the steamship Texas, got up steam, and proceeded to the scene of the disaster, hoping to be able to save the lives of the passengers, and perhaps the ship, but on arrival there, found the passengers and crew had all left and the ship had slid off the reef where she had first struck, and was nearly out of sight. The Captain of the port, together with two pilots and Customhouse officers, proceeded in the Texas, in order that should any necessity arise, he might be able to act in his official capacity. After being absent the greater part of the day, the Texas returned without having had an opportunity of rendering any service. The people of Vera Cruz are highly pleased with the establishment of this new line of mail steamers, and with the beautiful pioneer of the line - the Texas. Captain Lawless, in a card published in the Eco del Commerrcio, of the 19th instant invited the officials and inhabitants of the city to visit his ship, which invitation was accepted by very many, and all returned delighted with her. Santa Anna arrived in the city of Mexico on Sunday morning, the 17th instant, amidst the rejoicing of the inhabitants, who testified by their manner the great joy they experienced at his return. The whole city was brilliantly illuminated at night, and amid the booming of cannon and firing of rockets their new chief resumed his power.

Life in New Orleans. - The Delta says, that on Wednesday evening, (last week,) Agnes Anderson, living in Hercules street, gave herself up into the hands of justice, declaring that she had slain a man named William Taylor. It appears that she had been living with this person for some time, but latterly Taylor had become jealous, and Agnes says the he took a knife with him to bed for the declared purpose of killing her, which purpose he attempted to carry out, when she snatched the knife from him, and turned it fatally upon himself. Agnes is tolerably good-looking, was neatly dressed, but with a melancholy and dejected visage. Her hands were still bloody when in court next morning. She seemed to have no desire to conceal anything of the transaction. She said that she stabbed her victim a number of times, for until he fell exhausted, he made violent efforts to obtain a mastery over her.

Editorial Brevities. - It is said that the Government will shortly act upon the act of Congress, enabling them to purchase, at discretion, the United States stocks. The whole surplus revenue, not being wanted prospectively, will be invested without great delay. This will be of great effect on the money market, and will stimulate all enterprises.

United States District Court. - Hon. J.A. Campbell, presiding - Yesterday, says the Mobile *Tribune* the Grand Jury, in the case of the United States against Oliver S. Beers, upon the charge of embezzling public monies, came into court and ignored the indictment. Where upon, the court directed an order to be to discharge him and his securities from further attendance upon court.

We stated in Friday's Tribune that, in the case of the United States vs. Robert R. Harrison and twenty-four others, seamen of the ship Washington, Captain Paig, some of the men were convicted of creating a revolt on board of said ship and others for an attempt to do the same. Yesterday the man were brought into court and received sentence as follows: One for two years in the penitentiary; fifteen, for six months in the penitentiary; four, for ten days in the county jail.

The Leon (Texas), Pioneer learns that a Mr. Jones, who resided near the Navisoto in Rodger's prairie, Grimes county, was found shot in his own house a short time since. It is supposed that the deed was perpetrated by some one of his own family, as he had not been on good terms with his wife and others of them for some time. The accused parties, it is said, have been arrested and required to give bail for their appearance.

It is said that Hon. Hungford, residing near Watertown, N.Y., keeps five thousand hens in a ten acre lot, with large and suitable buildings all round for their lodging, setting and rearing chickens.

Arthur Spring, the Philadelphia murderer, attempted to commit suicide on the 26th ult., by sleeping with a quantity of tobacco under his arms, which physicians say is likely to cause death in a short time.

Lola Montez a Painter. - Lola Montez recently astonished the hands in the Cincinnati Nonpareil office, by going there and taking the "stick" and "rule," and setting up a communication made by the editor of the Sun. By the way we see that Lola was to start yesterday from New Orleans for California. She will subsequently take a tour of Mexico, and stop, as she comes back, at Havana.

We published yesterday says the Mobile Tribune, from the Marion Commonwealth with an account of the death of Mr. Knap. We are requested to say the story is not true - that his father exhibited symptoms of mental derangement, and has disappeared, but there is no evidence to show that he was drowned, or is not still alive.

Key West, April 22. - The schooner. J.F. Tobias, Capt. Hand, from Philadelphia, with an assorted cargo, bound to Mobile, arrived in distress on the 15th. The Tobias, when off Charleston, had a heavy gale of the wind, and was boarded by an ugly sea, which sprung the bowsprit, broke the jibboom, carried away the head gear and rails, topmast, split the foresail; put in repair damages. Will get off by the 28th. Consigned to Bowne & Curry.

In the United States Circuit court at Philadelphia, last week, Judge Greer refused a trial in the heirs of the Girard estate vs. the city of Philadelphia, which the jury had given a verdict for the plaintiffs. This decision gives to the heirs alive eleven tracts of coal land in Schuylkill county, valued at one million of dollars. The question involved was whether, under the law of Pennsylvania, a will devising all the real estate of the testator after the will is executed.

The Court has decided that it does not.

The State of Alabama, Autauga county, Special Court of Probate, May 2, 1853
This day came James and Thomas Underwood, administrators of the estate of Benjamin Underwood, deceased, and filed account and vouchers for the annual settlement of the said estate, which were examined and ordered to be filed for the inspection of all concerned . It is therefore ordered, that notice be given for forty days, by publication for three successive weeks in the Autauga Citizen, a newspaper published in said county, notifying all persons interested to be and appear at a court to be held on the 13th day of June next, to show cause, if any, why said account should not be stated and allowed. Henly Brown, Judge of Probate.

The State of Alabama, Autauga county, Special Court of Probate, April 28, 1853.
This day came Guilford W. Hadnot, one of the executors of the last will and testament of William S. Hadnot, deceased, and filed his account and vouchers for the annual settlement of said estate, which was examined and ordered to be filed for the inspection of all concerned. It is therefore ordered, that notice be given for forty days, by publication for three successive weeks in the Autauga Citizen, a newspaper published in said county, notifying all persons interested to be and appear at a court to be held on the 13th day of June next, to show cause, if any, why said account should not be stated and allowed. Henly Brown, Judge of Probate.

The State of Alabama, Autauga county, Special Court of Probate, May 2, 1853.
This day came William E. Boisseaw, guardian of G.A.F. Spratlin and M.C. Spratlin, minors, and filed their account and vouchers for the annual settlement of said wards' estate, which was examined and ordered to be filed for the inspection of all concerned. It is therefore ordered, that notice be given for 40 days, by publication for three successive weeks in the Autauga citizen, a newspaper published in said county, notifying all persons interested to be and appear at a court to be held on the 13th day of June next, to show cause, if any, why said account should not be stated and allowed. Henly Brown, Judge of Probate.

The State of Alabama, Autauga county, Special Court of Probate, May 2, 1853.
This day came Nathaniel Jeffrees a minor, and filed his account and vouchers for the annual settlement of said wards' estate, which was examined and ordered to be filed for the inspection of all concerned. It is therefore ordered, that notice be given for 40 days, by publication for three successive weeks in the Autauga citizen, a newspaper published in said county, notifying all persons interested to be and appear at a Court to be held on the 13th day of June next, to show cause, if any, why said account should not be stated and allowed. Henly Brown, Judge of Probate.

Administrators' Notice. - Letters of Administration upon the estate of Andrew S. Harris, deceased having been granted to the undersigned by the Hon. Henly Brown, Judge of Probate, in and for Autauga county, on this 2d day of February, 1853, all persons holding claims against said deceased are hereby notified to present them properly authenticated within the time prescribed by the law or they will be barred.

Vol. 1, Thursday, May 12, 1853, No. 15

Particulars in Fannin's Massacre. - Mr. Editor: The Muster Roll which you published last week, contained the names of 446 officers and soldiers, who were prisoners at Goliad when the Massacre took place, March 27, 1836. I have prepared a table showing what disposition was made of them. The number in the first column was detained by the Mexicans on account of their being surgeons or mechanics. The several companies are designated by the name of their captains:

Company	Detained	Escaped	Killed
1 Duvals	1	5	38
2 King's	2	0	20
3 Petus'	2	5	32
4 Bulloch's	9	2	26
5 Winn's	1	0	36
6 Wardsworth's	4	1	20
7 Ticknor's	3	0	36
8 Wyatt's	1	1	26
9 Westover's	2	0	42
10 Burke's	3	3	28
11 Shackleford's	0	3	52
12 Horton's	2	6	21
Field Officers	3	0	7
	33	26	385

As fitly succeeding the Muster Roll, I send you a letter which was first published in the Voice of Sumpter, (Livingston, Alabama), of November 28, 1839. Having formed the acquaintance of Mr. Brown soon after his return from Mexico, I suggested to him the propriety of publishing a narrative of his adventures, in the shape of a letter to Thomas Ward, Esq., or other of the late Col. Ward of the Texas army. He consented, and the letter came forth. Viewing it as a piece of history to be relied on, I desire you to give it circulation in your columns. Mr. Brown was a young gentleman of intelligence and vivacity. He is now dead. I always attributed to the kindness with which he was treated by the Mexican general to his rare personal beauty; his dark, piercing eyes, bronze complexion and graceful figure, giving him the appearance of a Spanish cavalier. He with a native of Georgia, and a nephew of Colonel Ward. Yours, respectfully, M. Livingston, Ala., November 1, 1837.

Dear Sir: Having been among the first who volunteered from Georgia in the service of Texas, under the command of your brother the late Colonel William Ward, whose name is destined occupy a place in history, I have thought that a communication of my adventure in a form you might preserve, would not be an unacceptable or improper. All I have in view is to give the facts which came within my personal observation and knowledge; and if they can be deemed of interest, as occurring to one of my years, (20 at the present time) I shall feel perfectly satisfied in having related them. About the 20th the of November, 1835, I left Macon in the stage for Columbus, where I joined Captain Ward's company, who had rendezvoused at that place, from whence we marched to Montgomery, Alabama, and took passage of the steamer Ben Franklin for Mobile. Remaining in Mobile five or six days, near which a public dinner was given us, we embarked on the steamer Convoy for New Orleans, where we halted about a week, and received some addition to our number - making the company about one hundred and fifty strong. Here Captain Ward laid in supplies for his men, and chartered the schooner Pennsylvania to Velasco, where we arrived on the 20th of December, 1835, and found Captain Wardsworth's company, fifty strong, and companies were organized into a battalion, of which Captain Ward's original company was divided into two equal parts, called the Georgia Battalion. Captain Ward's original company was divided into two more parts, the command of one of which was given to Capt. Uriah J. Bulloch of Macon, and that of the other to Captain James C. Wynne, of Gwinnette county. Major Ward lost no time in reporting his command to Governor Smith, at San Phillip de Austin. We encamped about two miles from Velasco, on the Brazos river, where they subsisted on the two month's provisions laid in at New Orleans. After a week's absence to the seat of Government, Major Ward return with the commission's of the several officers. We remained near Velasco until the first of February, 1836, when the batallion was ordered by the then acting Governor, Robinson, to repair to Goliad, on the San Antonio river, and it was forthwith transported by the schooner Columbus, U. S. vessel, to Copano, of Aransas Bay, after a five days' passage. There we were furnished with supplies by the government, and four pieces of artillery, two six pounders and two pounders. From Compano to Goliad the distance is forty-five miles, and about half way the batallion halted at the Mission, where we were joined by Captain Ticknor's company of Montgomery, Ala., making our ranks about two hundred and fifty strong. Thence we marched two Goliad, took possession and repaired the fort, and were joined by the Lafayette batallion, made up from north Alabama, Tennessee and Kentucky. Previous to this, the lamented, Col. Fannin had not taken any part in the service, but was actively engaged in collecting and diffusing information highly useful to the cause of Texas. At Goliad the two batallions were formed into a regiment, between five and six hundred strong, of which Fannin was elected Colonel, and Ward Lieutenant Colonel ; Dr. Mitchell, of Columbus, commanded the Georgia batallion, in place of Major Ward, promoted. For some purpose, Captain King, of the Lafayette batallion, had been dispatched by Colonel Fannin to occupied the Mission, about twenty-two miles off, who found himself annoyed by a party of Mexican Cavalry, and sent an express to Goliad for reinforcements. Lieutenant Colonel Ward, with one hundred and twenty-five men , myself among them, was directed by Col. Fannin to support Capt. King at the Mission. This was on the 12th of March, and the next day Lieutenant Colonel Ward's command reached the Mission, at which a large Mexican church, built of stone, made a very good fort, in which we took protection. The Mexican cavalry that reconnoitered the Mission, and tried to attack at, were estimated at two hundred; and the on the night of the 13th, a party of thirteen men, under Captain Ticknor, surprised their camp, a mile from the Mission, killing eight of them and putting the rest to flight. Among the slain was recognized a Mexican Lieutenant who had been with Colonel Fannin at Goliad, pretending to have joined the Texans with eighteen men. On the morning of the 16th, Lieutenant Colonel Ward and Capt. King differed as to who commanded at the Mission, the latter claiming it by being there first. A large majority of the troops, declared they would serve under Lieutenant Colonel Ward only, which induced Captain King with his original company of twenty - eight men, to withdraw, and was followed by eighteen of Ward's command, who had been detailed from Bradford's company at Goliad, leaving Ward one hundred and seven men. About ten o'clock in the morning, a party a fifteen, with myself, went to the river - about two hundred and fifty yards off - with oxen and cart, to bring two barrels of water into the fort. We had just filled the vessels, and were leaving the river, when we were fired on from an open prairie and other side, that Gen Urrea's army of eleven hundred men about a half mile distant. We made all possible speed for the fort, holding onto the water, except about a half barrel, which was lost by a ball piercing one of the barrel heads. The enemy kept firing as they crossed the river, and marched up within fifty yards of the church, when the order was given to fire, which drove the Mexicans back, and left the ground pretty well spotted with their dead and wounded. They made four regular charges, both cavalry and infantry, about half of each, and were often repulsed with great slaughter. About four or five o'clock in the afternoon they retreated, leaving four or five hundred of their dead upon the field. Colonel Ward had only three men wounded, one of them an Irish man, who resided at the Mission. When the attack was made in the morning Colonel Ward sent an express (James Humphrey, of Columbus, Georgia) to Colonel Fannin, at Goliad, and orders were received at twelve o'clock at night to abandon the church, and take a northeast course for Victoria, on the Gaudaloupe, twenty miles from Goliad where Colonel Fannin would join him. At twelve o'clock at night we left the fort, formed five deep, marched without a guide into the open prairie, and were only eight miles from the fort at daylight. For two days we had nothing to eat; the third we killed some cattle in the San Antonio, which revived us a good deal. On the twenty first of March, we reached Victoria, and had advanced to within one hundred and fifty yards of the town, expecting to find Colonel Fannin and his men there, when, to our utter dismay, it was in possession of the enemy, who fired upon us, causing us to retreat into the swamp. Colonel Fannin had set out to meet us in due time, but his whole command was captured by a large force within six miles of Goliad, and carried back to the fort. We had expended all our ammunition in the battle at the Mission, and very few of our army had a single cartridge left!

In this dilemma, we marched that night for Dimmit's Point, on the La Baca river, near Matagorda Bay, where supplies were landed for Texan troops. Next day, March 22d, we halted to rest, and concealed ourselves within two miles of our destination, sending two man to the Point to see who was in possession, and awaited their return. The remnants of the Mexican army that had attacked the Mission were hovering over this quarter, under Gen Urrea, took the two men prisoners, and surrounded us. The two men came within speaking distance of us, stated our situation and the power of the enemy, and desired Colonel Ward to see general Urrea of the terms of surrender; upon which he, in company with Major Mitchell and Captain Ticknor, had an interview with General Urrea, and returned making known to us the offer of the enemy, that if we surrendered prisoners of war, we should be marched to Copano without delay, and from thence to New Orleans, or detained as prisoners of war and exchanged. Colonel Ward addressed his men, and said he was opposed to our surrendering; that it was the same enemy we had beaten in the Mission, only much reduced in numbers, and that he thought the chance of our escape equally practicable as it was then. He proposed that the attack on us might be evaded until night, when we might possibly pass the enemy's lines and get out of danger. At all events, he thought it best to resist every inch, as many of us could save ourselves, and if we surrendered he had doubts of the faith and humanity of the Mexicans; that he feared we should all be butchered. The vote of the company was taken, and a large majority were in favor of surrendering upon the terms proposed; Colonel Ward informed them that their wishes should govern, but if they were destroyed, no blame could rest on him. The same officers as before, to wit: Colonel Ward, Major Mitchell and Captain Ticknor, again saw General Urrea, and I understood that a paper was signed by the Mexican General, to dispose of us in the manner above stated, on condition that we should never serve Texas anymore; one copy of the instrument in Spanish and the other in English. Then came the hour for us to see all of our hopes blasted. We marched out in order and grounded arms. Our guns were fired off, the flints taken out, and return to us to carry. When we left the Mission on the fourteenth of March, we had about a hundred men; at the time we surrendered we had only eighty five, the others having left this on the route from the Mission to Victoria, and most fortunate thing for them. We were put under strong guard, and the next morning, 23d March, proceeded to Victoria, where we were engaged the next day in bringing the baggage of the Mexican army across the Gaudaloupe, about four hundred yards from the town, and hauling it up. On the next morning of the twenty fifth we were marched toward Goliad, where we arrived late the next evening. Here we found Colonel Fannin and his regiment prisoners in the fort. All the Texan troops into the fort prisoners, belonging to Colonel Fannin's command, after we were brought in, amounted to four hundred and eighty men. Early on the morning of the 27th we were mustered into line and counted, and divided into four equal parties of a hundred and twenty each. That nearest the door of the fort was marched out first, being received by a strong guard, placed in double file, going we knew not where, or for what purpose. I was in this division, in the right-hand file. At the distance of half a mile from the fort, we were halted; the guard on the right then passed the left and instantly fired upon the prisoners, nearly all of whom fell, and the few survivors tried to escape by flight over the prairie and concealing themselves in the weeds. The firing continued, and about the same time I heard other firing towards the fort and cries of distress. At the time our division of prisoners were shot, Drury H. Minor, of Houston county, Georgia, immediately on the left was killed; and just before me, next in file, Thomas F. Freeman, of Macon, was also killed. As I ran off I observed several poor fellows who had been wounded, trying to hide in the clumps of weeds and grass, but were pursued, I presume, and killed. Soon after I made my escape. I was joined by John Duval and —— Holiday, of the Kentucky volunteers, both of whom were with me at the massacre, but not until after I had swam across the San Antonio river, about a mile from the butchery. For five days we had nothing to eat except wild onions, which abound in the country; on reaching the Gaudaloupe we found a nest of young pigs, and these lasted us several days, wandering at random over the open country, often wide from our supposed direction, we saw fresh signs of cavalry and withdrew to the swamp; the we had been perceived going there, and were taken by two Mexicans armed with guns and swords - that is, Duval and myself were captured; Holiday lay close and was not discovered. One of the men seized me and held on; Duval was placed between them to follow. He sprang off, and one of them threw down his gun to pursue him, but in vain; Duval made his escape; I have not seen him since. I was taken to their camp close by, when they saddled their horses in a hurry and rode off without me. From their actions, I judged they were of opinion a party of Texans was near, and some made off. I returned to the swap again, and found Holiday in his old position. Next day we came to a deserted house on the La Baca river, apparently that of an American settler, where we found plenty of provisions, such as meat, corn, lard, butter and eggs, and feasted upon these two days, camping at night a little way off. Taking a good supply of provisions along, we traveled quite refreshed, and in four days reached the Colorado. From almost constant rain and exposure I had lost the use of my right arm and shoulder, and could not swim the river, Holiday swam across with the provisions, promising to return and help me; but he was so exhausted by the cold and rapid current, that he was not able to do so. Thus we parted, and I never saw him again. I went up the river, and next day found a canoe, which I crossed, then wandered about until I came in sight of the Brazos, on the 10th of April, when I was taken by a party of twenty Mexican cavalry, who carried to me to the main armory under general Siesma, at Ford Bend, and put me under guard with other prisoners they had picked up. I can recollect the names of but three of them, and they had resided several years in Texas; Johnson, Leech and Simpson. Fort bend was about twenty miles from San Jacinto, where the battle was fought the next day, (21st of April). The night after the battle a Mexican officer who had escaped from San Jacinto, brought the news into camp, and army instantly retreated. When I arrived at the camp I pulled off my boots, to dry and relieve my swollen feet; my boots were stolen, and I had to March barefoot through mud and water, nearly knee-deep and over the prairies, the rain falling in torrents pretty much all the time. The army returned to Victoria, where I saw four of the Macon company who had been detained there after the surrender, on account of there being mechanics; W. Wilkinson, John Kinnmore, Banwell and Callahan. I was then taken to Goliad, where I remained five days, and saw the places where the four divisions of prisoners had been butchered, some of the carcasses remained, many burnt and others mangled; also disfigured that I could not recognize no particular person. A company of eighty two men from Tennessee, under Captain Miller, of Texas, who had been taken prisoners the moment they landed at Copano, than whom we left at the fort and Goliad at the massacre, still remained there on my return. One of its members, Mr. Coy, told me the particulars of Ward and Fannin's death, being an eyewitness. After the privates had been shot, the time of the officers came. Colonel Ward was ordered to kneel, which he refused to do; he was told if he would kneel his life might be spared; he replied that they had killed his men in cold blood, and he did not desire to live; death would be welcome. He was then shot dead. Fannin made an address to the Mexican officer in command, by an interpreter; handed him his gold watch, to be sent to his (Col. F.'s) wife, and also at purse to the officer to have him decently buried. He sat on a chair, tied his handkerchief about his eyes, and requested that he might not be shot in the head, and that the marksmen should stand far enough off for the powder not to burn him. Leaving Goliad in the month of May, with a dozen other Texan prisoners, under a guard attached to the main army, then three thousand and strong, we marched to San Patricio, on the Nueces river, where Colonels Teale and Carnes, of the Texan service, came under a flag of truce, and obtained passports to go to Matamoros, at which place Colonel Teale told me I should be discharged. I was kept with the main army until Gen. Filisola received orders from Mexico to hasten there. He took with him a bodyguard through the Indian country, about fifty cavalry, who in charge of it ever since I left Goliad, and they still held on to me. Gen. F. Left his body guard at Saltillo, that took the stage for the city of Mexico, where the cavalry arrived with me, their only prisoner, in August, 1836. I was then confined in the Quartedo, or barracks, until the first of February, 1837, and about that time Gen. F. expected to leave the city, to take command of the army at Matamoros. His interpreter, an Italian named Quarri, often visited the barracks, he treated me with great humanity. He said that he would get my release, and to come to Gen Filisola's house, to accompany him to Matamoros. From some delay he did not start until the 28th of March, during which time I was a member of his family, and treated with perfect kindness - under orders, however, for my own safety, it was said, not to leave the guard alone. Whilst in confinement in the city of Mexico, I was kept in the barracks with the number of Mexican prisoners, who were confined for various offenses, and from the time I entered, in August, 1836, until I went to Gen Filisola's house, in February of the following year, I had no food and then boiled beef the water was fresh and pure brought there by an acqueduct which supplies the whole city from the mountains twelve miles distant. On the 20th of March last, I left the city of Mexico in company with General Filisola, his staff and a small guard, and arrived at Matamoros the first of June - a distance of nine hundred miles from one place to the other. On the 17th of June, Gen. Filisola gave me a passport, and on the first of July I embarked for New Orleans, where I arrived in due time. The unpretending narrative is at your service, with my permission to make what use of it you may think proper. I am, very respectfully, your most obedient servant, S.T. Brown., Thos. Ward, Esq., Sumter Co., Ala..

Mr. Thos. De Wolf has retired from the Montgomery Advertiser and Gazette - having sold his interest to Mr. M.P. Blue, of that city. Col. Seibels, who has been connected with the editorial department, also vacates that "hide bottom chair." Mr. Britttan - whom there is not, in the whole press gang of the South, they more amiable gentleman - continues, with Mr. Blue, the conduct of the paper, which we have the means of knowing, is in a flourishing condition; that it may long continue so, is our hearty wish. We shan't bid Mr. De Wolf "good-bye yet a while. Guess he'll turn up again, e're long, in the" same old trade; "he can't keep still - don't know how "to do nothing".

Railroad Improvement! I speak to the public whom it concerns or feeling interested in those important security if I may call it secure to prevent locomotives running off the track and grinding our bodies into the earth. Beng. A. Rogers, Inventor, Prattville, Ala.

We have the pleasure of examining the invention of Mr. Beng. A. Rogers, to which the above communication refers, which, by the way, we have inserted *verbatim et literatim*, and have come to the conclusion, with many others, that it is the very thing to keep trains from running off the track, or at least prevent them from "grinding our bodies into the earth." It would be awful *cat-as-tro-phe* to have one's self *grinded* up by the ponderous wheels of a train of cars, and when this is taken into consideration, no doubt the invention will be held with joy by all the world "rest of mankind" - but more particularly by railroad companies. We are not allowed the liberty of making known the principle upon which it works, but the inventor, we doubt not, will soon give the public all the necessary information concerning this *new-fangled, rip-snortin'* invention, and demonstrate, most *emphatically*, the extreme folly of traveling on trains that are liable to "grind our bodies into the earth." *Vive la neumphschulle!*

Southern Planters' Convention. - Second Day's Proceedings-Afternoon Session. The Convention assembled at 4 o'clock, when Mr. Nelson, of the Troop Hill Nursery, Georgia, delivered an interesting and practical address on Horticulture and Fruit Culture at the south. After which, Colonel James M. Chambers, of Georgia, addressed the Convention. His subject was the Agricultural Press.

Third Day's Proceedings. The association convened of as per adjournment, when, on motion of Dr. Daniels, of Georgia, the Constitution was taken up an revised and some of the sections. After which, their reports of committees (on documents and Agricultural Institutes) were received. These reports were laid on the table temporarily, to hear the address of the Hon. Robert Toombs, of Georgia. Col. Toombs was introduced the association, an interested the assemblage, consisting of a crowded hall of ladies and gentlemen, with an address forcible and learned, setting forth the duty and objects of the association. The association then proceeded to the election of officers, which resulted as follows:

President-George R. Gilmer, of Georgia.

Vice Presidents-H.W. Vick, of Mississippi; B.F. Glover, of Virginia; Dr. J.A. Whetstone, of Louisiana; and Dr. R.W. Withers, of Alabama.

Secretary and Treasurer-N.B. Cloud, of Alabama.

The association then adjourned to assemble in the hall of the Mechanic's Institute, at 3 o'clock.

Afternoon Session. The association met as per adjournment, when, after the appointment of various committees, &c, the Executive Council was appointed, composed of the following gentlemen: M.A. Holt, Dr. C. Bellinger, B.S. Bibb, Alabama; Col. Young, Mississippi; Walker Anderson, Florida; A.S. Summer, South Carolina; and James M. Chambers, Georgia. The association then fixed on Columbia, S. C. as the place for its next meeting in November next. After the usual resolutions of thanks, &c, to the citizens of Montgomery for hospitality and attentions, the association adjourned *sine die*. - *Journal*

Editorial Brevities. - The New Orleans Bulletin says that it is not generally known that there was at one time a State in this country which for the name of *Franklin*. It lay west of Alleghanies, an original eight was that portion of North Carolina, now a part of Tennessee, lying between the Alleghanies and the Cumberland mountains. It parted from North Carolina in 1784, and maintained its separate existence and government until 1788-more than three years. These facts are gathered from the work of Dr. Ramsay, the historian of Tennessee.

Louis Napoleon recently bought for the Empress a piano exhibited at the London exhibition, for forty thousand francs.

The Washington rumor that Chief Justice Tancy intends resigning his seat in the Supreme Court, is denied. He has recovered from his late sickness, and has resumed the discharge of his duties.

Mr. Thackery. - the Richmond (Virginia) Mail, in noticing the departure of this distinguished author, says: "We are pleased to learn, from good authority, that Mr. Thackery's visit to the Southern States impressed him with a very different opinion of our institutions from that expressed by the Prince of snobs, Charles Dickens."

It has been stated in the papers that the 4th of March was selected for the inauguration of the President, because it will not fall on Sunday for 300 years from the time of its selection. General Taylor, we believe was inaugurated on the 5th, because the 4th was Sunday.

An election was held on Monday of last week for Judge of the 2d Judicial Circuit - the candidates being Judge N. Cook, of Lowndes, and J.D. Jenkins, of Wilcox. From the returns we have seen, it is certain that Judge Cook is re-elected by a large majority.

"Ion," the Washington correspondent of the Baltimore Sun, says: "The new territory of Washington, so fertile and salubrious, and so inviting to agricultural enterprise, is opened by the liberty of Congress, for the reception of Southern immigrants, with their slaves. A considerable number of citizens of Missouri and Kentucky, and probably Virginia, will avail themselves of the boon, and of the opportunity thus unexpectedly afford it for the introduction of another great slave State into the Union. Messrs. Chase, Hale and Sumner were so wholly ingrossed by their admiration of the works and triumphs of Mrs. Stowe, that they suffered the bill establishing the magnificent territory of Washington to pass without the usual recognition of the ordinance of '69-zero or the Wilmot proviso.

The dwelling house of Mr. W.J. Wagoner, Nashville, Tenn, was burnt on the night of the 26th inst. Horrible to relate, three of the children were consumed in the flames. Both mother and father were badly burned in attempting to save their dear ones, and they saved two.

Governor Stevens will probably locate the territorial government of a new territory of Washington at Olympia, the thriving village at the head of Puget's Sound, which, it is thought, is shortly to become a great commercial capital of our northern Pacific coast possessions.

Rattle Snake Bite Cured. - The *Southern Medical Journal* contains the description of the case by Dr. T.A. Atchison, in which a girl seventeen years of age, bitten on the left instep by a rattle snake, was cured by being placed in a hot bath, and whiskey and carbonate of ammonia administered to her, until she had taken three pints of the former and eighty grains of the latter. It was two hours and a half after that Dr. A. visited his patient, when her mind was wandering. The liquor caused no intoxication, and the cure was complete.

The President has appointed Colonel Alfred Cummings, formerly of Georgia, and now of Missouri, to be superintendent of Indian affairs for the central superintendency.

Obscure Birth. - It appears from the biographies of the Duke of Wellington, that the exact time and place of his birth is not known, there being no record and no evidence to fix it with precision.

President Pierce's Personal Habits. - The Washington correspondent of the New York Courier says of General Pierce, "that he drinks no wine, and those who enjoy and intimate acquaintance with him, say that the bereavements and afflictions of his later years and the pressure of the onerous public duties since his election, have impressed him with a deep sense of religious responsibility, and given a tinge of gravity to his character which forms an observable contrast with the ardor and vivacity of his temperament at earlier periods of his life."

Inspector General. - A dispatch to the New Orleans Picayune says that Capt. Scott, son-in-law of General Winfield Scott, has been appointed Inspector General of the Army, by the President.

"The Lost Bourbon". - The New Orleans papers said that fresh evidence of the identity of the Rev. Mr. Williams with the Dauphin of France has been discovered. The Delta says: "In substance, this evidence is as follows: In the northeastern part of New Orleans, an old lady has resided for many years past, who, in early life, with own terms of the intimacy with the Bourbon family, her husband having been secretary to the Count d'Artola. She possessed, therefore, opportunities of information which few could enjoy. She makes oath that she heard, from the sister of the Dauphin, as long ago as 1807, that her brother was safe in America, and that she learned from a member of the Royal household, in 1817, that the exiled Prince was an Indian missionary in the United States, named Williams; and in proof that these declarations are not based on recent publication, there is responsible testimony that she has made them for at least twelve years."

We see it stated that the famous abolitionist Gerrit Smith gave away thousands of acres, in small tracts, in Western New York, to free negroes and refuge slaves. Most of these lands are now being sold for the taxes, the darkies being too lazy to work them. Smith is now a member of Congress, and purchased a residence in Washington.

(?) Affair. - the Cumberland, (?), Journal relates the following occurrences: On Wednesday of last week, the dead body of a young man was found in the Potomac river near the Big Tunnel on the Chesapeake and Ohio Canal. From a fracture of the skull, and other injuries, he was supposed to have been dealt foully with. Various surmises as to the identity of the corpse were entertained, when Capt. Henry Troutman, of the Cumberland Night Watch, again convinced that it was the body of his son James, who had been at work in the vicinity, and was missing at the time. A coroner's jury was summoned from Cumberland and the body was fully identified by Capt. T. and others as that of his son. Particular marks were pointed out by the distressed father, and there seemed to not to be the slightest doubt on the subject. The jury returned an unanimous verdict based upon the facts as thus set forth. The body was consequently decently interred by Capt. T. who forthwith arrayed himself into the garb of mourning, and engaged the services of a minister of the Gospel to preach a funeral discourse on the occasion. It turned out, however, that on Sunday morning last the dead son of Capt. Troutman deliberately walked up to his astonished father and informed him that he was not dead! The mingled surprise and the delight of the father may be imagined. The fact is, the young man had been at work in another direction, and upon hearing of his reported demise returned to Cumberland to relieve the apprehensions of his parents. The dead man is supposed to have been a boat man on the Canal, who was murdered and thrown into the river. Some persons suggests that he was a German named John Burn, of Cumberland, but there is no certainty about the matter.

The State of Alabama, Autauga County, Special Court of Probate, May 16, 1853.
This day came Berry Tatum, guardian of Henry Fralick and Mary Fralick, minors, and filed his accounts and vouchers for the annual settlement of the said guardianship, which was examined and ordered to be filed for the inspection of all concerned. It is therefore ordered, that notice be given for forty days, by publication for three successive weeks in the Autauga Citizen, notifying all persons interested to be and appear at a Court to be held on the twenty first day of June next, to show cause why said account should not be stated and allowed, and said settlement be made. Henly Brown, Judge of Probate.

Notice. Letters of Administration on the estate of Joel Floyd, deceased, having been granted to the undersigned, on the 19th day of April, 1853, by the Hon. Henly Brown, Judge of Probate in and for Autauga county, Ala., all persons having claims against said deceased are hereby notified to present them properly authenticated within the time prescribed by law, or they will be barred. G.W. Floyd, Adm'r.

The State of Alabama, Autauga County, Special Court of Probate, May 5, 1853.
This day came Elizabeth Cheek, Administratrix to the estate of Brantly J. Cheek, deceased, and filed her account and vouchers for the annual settlement of the estate of said deceased, which was examined and ordered to be filed for the inspection of all concerned. It is therefore ordered, that notice be given for forty days, of publication for three successive weeks in the Autauga Citizen, notifying all persons interested to be and appear at a Probate Court to be held on the first day of July next, to show cause why said account should not be stated and allowed. Henly Brown, Judge of Probate.

Vol. 1, Thursday, May 19, 1853, No. 16

Thos. H. Watts, Esq., has been nominated by the Whig convention as a candidate to represent the Autauga and Montgomery counties in the State Senate. James E. Belser and Thos. J. Judge are the candidates of the same party to represent Montgomery in the lower house.

We have been requested to publish the following letter from Col. Winston, the nominee of the Gubernatorial Democratic Convention, held a couple weeks since in Montgomery: Mobile, May 10, 1853. Gentleman: Your note informing me, officially, of the nomination made by the Democratic Convention, has been received. Having through life and an ardent supporter of the principles of the Democratic party, and having followed the fortunes of the Democratic colors through good and adverse fortune, I feel deeply the honor which has thus been conferred upon me on my political brethren and shall endeavor to justify the selection in conducting the canvass, and in discharging the office, should the people confirm the nomination. We have arrived at a period of peculiar interest in the history of the State. Emerging from a state of pecuniary embarrassment, (the necessary result of the hasty and visionary legislation) we are, as a people, in a condition of financial prosperity. It will become those having the destiny of the State in charge, to so direct the legislation of the country as to promote such system of internal improvement as will advance the commercial and agricultural interest, without involving the State again in heavy debts for we are free of those of the past. It will belong more particularly to the legislature body to digest and enact such measures as will ensure ends so desirable, to which I shall give my hearty cooperation. I thank you, gentleman, and through you the convention, for the distinguished honor you have done me. Very respectfully, etc. John A. Winston

Messrs. John H. Garner, Robt. E. Coxe, B.F. Wilson, S.M. Strong, Jas E. Francis.

Hon. David Meriwether, of Kentucky, has received the appointment of Governor of New Mexico, *vice* Wm. Carr Lane.

Editorial Brevities. - Tennessee. The two political parties in Tennessee have recently held State Conventions, for the nomination of candidates for the Governor ship. Mayor Gustavus Henry is the nominee of the Whig Convention, and Hon. Andrew Johnson, of the Democratic.

The Boston papers record the death of Robert G. Shaw, Esq., aged 76 years, well known for many years as an active an enterprising merchant of that city, and one who knew was much esteemed for his probity and private benevolence. He leaves an estate worth nearly a million of dollars.

Hon. N.P. Tallmadge, formerly U.S. Senator from New York, writes to the National Intelligencer a letter expressing his firm belief in the spiritual rappings and other similar demonstrations. He says he has had frequent communications from Mr. Calhoun, being, "both in style and sentiment, worthy of him in his palmiest days in the U.S. Senate."

Ruben C. Shorter, Jr., Esq., of Montgomery, died in that city on the 14th inst.

Mr. Ericsson, finding that in order to obtain a patent for his invention in France, a caloric engine must be in actual operation in that country before the 20th the next month, has arranged with the proprietors of the New York evening post to take for the purpose the engine constructed for that paper, which is the only one that can be got ready in season. It will accordingly be sent out by the steamer Humboldt. Capt. Ericsson is, just now, one of the most notorious men in England; his ship is being discussed in the leading journals of the country. At a great meeting of scientific gentleman, Lord Radstock entered it into a detailed statement in relation to this marvel of the age.

The Atmospheric Express. We noticed the other day, says the Baltimore *Patriot*, that a company was about to be formed in Boston, to lay down a line of tubes or pipes between cities, through which by the aid of atmosphere, mails and packages were to be dispatched with the speed of wind. The invention in Boston is claimed by Mr. J.O. Richardson. In the Richmond (Va.) *Enquirer*, Lorenzo Sibert, of Shenandoah county, claims that the invention is his; but we see by a Philadelphia paper that it is claimed that James Spicer, of Philadelphia, first invented it, and exhibited models in that city in 1851. We doubt if any of these gentlemen are entitled to the credit of original invention, any more than T.C.H. Smith, Esq., well known and the efficient carrier through and promoter of the Western Telegraph, does not however, we believe, pretend to be the great original. The idea, amongst some people, was obtained from the atmospheric railway project, in England, some years since. It may be a feasible one. It looks so, and we wish it all success. But, if a package containing an immense amount of money, or valuables, should lodge at some indefinite and indefinable place among the tube, it might be productive of no inconsiderable degree of inconvenience. Science, however, may be enabled to obviate all difficulties. It would be a magnificent triumph of art.

Ex-president Martin Van Buren took his departure for Europe at 12 o'clock, on Saturday last, in the government steamship Arctic. A large number of his personal friends were present, on board with him for several hours previous to the ship's sailing. Amongst the number were Benj. F. Butler, Dudly Field, and several of his old political associates and adherents. Mr. Van Buren is accompanied by his son Martin, whose extremely delicate health has been the chief cause of his present trip to Europe. He is the first President of the United States who has paid a visit to the old country and will of course create a sensation. He visited England and number of years ago, having been appointed Ambassador to London by General Jackson; that this appointment having been defeated in the Senate, he was recalled. This was before he was elected President. Before his return Mr. Van Buren designs visiting the Courts of England, France, Spain, and other European countries.

Wm. A. Ashly, of Conecuh, has been nominated by a Whig convention, held at Andelusia, for the State Senate, from the counties of Covington, Coffee and Conecuh.

Letters from Paris of the 21st ult., state that our Minister, the Hon. William C. Rivers, was expected to take his departure in 3 weeks, and that no advices had been received as to his successor.

Whig and Democratic Conventions have just been held in Mobile, to select candidates for Congress. The Whigs nominated E. Lockwood, and the Democrats Col. P. Philips.

A meeting of the "Southern Rights Party of Dallas County" was held at Selma on the 9th inst, as we learn from the Dallas Gazette, when and where Col. Geo. W. Gayle offered the following resolution, which was unanimously adopted: "Resolved, That as members of the Southern Rights Party, we will vote in the next State election in August, for the man or men, who entertain principles nearest those advocated by the Southern Rights Troop and Quitman party in the late at the last Presidential election, and recommended the same course to be pursued in by every friend of the South."

Shooting Affray At Shasta, California. - *The Murderer hung by the people.* The Union contains an account of a shooting affair at Shasta, and the execution of the murderer by the people: On Wednesday morning last, James Noland, gambler, and a Mr. Murdoch, trader, were engaged in a game of Monte at the Trinity House, the former dealing and the latter betting at the game. During the progress of the game, Noland pulled 2 cards, which Murdoch detecting, grabbed the money of the bank in 1 hand, while the other he reached across the table and collared Noland. High words ensued between them, in the roots of which they scuffled and worked themselves off from the table. Murdoch, in the meantime, drew his revolver, cocked it, and letting the muzzle hang down, threatened to shoot Noland unless he delivered over the money won. Having gained a position near the counter of the bar in the scuffle, Noland reached over it, or under it, and procured a pistol, which he cocked silently and rapidly, and presenting it at the breast of Murdoch, exclaimed: "You have drawn a pistol on me and threatened to shoot; now shoot and be d—d!" saying which he fired; the Bulloch passing into the neck of Murdoch, immediately above the collar bone, and killing him instantly. Sheriff Cozart arrested Noland and placed him under guard. News of the affray and its consequences having traveled with lightning speed among the miners, during the day many of them crowded into Shasta from Whiskey Creek and the surrounding region, and demanded Noland to be given up. The Sheriff resisted their demands as long as it was safe to do so, when he relinquished Noland into their hands. A jury was formed, a trial held in the prisoner found guilty. At 7 o'clock in the evening he was hung by the neck until he was dead.

Administrator's Sale. Will be sold at the Court House door in Kingston, on Monday, the 20th day of June, 1853, Land Warrant No. 37,776, for eighty (80) acres of land, issued in favor of Mathew Luter - and of belonging to Mathew Luter, deceased - a credit until the first day of January next. John W. Hollon.

Notice. Letters of Administration was this day granted to the undersigned by the Honorable Judge of Probate in and for the State of Alabama and the county of Autauga, on the estate of Mathew Luter, deceased. All persons having demands against the said estate will present them within the time prescribed by law, or they will be barred. John W. Hollon

The State of Alabama, Autauga County. Taken up, by Greene B. Barber, and posted before A.T. Love, a Justice of the Peace in and for said county, a Brown Bay Horse, about sixteen hands high, about ten years old; has a not upon his left pastern-joint, and a small white spot in the forehead. Appraised by H.C. Lane and H. Booth, at seventy-five dollars, the 30th day of April, 1853. Henly Brown, Judge of Probate

Vol. 1, Thursday, May 26, 1853, No. 17

We regret to announce the death of Col. Claiborne Myers, and esteemed and much beloved citizen of this county, who died on board the *Cherokee*, on his way from New Orleans to New York. Col. Myers had been, for some time, in bad health, and it was thought, by his physicians, that a trip to Havana and New York would be the means of saving his life - but, alas, death had a fixed upon, and claimed him as his victim. He leaves a family and many friends and acquaintances to mourn his irreparable loss.

Autauga Mercury. We have received the second number of the above named the paper, edited and published by N. J. & L.T. Blome, Autaugaville, Ala. The number before us presents a neat appearance, and is edited with much spirit and energy. We believe it is to be independent in politics. Success, say we, to the Mercury.

David Pollard, another victim to spiritual rappings, committed suicide in Clinton county, New York, last week.

Editorial Brevities. Central Route to the Pacific. Mr. Elisha Riggs, of the firm of Corcoran & Riggs, and his young brother, William Henry, and H. Rodgers, Esq. member of the bar at Washington city, left St. Louis on the 10th inst., for Kansas, to join Superintendent Beale in his new route to California. As the Superintendent will have left the Kansas when these gentlemen arrives there, they will take a light carriage drawn by six Mexican mules, and run fifty miles a day until they overtake him. These gentlemen are not employed by government, but go as amateur travelers to see the country and to form their own opinions of the practicability of the route. Col. Benton accompanied Mr. Beale to Kansas.

By the decease, of a certain Absolom Sharp, late of Mississippi, a very large fortune has fallen to the brothers and sisters, or their heirs, who are supposed to reside in Western Pennsylvania. Besides property in Mississippi, the deceased to left an estate in Louisiana, appraised at the sum of $70,000.00. His brother's were John, Henry and Levi Sharp.

U.S. District Court. The U.S. Court for this District commenced in session on Monday, at Montgomery, Judge Gayle presiding, and will probably continue for several days. We learn that the docket is not important. - *Journal*

We regret to see it stated by a writer in the Greenville (S.C.) *Patriot*, that since the death of Juniuus W. Smith, Esq., his tea plantation is a on the road to ruin. Mr. Smith spent much of his time in efforts to introduce the tea culture in the South.

Governor Foote, of Miss., has challenged of all his competitors for U.S. Senator to meet him on the stump and discuss their claims before the people.

Senator Pearce, of Maryland, has accepted the invitation to deliver the address at be Ohio State Fair, at Dayton, in September next.

A monument to Daniel Webster, to cost ten thousand dollars, has been determined on by the Legislature of Massachusetts.

The English commission to the New York World's Fair, headed by Lord Ellesmere, will include sir Charls Lyell and Henry de la Beche, Esq., the distinguished geologists.

In Lauderdale, Mr. Robert Pattou is a candidate for the Senate, and General L.P. Walker for the House - strong men both - the first a Union Whig, and the latter, an secession democrat.

Arrest. We learn from the N. O. True Delta, that a man who calls himself John Richards, but whose real name is supposed to be Norris, was arrested in that city on Wednesday, on suspicion of being absent without leave from the Alabama penitentiary. The prisoner answers the published description of Norris, and news of his arrest has been telegraphed to Wetumpka.

Railroad Jubilee. From accounts in the Columbus (Ga.) Times, there was a pleasant occasion in Columbus on Thursday last, being the Festival of the completion of the Muscogee road, and the union of the Chattahoochee with the waters of the Atlantic and Savannah. On the arrival of the guests from Savannah and Macon, &c, the banquet commenced, and the assemblage was addressed by Maj. J.H. Howard, J.M. Berrian, R. Toombs, Seaborn Jones, Cuyler, Pierpont, and others. The *reunion* was most pleasant, and according to the papers, the fun and excitement was fast and furious. We trust to see another such here when the Prattville and Montgomery branch of the Selma road is completed!

Gen. Arista Banished. Gen. Arista, late President of Mexico, arrived at Havana on the 6th inst, in the English mail steamer from Vera Cruz, and proceeded in her to England. It appears that he has been banished by Santa Anna, ordered to go to Europe, and there remain, where he will be allowed to retain his rank in the army and pay pertaining to it. A desire to maintain public tranquility is alleged as the reason for his banishment. Arista publicly protested against the decree and tyrannical reparation for injuries. He avows his sympathy for the North American institutions, a desire for the establishment of federal institutions in Mexico, and, if possible, annexation to the United States, which, he predicts, will yet happen.

General Intelligence.
England. Kossuth had been fully exhonorated from all implication in the rocket affair.
France. The Empress Eugenie had recovered from her late misfortune - a miscarriage, the consequence of fatigue and over exertion during the coronation of the Emperor.

More from the Gold Regions. after a rather unaccountable silence on the exciting topic of the Texas gold diggings, the Austin Gazette now gives the following strong endorsement to the most favorable reports. The public have looked to the Austin papers for information, and they finally give it, would be very praiseworthy assurance that they will "practice no concealment to gratify the avarice of speculators. The Gazette says: A considerable excitement is prevailing throughout Western Texas on the subject of the gold discoveries in our neighborhood; and we have had several letters, and observe notices in our exchanges, asking information on the subject. That there is gold, and in great quantities, on the tributaries of the Colorado, a short distance above this city, we can no longer entertain a doubt, for some specimens shown us are of the most beautiful character. We understand, upon good authority, that one specimen have been found with twenty-four dollars worth of gold. This report we have no hesitation in crediting, as it was brought a a gentleman of the undoubtedly veracity. The number of persons now at the mines is very considerable, set down by reports from 200 to 500, most of whom are greatly encouraged by their success. Persons are flocking into the mining districts from all parts of the country, and we shall not be surprised to hear soon of discoveries equaling in importance the golden stories of California. The Indianola Bulletin says that Mr. Wm. N. Varnell, of that place with several persons from Port Lavaca and elsewhere, will soon leave for the mines by way of Gonzales, Austin, &c. The district of country in which gold has been found is very extensive, an easy of access from the city. Our readers may rely upon it, that we will give them, from time to time, such information, and such only, as can be relied upon. We shall practice no concealment to gratify the avarice of speculators, nor unduly magnify the extent of the gold discoveries, to mislead the unwary.

The State of Alabama, Autauga County, Special Court of Probate, May 20, 1853.
This day came William L. Knox and Harriet D. Knox, guardians of Robert E. Durden and Lawrence A. Durden, minors, and filed their accounts and vouchers for the annual settlement of said wards' estate, which was examined and order to be filed for the inspection of all concerned. It is therefore ordered, that notice be given for forty days, by publication or three successive weeks in the Autauga Citizen, a newspaper published in said county, notifying all persons interested to be and appear at a Court to be held on the 2nd day of July next, to show cause, if any, why said account should not be stated and allowed. Henly Brown, Judge of Probate

The State of Alabama, Autauga County, Special Court of Probate, May 20, 1853.
This day came Harriet D. Knox, formerly Harriet D. Durden, guardian of Georgianna W. Durden and Charles W. Durden, minors, and filed her account and vouchers for the final settlement of said wards' estate, which was examined and ordered to be filed for the inspection of all concerned. It is therefore ordered, that notice be given for forty days, by publication for three successive weeks in the Autauga Citizen, a newspaper published in said county, notifying all persons interested to be and appear at a court to be held on the 2nd day of July next, to show cause, if any, why said account should not be stated and allowed. Henly Brown, Judge of Probate.

The State of Alabama, Autauga County. Taken up, by Thomas Hogg, and posted before A. Samples a Justice of the Peace in and for said county, a light colored grey mare, five feet one inch high, supposed to be eleven years old, and far it advanced in foal; has marks of the saddle and collar. Appraised by Wm. N. Peeples and Wm. Samples at sixty-five dollars, the 7th day of May, 1853. Henly Brown, Judge of Probate.

Vol. 1, Thursday, June 2, 1853, No. 18

On the 23rd ult, a batch of foreign appointments by the President was announced. Among them we notice the following: Ministers. To Prussia, Peter D. Vroom, of N. J.; Brazil, Gov. Wm. Trousdale, of Tenn.; Chili, Sam'l Medary, of Ohio. Col. J.J. Seibells, late editor of the Montgomery Advertiser and Gazette, goes to Belgium as Charge de Affaires. J.M. Tarleton, of this State, is Consul at Panama, and Donald G. Mitchell (" Ik Marvel") Consul at Venice. **Look Out for the Scamp!** Several citizens of Lawrence District (S.C.) and of Franklin county (Geo.), publish a chap named Alfred Owens, who suddenly left the first named place, leaving also, and Miss Kennedy to take care of a pair of twins; he had *promised* to marry her. He turned up in Franklin, stopped at his aunt's house, gained the affections of her only daughter, seduced her, and then ran way - after, in addition, borrowing all of the money he could, and buying one thing and another where every he could, "on a cred." He is supposed to have made tracks for this State, where he has numerous relatives. Here is Master Owen's picture: "He is about 28 years old, 5 feet 6 or 8 inches high, dark complexion, black hair, a heavy beard, square built, bow-legged, of low Dutch appearance, a dull, in 6 countenance, very surly and sour looking; has thick lips, yellowish grey eyes, is exceedingly secluded and selfish in his habits, niggardly and proud; but has little to say, he never speaks well of anybody but the vulgar. He professes to be a great blacksmith, carriage trimmer and a painter."

Washington Items. The correspondent of the N.Y. Journal of Commerce, after stating that the Cabinet agreed upon all the following appointments, says: It is understood that for every place - even those of the obscurest character, where disease and danger must be braved, without the hope of any pecuniary reward, - there were at least forty applicants. This administration is remarkable for the secrecy of its councils. It is still doubtful whether Mr. Dix, or some new man, will be sent to France; so on through the whole catalog of minor appointments. Gov. Marcy has been untiring in his efforts to reconcile conflicting interests, and, looking at his merits in every branch of official duty has not been excelled by any of his predecessors in the Department of State. Mr. Clay may have been more brilliant, Mr. Calhoun more philosophical, and Mr. Adams may have possessed more varied learning, but for keen, practical sense, vigorous and logical thought, and industrious application to business, Mr. Marcy has never had a superior in the Department which he occupies. He will make his mark on the foreign policy of this government, and inaugurate a new era in American diplomacy. And this, without any adoption of wild and vague theories, for he is eminently conservative, as well as bold and decisive. The ideal that in this administration any foreign minister will be granted a *carte blanche* to conduct affairs as to him seems best, is entirely absurd. No government could be sustained on such a principal. - There must be a unity in the management of affairs, which is only possible when the direction comes from the central point. No man of common sense can suppose for a moment that Mr. Soule is to do as he pleases in Spain, or that Mr. Buchanan, in England, is to follow a similar independent course. All negotiations with foreign powers are relative, and have a bearing on each other. In a few years more, treaties between states will be made at Washington, - not at London and Paris, as heretofore.

Miss Macy, of Boston, daughter of the late John D. Williams, Esq., and heiress in her on to over a quarter million of dollars, was wedded, on Wednesday last, to Mr. T.R. Frothingham, son of the Rev. Dr. Frothingham.

Editorial Brevities.
Dr. Joseph Leidy has been elected Professor of Anatomy in the University of Pennsylvania,

in the place of Dr. Horner, deceased.

The Alabama Journal says: We learn from direct and reliable authority from Huntsville, that Senator Clemens will not, as has been announced, take the field for the office of Governor. His health renders all exertion, at the present moment, utterly impossible.

Robert Owen's 82d birthday was celebrated last week in New York I have few of the "strong-minded" women and differently minded men. Mrs. Rose and Lucy Stone (en costume) were present. Dancing, feasting, and speeches, where the order of exercise.

The Road Complete. The whole line of railroad, from the city to Fort Valley, is now finished and there remains no gap between here and Savannah. Situated as we are, nearly three hundred miles apart the fiery steed that puffs and whirls along on the iron track, brings us almost in speaking distance of our friends on the seaboard. In a short time the trains will pass from one point to the other between the rising and setting sun. Who would have dreamed of such a thing, twenty or even ten years ago? [Columbus (Ga.) Enquirer]

Our Circuit court was engaged all the past week, says the Montgomery Advertiser of yesterday, in the trial of criminal cases. Two negroes were found guilty of manslaughter (on slaves). Chas. H. Parmer was convicted of the murder of W. F. Richbourg, and condemned to the penitentiary for life. This murder was committed in Pike county - the venue having been charged by the prisoner to this county. The conviction was made of circumstantial evidence of a very strong and overwhelming nature.

A negro woman in Bowling Green, Ky., was delivered at a few days since of twins, one of whom was perfectly white, the other a pure African.

Important Decision. Judge McLean has decided in the U.S. Court at Columbus, Ohio, that Railroad Companies have a legal right to build bridges over navigable streams in such a way not to obstruct navigation.

Judge Thomas, an old an respectable citizen of Mount Vernon, Ohio, committed suicide on the 2d inst. He was the first United States Senator from Indiana, and author of the celebrated Compromise law which Henry Clay carried through Congress.

M.A. King, Esq., who recently announced himself a candidate for Congress in the 6th district, now announces that he declines to run, and says that "circumstances have recently transpired which, in his judgment, render it necessary and proper for him to decline."

Funeral Notice. The Funeral of Mrs. Elizabeth Whetstone will be preached by the Rev. D.B. Smedley, on the Third Sabbath in the month (June), at Autaugaville Protestant church.

Notice. Letters of administration having been granted to the undersigned on the estate of George Laycock, deceased, on the 17th day of May, by the Hon. Henly Brown, Judge of Probate of Autauga county. All persons having claims against said estate will present them within the time prescribed by law, or they will be barred. Malcom Smith.

Administrator's Sale. Will be sold in the town at Autaugaville, on Thursday, 30th of June, all the perishable property be longing to the estate of George Laycock, deceased, (except the negro property), on a credit of six months, the purchaser required to give small notes with approved security. Malcolm Smith.

The State of Alabama, Autauga County, Special Court of Probate, May 27, 1853.
Ordered, that notice be given to the creditors of Benj. F. Tarleton, deceased, by publication in the Autauga Citizen, a newspaper published at Prattville, once a week for six successive weeks, that Thomas J. Tarleton, administrator of said estate, has this day filed his report and statements, setting forth that said estate is insolvent, and that the 12th day of July next has been appointed to hear and determine the same, at the Probate Court room in Kingston, in said county. Witness - Henly Brown, Judge of Probate, of said county. Henly Brown, Judge of Probate

Sheriff's Sale. Will be sold to the highest bidder, for cash, at the courthouse door in Kingston, on the first Monday of July next, between the legal hours of sale, the following town lots, known and described in the plan of the town of Wetumpka by numbers one hundred and forty-nine, one hundred and fifty one, one hundred and fifty three, one hundred and fifty four: Levied on as the property of Edmond J. Felder and Epaphras Burrows, to satisfy two executions in my office from the Circuit Court of Autauga county, one in favor of Begelow & Clough, and against the said Felder, and the other in favor of the Branch Bank of the State of Alabama at Montgomery, and against the said Burrows. James A. Lawler, Shff of Autauga Co.

Sheriff's Sale. Will be sold to the highest bidder, for cash, at the court house door in the town of Kingston, on the first Monday of July next, within the legal hours of sale, a house and lot, in the town of Autaugaville, known and described in the plan of said town as lot number two, in fractional block number one, east of Picket street, with a front of thirty feet; which is now occupied by Messrs. B.F. & T.A. Davis, druggists. Levied on as the property of Edward D. Jarrete, to satisfy an execution in my office from the Circuit Court of Autauga county, in favor of William Walker and against Edward D. Jarrette. James A. Lawler, Shff. Autauga Co.

Sheriff's Sale. Will be sold to the highest bidder, for cash, in the town of Prattville, between the legal hours of sale on Saturday, the 4th inst., a (?) harness and saddle horse, (large bay), levied on under two attachments in my office against the estate of C.N. Knox, where in Wm.(?) Knox and Harriet D. Knox, are plaintiffs. James A. Lawless, Shff. Autauga Co.

Vol. 1, Thursday, June, 9, 1853, No. 19

The First of the Season. Mr. F.P. DeBardelaban has left that our office the first cotton bloom that we have seen or heard in this vicinity, or in the State. We learn that the crops in this county are generally good, but suffering very much from drought. Weather dry, and distressingly hot at this writing, with but little prospect of rain.

The Charleston papers note a sad railroad catastrophe which occurred on the Columbia road about midnight on Monday last. The train, when within the vicinity of Cattle Creek, about six miles from Branchville, came in contact with a portion of the track from which the railing had been torn off, the iron being placed crosswise, in a manner intended to divert the course of the car. By this means the car was immediately thrown from the track, striking the cross-tree trussel, and instantaneously killing Mr. Winter, the engineer, and one fireman; another was also seriously injured. Three of the cars were much broken up, that none of the passengers were injured. The two unfortunate victims were men of family, who were all together dependent upon their industry for a livelihood. The calamity was occasioned by design. The company offers a reward of $1,000.00 for the apprehension of the murderers.

Editorial Brevities.
Cotton Trade. We have been shown an important letter addressed to C.G. Baylor, Esq., late United States Consul at Amsterdam, and editor of the Cotton Plant, by the President of a powerful and wealthy European Commercial Company. This letter is in conclusion of a correspondence which has been going on for some time between Mr. Baylor and European influences in regard to the importance of a Continental Depot for cotton. From the language and tone of the letter before us the most favorable disposition is manifested, and the President has notified Mr. Baylor that one of the company was to sail for America in time to be at the Memphis Convention. At Memphis the plan of a tour will be agreed upon. His tour is to enable this gentleman, as the confidential friend and agent of the European Company, to inform them of the cotton growers, and their disposition to participate in any general movement such as is contemplated by direct trade. The object will also be to give certain assurance to the planter of the determination of European capitalists to cooperate in the formation of a Continental Depot of Cotton. This tour must prove interesting, not only on account of opportunity it will give intelligent European society to judge of our Southern friends, at also in regard to a changing the destination of that portion of the cotton crop which now goes circuitously to the manufacturers of the continent. Nat. Int.

A locomotive, it is said, dispatched from Laporte Indiana, to Chicago, for physicians to attend Robert B. Toxander who died at Laporte of apoplexy, ran the entire distance and back, in one hour and forty five minutes. This is fully up, if not superior, to the speed daily attained on the English Great Western Railroad between Paddington and London.

A new Safety-Lamp has been invented by C.J. Conway of New York City. For his invention Mr. C. Forms a reservoir at the base of the lamp, into which the fluid is poured without bringing the fluid can near the burning lamp.

The Earthquake, a shock of which has been noticed as having been felt at Washington and Wheeling, was quite severe at Lynchburg, Va. At the railroad depot it shook the desk of which M.F.G. Morrison, the Secretary and Treasurer, was writing, to such an extent that he was compelled to stop. A glass filled with water, on the same desk, had the water almost thrown out of it. It lasted about a minute and a half.

Southern Rights Club. For the Autauga Citizen. At a called meeting of Mulberry Southern Rights Club, held on Saturday, the 4th inst., at Mulberry P. O., the following resolutions were offered by H.D. Holmes, and adopted: *Resolved*, That it is the opinion of this Club, that the Southern Rights party of Autauga county should have a candidate for the lower branch of the Legislature in the coming election; and to secure united action, and thereby success, we recommend to the party the propriety of holding a meeting in Autaugaville, on Saturday, the 18th inst. *Resolved*, That the Chairman appoint ten delegates to represent this Club in said meeting. In compliance with the second resolution, the following gentlemen were appointed, to which the Chairman was subsequently added: A.D. Holmes, C.C. Dickerson, L. Howard, S.E. Macon, A.C. Taylor, Charles M. Howard, Wm. C. Love, D. Lamar, C.G. Lanier, A.C. Love and A.C. Houston. On motion, the proceedings of the Club be signed by the Chairman and Secretary, and sent to our county papers, with a request to publish them. A.C. Houston, Ch'm. Chas. M. Howard, Sec'y.

From the Montgomery Journal **Proceedings of Whig State Convention.** The Whigs State Convention that at Montgomery on the first inst. J.D. Hopper, Esq., was called to the Chair, and Benj. Gardner, Esq., acted as Secretary - when, on motion, all Whigs present were requested to enroll their names as delegates. Macon, Lowndes, Mobile, Montgomery, Pike, Talledega and Autauga counties, were represented - the last named by Messrs. Edmond Shackelford, Caleb Moncrief, Jessee R. Jones, J.D. Whetstone, A.H. Whetstone, J.H. Huie, Lewis Tyus, John C. Reid, E.G. Carew and J.M. Clay. A committee of five was appointed to select officers of the Convention, who reported the following:
For President, W.H. Fielding, of Mobile.
For Vice Presidents, G.S. Coxe, of Lowndes, B.S. Bibb, of Montgomery, Lewis Tyus, of Autauga, J. Perine, of Mobile, J. McCaleb Wiley, of Pike, H.H. Armstrong, of Macon.
Secretaries, Daniel Sayre, of Macon and Benjamin Gardner, of Montgomery.
On motion, a committee of fifteen was appointed to draft "resolutions embodying a Platform as principles and policy as the basis of organization for the Whig party of Alabama," and the also, to inquire into the expediency of nominating a candidate for Governor - which committee reported as follows: The committee on resolutions have the honor to report for the consideration of the Convention, the following outline of principles of policy, which, in their opinion, should form the basis for a thorough organization of the Whig party of Alabama. Believing that gravity and point are of great importance in articles of party faith, the committee have sought to condense as much as possible, while endeavoring to express in unmistakable terms the object we, as a party, desire to accomplish. The resolutions are believed to correspond with the convictions of the great majority of the Whigs of the State, and the committee deem it unnecessary, in this place, to submit an argument in favor of their adoption... The preamble resolutions were read seriatum and adopted, and afterwards were unanimously passed as a whole, as the principles of policy of the Whig party of Alabama. Mr. Gardner than advocated the necessity of nominated and Whig candidate for Governor, and the completion of his remarks nominated the Hon. Henry W. Hilliard. Mr. Hilliard immediately arose and to eloquently addressed the Convention, announcing his unfaltering devotion to the Whig party and its principles, but earnestly requested to be excused excepting the nomination. Mr. Gardner then withdrew the name of Mr. Hilliard - when Mr. Hilliard nominated Richard W. Walker, of Lauderdale - which was confirmed by acclamation, and Mr. Walker declared the candidate of the Whig party of Alabama for Governor. Mr. Clark, of Mobile, then offered the following preamble and resolutions for the more effectual organization of the Whig party in the State: Whereas: It is the opinion of this Convention that a more thorough and perfect organization of the Whig party in the State is essential to its prosperity

and appropriate influence of, and whereas, it is expected of the delegates here resembled to recommend a suitable plan for such organization: Be in there for, *Resolved*, That a committee of twenty one, to be called "The Whig State Central Committee" comprising at least one member from each Congressional District in this State; and a majority of whom shall reside within convenient access to the city of Montgomery, show be elected by ballot by this Convention, whose duty it shall be to superintend the general affairs of the party in the State; counsel their fellow Whigs as to the best method of conducting canvasses for State and national offices; correspond when thought expedient, giving adequate public notice of the time and place for holding said Convention, and discharge such other duties as a general supervision of the interests of the party may require, or as may properly belong to such a committee... The committee then proceeded to elect the committee under the first resolution, when the following gentlemen were elected: Jack Thorington of Montgomery, A.R. Manning of Mobile, L.F. Parsons of Talledega, George P. Blevins of Dallas, R. Jemison, Jr., of Tuscaloosa, N. Davis of Limestone, A.E. Mills of Madison, J.H. Clinton of Montgomery, A.G. McGee of Lowndes, J. McCaleb Wiley of Pike, W.W. Echols of Macon, J.C. Reid of Autauga, A.M. Sandford of Barbour, Alexander Carter of Montgomery, Daniel Pratt of Autauga, W.S. Kyle of Coosa, S.F. Hale of Green, T.S. Tate of Russel, Sidney A. Smith of Henry, C.W. Gazzam and R.H. Smith of Mobile. On motion of Mr. Sayre, the following gentlemen were appointed a committee to notify Mr. Walker of his nomination; H.W. Hilliard of Montgomery, W.G. Clark of Mobile, J.M. Wisey of Pike, Lewis Tyus of Autauga, J.E. Belcer of Montgomery, A.G. McGehee of Lowndes. On motion of Mr. Hilliard, it was *Resolved*, That in case Mr. Walker should decline in nomination, the Central Committee be instructed to select a candidate and present him to the people. On motion of Mr. Clanton, Mr. A.G. McGehee in the Chair, it was *Resolved*, That the thanks of this Convention be tendered the Chairman for the prompt and satisfactory manner in which he has presided over the deliberations of this convention, and to the Secretaries for the faithful manner in which they have discharged their duty. On motion of Mr. Wiley, all papers in this State, friendly to the principles and policy of this Convention, be requested to publish these proceedings. On motion of Mr. Sayre, the Convention then adjourned *sine die*. Wm. H. Fleming, President. Daniel Sayre, Benj. Gardner, Secretaries.

Administrator's Sale of Real Estate. Will be sold to the highest bidder, before the court house door in Kingston, Autauga county, on the 12th day of July next, within the legal hours of sale, the following described lots of parcels of land in the town of Washington, in said county, viz. lots No. 1 and 6, bounded north by three acre lots No. 1 and 4, east by Warren street and for acre lot No 3, south by for acre lot No. 3 and Hancock street, and west by the line dividing sections 32 and 33 of township 17, range 16. Also, and undivided half interest at lot No. 8, of square No. 9; and one undivided half of three-fourths of lot No. 5 of square No. 9. Sold as the property of the estate of Benj. F Tarleton, deceased, by virtue of an order from the Probate Court of said county. Terms - A credit until the first day of January next, the purchaser giving notes with two good securities. Thomas J. Tarleton, Admr.

The State of Alabama, Autauga county, Special Court of Probate, May 28th, 1853.
This day came William Montgomery, Administrator of the estate of Abner Hill, deceased, and filed his account and vouchers for the annual settlement of the estate of said deceased, which was examined and ordered to be filed for the inspection of all concerned. It is therefore ordered, that notice be given for forty days, by publication for three successive weeks in the Autauga Citizen, notifying all persons interested to be and appear at a Probate Court to be held on the 12th day of July next, to show cause why said account should not be stated and allowed. Henly Brown, Judge of Probate

The State of Alabama, Autauga county, Special Court of Probate, May 28, 1853.
This day came William Montgomery, guardian of George W. Dismukes, a minor, and filed his accounts and vouchers for the annual settlement of his said guardianship, which was examined and ordered to be filed for the inspection of all concerned. It is therefore ordered, that notice be given for forty days, by publication for three successive weeks in the Autauga Citizen, notifying all persons interested to be and appear at a court to be held on the 12th day of July next, to show cause why said account should not be stated and allowed, and said settlement be made. Henly Brown, Judge of Probate.

Vol. 1, Thursday, June 16, 1853, No. 20

Autauga County. We tender our thanks to Mr. Dorsey for the interesting paper which accompanied the following note:

Office State Guard, Wetumpka, June 8, 1853.

Messrs Howell & Luckett, Gentleman: In looking over some old papers and my office, I found the enclosed manuscript, in which, as it appertains exclusively to your county, I take the liberty to send you. I am confident it has never been published, and I also feel assured that it will prove of interest to your readers. Very respectfully, your friend, &c. D.W. Dorsey. Members of the General Assembly elected from Autauga county since its organization, and County Court Judges from the organization of the court, in June, 1821, up to the time it was superseded by the Probate Court, in May, 1850: [From "Cleveland's Alabama Register," and unpublished volume, compiled by James A. Cleveland, Esq., of Limestone county.]

Years.	Judges	State Senators.
1819	-	Howell Rose
1820	-	"
1821	John Ashley	"
1822	"	Dunklin Sullivan
1823	A. A. McWhorton	"
1824	"	"
1825	Eli Terry	James Jackson
1826	"	Jack Shackelford
1827	"	"
1828	"	Wm. R. Pickett
1829	"	"
1830	"	"
1831	"	"
1832	"	"
1833	"	"
1834	Henly Brown	Robert Broadnax
1835	"	"
1836	"	"
1837	"	Sam'l S. Simmons
1838	"	"
1839	"	"
1840	"	Dixon Hall
1841	"	"
1842	"	"
1843	"	William L. Yancey
1844	"	Samp W. Harris
1845	"	"
1846	"	"
1847	"	Seth P. Stors
1848	"	"
1849	"	"
1850	6	"
1851	"	"

[Previous to 1850, the Judges were elected by the Legislature - in that year they were elected by the people, for the term of six years. - Eds Citizen.]

Members of the House of Representatives.

1819-Phillip Fitzpatrick, Charles A. Dennis
1820-Philip Fitzpatrick, James Jackson
1821-Wm. R. Pickett, John A. Elmore
1822-Philip Fitzpatrick
1823-Wm. R. Pickett
1824-Wm. R. Pickett
1825-Robt. Broadnax, John McNeill
1826-Robt. Broadnax, Eli Terry
1827-Robt. Broadnax, Eli Terry
1828-Robt. Broadnax, Eli Terry
1829-Robt. Broadnax, William Hester
1830-Robt. Broadnax, Dixon Hall
1831-Robt. Broadnax, Dixon Hall
1832-Robt. Broadnax, Saml. S. Simmons
1833-S.S. Simmons, Dixon Hall
1834-S.S. Simmons, Jas B. Robinson, Wm. Burt
1835-S.S. Simmons, Dixon Hall, Benjamin Davis
1836-S.S. Simmons, John P. DeJarnett, William Burt
1837-T.W. Brevard, John P. DeJarnett, William Burt
1838-John W. Withers, Dixon Hall, Thomas Hogg
1839-John W. Withers, Dixon Hall
1840-Benjamin Davis, Absalom Doster
1841-William S. Morgan, John Steele
1842-Wm. S. Morgan, John E. Mitchell
1843-C.M. Jackson, John Steele
1844-C.M. Jackson, John Steele
1847-C.M. Jackson, John Wood
1849-Bolling Hall, John Wood
1851-Bolling Hall, C.C. Howard

Singular Tragedy. On Wednesday two weeks ago, at the lunatic asylum in Somerville, Mass., Mrs. Strong, an aged lunatic, was found dead beside a bed in the room of Mrs. Jameson, another lunatic, who, at the time of the discovery, was kneeling on the bed, an attitude of prayer. Both the deceased and the insane murderer were very respectably connected. Mrs. Jameson, on being questioned as to the death of Mrs. Strong, gave the following account: I heard Mrs. Strong asking for light-this was her constant habit-it occurred to me that the Lord had delivered her into my hands, and that if there was any more light in the other world, she should see it. She had been plaguing for many months with this inquiry, and now, one of the attendants had gone out, and the other preparing dinner, I determined to be rid of the annoyance. I accordingly slipped out into the gallery and invited Mrs. S. into my room. She came with me willingly; she had on two caps; I took them off and tied them a round her neck; the string broke. She stood still, close to me, making no resistance, so I knew the Lord had given her to me. I've then put my hands around her and choked her. I then laid her down on the floor softly, so as to make no noise, and took off one of my stockings and put it around her neck, pulling it as hard as I could-but it was no use, she was already dead; I felt her pulse and I knew it. While I was doing this I said my prayers, and thanked the Lord that he had thus permitted me to glorify His name.

Editorial Brevities.
Casualty - Almost. Mr. Glackmeyer, of the firm Jones & Glackmeyer, Druggists, and the

others present, says the Montgomery Journal of Monday, made a narrow escape yesterday from the effects of the explosion of a Soda Fount which was in the process of being charged in the court in the rear of their tenement. The workman had just completed charging it with the customary number of feet of gas from the gasometers, when it exploded with immense force prostrating Mr. G. And driving the fount several hundred feet in the air. The sound was like that of the discharge of a six pound cannon, and in its accent, destroyed a balcony which was over it, and in falling struck and demolished the parapet of a neighboring building, and rolled inwards on the roof, where it now lies. It fortunately exploded from the bottom, which projected it upwards like a rocket. If the sides or top had given away, loss of life must have ensued. We can graduate our friends on their fortunate escape.

The Boston Post says: "Charles Fernald, Esq., a talented and energetic young printer, who four years ago was a compositor upon the Boston Post, has been appointed by the Governor of California, county judge for Santa Barbara, of that State. The position two which he has been elevated is an extremely responsible one, embracing criminal, civil, and appellate jurisdiction. The appointment is a very judicious, and displays a commendable appreciation of merit. It will be recollected that George H. Campbell, Esq., another Boston printer, was made judge of Calaveral county, California, a year or two since; and this latter appointment is another complement to the intelligence of the craft.

The late Democratic State Convention in Mississippi nominated John J. McRae, of Clark county, as candidate for Governor.

Sailing of the Pacific Expedition. The expedition under Commander Ringgold, United States Navy, for the exploration and survey of the China and Japan seas, North Pacific Ocean, sailed from Norfolk on Monday for its destination. It is supposed that the expedition will dispatch to the East Indies, via Cape of Good Hope, touching at Cape de Verde Isles for water and, rendezvous at Batavia, preparatory to a careful reconnaissance of portions of the lower part of the Chinese Seas. This (says the Union) is an important enterprise-one worthy of the Government, and from which valuable results may be anticipated. Expeditions of this kind suit the taste and genius of our people, and form good schools for our young officers.

Victor Hugo, in a speech delivered over the grave of his exiled compatriots, used the following bold figure: "God is throwing years upon thrones as we throws spades full of earth upon coffins."

An unfortunate rencounter occurred in this place on Friday evening late between Dr. A.T. Daniel, and Irishman by the name of Harold (who was strongly under the influence of liquor) in which the former received a severe wound on the side by a knife in the hands of the latter. Dr. Daniel survived until about six o'clock on yesterday morning when death came to his relief. Harold had been committed to jail to await his trial at the next term of our circuit court. - Recorder, Camden, Willcox county.

Editors for Congress. Mr. Snowden of the Alexandria Gazette; Mr. Sterrett, of Parkersburg News, all Whigs, are candidates for Congress in Virginia.

Final Adjournment. The Convention met the morning of the 9th pursuant to adjournment, when it was addressed in an eloquent speech by the Hon. John Bell, of Tennessee. At the conclusion of Mr. Bell's address, it was moved to that when the Convention adjourned it will be to meet and Charleston, S.C. on the second Monday in April, 1854. The motion was carried. After some further business of little importance, the Convention adjourned to meet in Charleston at the time above stated.

California News. The New Orleans mail yesterday brought us some papers from California and our files of Panama papers. The advices thus received our only to the 8th inst. from San Francisco, and the 31st from Panama. The fire in San Francisco, noted in our dispatch yesterday, was very rapid. Many persons, including women and children, escaped from the flames only with their lives. A Mr. Hubbard, of Ohio, (an invalid) and several others were supposed to have been burned.

Adams & Co.'s express office at Mormon island was robbed at on the night of the 29th ult., by eight men, who seemed to be perfectly acquainted with the office, and succeeded in overpowering and gagging the two clerks who slept in the front office, without alarming Mr. Nicolls, the agent, who slept in a back room. Finding that Mr. N. had the keys of the safe, they ordered one of the clerks, Mr. Ryan, to call Mr. Nicolls and tell him he was sick and wanted some brandy. This they compelled him to do with drawn knives. He then called Mr. Nicolls' name, and without giving him an opportunity to say more, they gagged again, and springing upon Mr. Nicolls, secured him also. They then opened the safe, and seized the contents some $10 or $15,000 in coin and dust, part of the latter was special deposit, belonging to miners. They also took the watches and even the rings from the fingers of the clerks, and escaped with their booty. They were followed as far as the 12 mile house near this city, and then they were lost track of. One of the robbers was subsequently caught.

A difficulty occurred at Santa Barbara on Saturday, 23d ult., in which the sheriff of the county, named Twist, was dangerously shot. He had summoned all the men of the county to act as a *done* to assist, him in serving a writ against a squatter named John Power, and, when assembled with a large party in the Plaza, a disturbance arose, in which a Californian stabbed Twist, who immediately turned, drew his revolver, and shot the Californian dead, at the same time ordering his party to fire. Here ensued in a general melee, and pistol bullets were rattling in all directions. The Californians, understanding the sheriff to fire on the Americans, immediately selected a very prominent and much respected citizen, J.A. Vidall, Esq., formerly a Justice of the Peace in the county; and so determined where they to kill him, that when his body was examined, it was found to be completely riddled with pistol bullets. Great excitement prevailed until next day when the arrival in port of the U.S. revenue cutter "Ewing" gave anewed assurance to the authorities. The writ had not yet been served.

List of Letters. Remaining in the Post Office at Robinson Springs, on the 8th of June, 1853; Paten Ziegler, Miss Caroline Bassel, Wm. Miles, Henry Trammell, Wm. Hogan, Joseph A. Johnson, John Jackson, Thomas M. Stewart, Robert Glenn. M. Spigner,P.M.

The State of Alabama, Autauga county, Special Court of Probate, June 6, 1853.
This day came Reuben P. Turner, administrator of the estate of Abram Bishop, and filed his accounts and vouchers for the final settlement of the estate of said deceased, which was ordered to be filed for the inspection of all concerned. It is therefore ordered, that notice be given for forty days, by publication for three successive weeks in the Autauga Citizen, a newspaper published in said county, notifying all persons interested to be and appear at a court to be held on the 18th day of July next, to show cause, if any, why said account should not be stated and allowed. Henly Brown, Judge of Probate

The State of Alabama, Autauga county, Special Court of Probate, June 2, 1853.

This day came Abram Martin, Administrator of the estate of the Aaron Ready, deceased, and filed his petition, setting forth that said deceased died seized of lots no. 16, 17, and 18, of original lot No. 182, in West Wetumpka, and a tract or parcel of land situated northwest of Three Mile Creek, in Mobile county, bounded south by the lands owned by Thomas Herndon, west by lands by David Clegg, north by lands conveyed to James B. Bates, and east by the St. Stevens road containing 19 acres, and 12 shares in the Tuscaloosa Manufacturing Company, situated in Bibb county, and two-thirds of fifty shares of the Central Plankroad Company in Coosa and Talledega counties; and that the estate of said Ready has been declared insolvent, and prays a decree to sell said lands and the lots, and shares of the capital stock in the Tuscaloosa Manufacturing Company and Central Plankroad Company, to pay the debts of said Aaron Ready. It is therefore ordered by the court that notice of said petition be given by publication in the Autauga Citizen, for three successive weeks, to all persons concerned in the premises to appear at a regular term of this court to be held on the 2d Monday of July next to contest said petition. Henly Brown, Judge of Probate

Vol. 1, Thursday, June 23, 1853, No. 21

Our friend, Mr. Merril Pratt, will accept our thanks for the fine water melon that he presented us a few days ago.

We learn, from the Alabama Journal, that Richard W. Walker has accepted the nomination of the Whig Convention for Governor.

Homicide. We learn that Mr. Alpheus Jones, residing near Butler's Mills, in this county, was killed on Wednesday by Dr. Miller, of the same neighborhood. The circumstances, we learn were these: John's suspected the seduction of his wife by Miller, and on watching detected them in the act, and rushed on Miller, who killed in with the Bowie knife. Miller has escaped. If these are the facts as stated, he becomes the Governor and State authorities to offer a reward sufficient to secure the person of the adulterer and assassin. - *Journal*

On Tuesday the trial of Agnes Anderson for the murder of W.B. Taylor, took place before Judge LaRue. The reader will recollect that Taylor was killed in his bed, and that the parties lived together illicitly. The Picayune thus describes her appearance: The prisoner is apparently about twenty years of age, rather under a medium height, prepossessing in her personal appearance, and was neatly dressed, having on they changeable silk dress, a white silk mantilla and a straw bonnet with blue trimming and a black and green veils. The prisoner appeared somewhat nervous but acted generally with much decorum, weeping on one or two occasions during the trial. We should judge from her appearance that she was a person of the sanguine and impulsive temperament, and that she belongs to the middle walks of life. The jury was out about fifteen minutes and returned a verdict of not guilty.

Editorial Brevities.

The widow of Gen. Harrison still occupies a portion of the old mansion at North Bend, (on the Ohio river, in the state of Ohio,) where she is watched over by the filial care of the family of Col. Taylor. She is in the serene evening of a long an eventful life, and though bearing the weight of many years, is still able to move about her room carried the present Harrison estate consist of 800 acres at North Bend and 420 at the mouth of the Miami. The property is as yet undivided, but it is the intention of the heirs to effect a division the coming season. The estate formally embraced a large tract of intervale land to the northward, but is now mostly composed of high rolling lands near the Ohio.

Desperate rencounter. On Saturday last an affray occurred at Taylor's Springs, in this county, between four men-the Hills and Kings, two brothers on each side, which resulted in the murder of two of them and severely wounding of the third. It seems Lewis B. Hill and Alex King were engaged in a fight when the latter drew his knife and inflicted a severe wound in the breast of Hill, cutting him to the hollow and severing part of the liver, although morally wounded, Hill drew his knife and stabbed his antagonist inflicting wound in the abdomen, through which the bowels of King, protruded felt upon the ground and in the dirt. King died six hours after the fight, and Hill lived until Monday morning last. During the affray the brother of each party endeavored to interfere, which resulted in a fight between them, during which time King was knocked down and Hill seriously, but not dangerously, stabbed in the thigh. [Florence (Ala.) Gazette, 11th inst.]

The Paris correspondent of the Boston *Atlas*, writing to that journal under the date of the 16th ult., says that he saw Mr. W.M. Thackery a day or two previously strolling along the

Boulevard des Italiens looking very well and in fine spirits, and that he speaks in a most enthusiastic manner of the United States, and contemplates returning there very shortly to reside permanently.

No More Bachelor's Reveries. Charleston papers announced the marriage of Donald G. Mitchell, ("Ik Marvel") the author of the Reveries of a Bachelor, and other popular productions, to Miss Mary F. Pringle, daughter of William B. Pringle. Mr. Mitchell was a few days since, appointed Consul to Venice.

The New York Tribune says that the place of DeLeon, who is Consul to Alexandria, is worth $5,000.00 a year. Mr. DeLeon was one of the editors of the Southern Press.

Execution of Arthur Spring. The New York and Philadelphia papers are gloating over the particulars of execution of Arthur Spring, in the jail yard at Philadelphia, on the morning of the 10th inst. He died apparently without a struggle. A few moments before the execution took place, the Rev. Dr. who was in attendance, put the following question to the prisoner: "Is young Arthur, your son, guilty of the murder of Mrs. Shaw and Mrs. Lynch?" To this the culprit made the following answer: "He is no more guilty of their murderer than I am." The last words of Spring where: "I went to bed at night-I mean the night of the murder-at seven o'clock, and did not rise until breakfast time the next morning. I knew nothing of the murder until the officers arrested me." Spring denied those positively and earnestly his having committed the murder for which he had been convicted. He also protested his incurrance of the murder of Rink, with which he had been charged. Of these he alleged, just before passing from time to eternity, that he was wholly guiltless. He passed the night with the apparent composure, and the next morning ate a hearty breakfast, remarking whilst he ate it that it was the last breakfast, he would ever have. Whilst on the gallows he stood up firm, not the slightest tremor was visible. Quite a large number of persons witnessed the execution, which has created a great sensation throughout the city. Before ascending scaffold, Spring asked for some liquor, which the sheriff refused to give him. Thousands of persons witnessed the execution. An immense heterogeneous mob, or concourse of persons, all colors and sexes, surrounded the prison. The neck of the culprit was broken instantly upon the falling, which is the reason of his not struggling. He was allowed to hang 27 minutes, and then cut down, and the body taken by Doctors Kirkbride and McClintock for examination of the brain, after which it was handed over to the Rev. John Street, or burial everything passed of orderly.

Isaac Crandall, of Cherry Valley, N.Y., has made certain improvements in the construction of wagons. His invention relates to a novel method of arranging many of the parts of the common double wagon and of making its upper reach elastic, so as to yield when the front axle and tongue are moved out of a straight line with the direction in which the carriage is moving so as to accommodate itself to the movement of the horse.

The State of Alabama, Autauga county, Special Court of Probate, June 17, 1853.
This day came Jessee R. Jones, guardian of Frederick H. Brown and Jesse R. Brown, minors, and filed his account and vouchers for the annual settlement of said wards' estate, which was examined and ordered to be filed for the inspection of all concerned. It is therefore ordered, an notice be given for forty days, by publication for three successive weeks in the Autauga Citizen, a newspaper published in said county, notifying all persons interested to be and appear at a Court to be held on the 30th day of July next, to show cause, if any, why said account should not be stated and allowed. Henly Brown, Judge of Probate.

Masonic. There will be a celebration of Anniversary of St. John's Day (Being 24th June,) by Prattville Lodge No. 89, at which time the officers will be installed, and an address suitable to the occasion delivered by the Rev. S.O. Capers, at half-past ten o'clock, at the Baptist Church. Sister Lodges, transient brethren, and the public are respectfully invited to attend. J.M. Smith, Thos. W. Hutchinson, Wm. Walker, Committee.

We are authorized to announce Major Bolling Hall as a candidate for representative in the next Legislature.

Warner Hurst is a candidate for Tax Collector of Autauga county.

The friends of John W. Clarke announce him as a candidate for Tax Collector of Autauga county, at the ensuing August election.

Col. John A. Winston, the democratic nominee for Governor, will please answer the questions propounded to him by "Autauga," which will be found in another column.

At a public meeting held at Santa Fe on 11th May, H.N. Smith presiding, resolutions were passed sustaining Gov. Lane in proclaiming the Mesilla Valley a portion of the territory of New Mexico. The Santa Fe Gazette publishes a letter from Antonio Jacques and Thomas de Zuluago, Commissioners of the State of Chihuahua, to Gov. Lane, contending that the Mesilla Valley does not belong to the United States. A communication from the Governor, in reply, sustaining the position taken in his proclamation, is also published.

The Capital Extension. Professor A.D. Bache, United States Coast Survey; Professor J. Henry, President of the Smithsonian Institution, and Capt. Meigs, United States Engineers, the committee appointed by Congress to superintend the enlargement of the Capitol, are now in New York, and had visited Metropolitan Hall, Niblo's Saloon and Concert room, as well as several churches and public buildings, or the purpose of ascertaining the acoustic merits, and viewing the architectural beauties of each, to enable them to attain the greatest perfection in the construction of the new Congress Hall, new building in Washington.

Recent advices from Washington, announce that Hon. Robert J. Walker, of Mississippi, has been selected to supersede concrete Humphry Marshall, Esq., as Commissioner to China. No better selection could have been made, and choice of such a man as Mr. Walker is sufficient evidence that the nation as well appreciated by the administration. As farseeing and sagacious statesman, Mr. Walker has no superior. As Secretary of the Treasury under Mr. Polk's administration, he distinguished himself by the masterly ability with which he conducted the finances of the country; and we are now reaping in the soundness of our currency and the solvency of the states, a good fruits of his consummate abilities. His intimate acquaintance with our commerce and its wants, peculiarly fit him for the Chinese mission.

Editorial Brevities.
Departure of Gen. Garland for New Mexico. The St. Louis Intelligencer of the 13th says: "Gen. Garland, USA, whose arrival has been expected here for nearly a week, reached the city yesterday, on his way to New Mexico, where he will take command of the U.S. troops stationed in that Territory. He will leave tomorrow for Fort Leavenworth, where he will be joined by Gov. Meriwether and a number of private citizens, who will avail themselves of the opportunity for a safe and agreeable escort across the Plains. About three hundred troops will accompany Gen. Garland from the same point, designed as a reinforcement of the army now stationed in New Mexico. Major Nichols, who is now here also, goes out as adjutant General.

Acquitted. Miss Mary Ann Wheeler, on her second trial at Milwauki, Wisconsin, for the murder of her seducer, has been acquitted. The law of Wisconsin seems to authorize a verdict of that sort, and imposes upon the Judge in such cases, the duty of inquiring whether insane persons are dangerous to the community, and if so, in Ms. Wheeler's case, however, thought no precaution of that kind necessary, and is charged the prisoner from custody.

Death of Gen. Riley. This gentleman, a distinguished officer of the United States Army, died at Buffalo, N.Y., on the 9th inst. He served with distinction in the war of 1812, and also in the Mexican war, and was subsequently appointed Military Governor of California by President Polk.

Proceedings of the Southern Rights Convention. In pursuance of previous notice delegates from the Southern Rights Clubs of Autauga county assembled in convention at Autaugaville, on Saturday, 18th inst., for the purpose of selecting a candidate for the House of Representatives of the next Alabama Legislature. The convention was organized by calling Malcom Smith to the chair. On motion of Wm. P. DeJarnett, Dr. C.A. Edwards, of the Prattville Club, was requested to that as Secretary-declined. James A. Lawler move to that Albert Elmore the requested to act as Secretary to the convention-carried. On motion of the Secretary the roll of the Clubs was called, and delegates requested to come forward and enroll their names. A.C. Love inquired of the chair if a delegate should register his name, would be bound, in honor, by the action of the convention. The chair decided in the affirmative. The following delegates came forward and enrolled their names. From the Autaugaville Club: J.B. Wilkinson, J. Paris, D.B. Smedley, J.A. Lawler, W.P. DeJarnett, B.F. Davis, E.P. Jarrott, J.W. Gholson. From the Mulberry Club: L. Howard, A.C. Taylor, C.M. Howard, W.G. Love, C.C. Dickerson, H.P. Holmes, A.C. Love. From the Prattville Club: J.B. Carpenter, W.D. Smith, C.B. Durden, J.M. Gordon, O. Tatum, P.G. Hall, A.Y. Smith, M.P. Smith, C.A. Edwards, H. Gardner, John T. Hamilton, Wm. H. Northington. From the Wetumpka Club: B.W. Saxon, S.S. McWhorter, A. Elmore. Dr. Edwards moved to that the delegation from the Wetumpka Club be excluded from a voice in the convention, on the ground that the Wetumpka Club embraced the citizens of Coosa as well as Autauga county. Where upon, S.S. McWhorter produced the proceedings of the meeting of the Club, which showed that said Club was held in Autauga county, and that those members of the Club only, who resided in said county, were present and participated. The motion was lost. After some discussions between L. Howard, W.P. DeJarnette, W.H. Northington and C.M. Howard, as to the rule which should govern the conversation and allowing the ratio of representation to the different Clubs, C.M. Howard moved that a committee of one from each Club be selected by the convention to report what number of votes each Club should be entitled to cast in the convention. E.P. Jarrott, W.D. Smith, L. Howard and B.W. Saxon were appointed said committee. On motion, W.H. Northington was added to said committee. S.S. McWhorter offered the following resolution: Resolution of the Southern Rights Convention, which met in Montgomery, September 13th, 1852, for the adoption of the convention. The substance of the resolution was, "That the Southern Rights party will coalesce within neither national party, that may cooperate from time to time with either, as their principles best accord with our own." After some discussion on this resolution, the ayes and noes were called for, which resulted as follows-ayes 25, noes 3. The committee on representation of Clubs made the following report through their chairman, E.P. Jarrott. That one vote be allowed for every ten members of a Club, which ratio gave to Autaugaville 12 votes-to the Prattville Club 13 votes-Mulberry Club 6 votes-Wetumpka Club 7 votes. The report of the committee was adopted. W.H. Northington offered the following resolution: *Resolved*, That this convention deem it in expedient to make in nomination of a candidate to represent Autauga county in the next Legislature. The vote on this resolution was taken by Clubs, a majority of the delegation casting a vote of the Club, which resulted as follows: In favor of the resolution 34-against it 6. The Clubs that voted in the affirmative were in the Wetumpka Club, Prattville Club, and Autaugaville Club. Negative, Mulberry Club. On motion of W.P. DeJarnette, it was resolved that this convention desire opposition to the present done Union candidate for the Senate. Whereupon, J.A. Lawler move that this convention solicit the Hon. W.L. Yancey to become a candidate for that office, which was carried unanimously. On motion of kernel. J.B. Wilkinson, it was resolved at the proceedings of this convention be published in the county papers. On motion of A. Elmore, the convention adjourned *sine die*. Malcom Smith, Ch'm., A. Elmore, Sec'y, Mercury copy.

Physical Phenomenon. A Sleeping Giant-A Rip Van Winkle. The Rochester Democrat gives the subjoined account of a Rip Van Winkle in its neighborhood: Our attention was called yesterday to a most extraordinary phenomenon. A full grown man, six feet two inches tall, thirty seven years of age has slept for nearly five years, with only occasional and brief intervals of wakefulness. The name of this man, subject to so remarkable of suspicion of the ordinary faculties of the race is Cornelius Broomer area he is the son of a farmer living in the town of Clarkson, in this county, in whose family only this single and singular instance of somnolency as ever occurred. The subject of notice first fell into this long sleep on the 19th of June, 1848, and since that time has been awake, at different periods, from a few hours to four months at a time. It is remarked that when it comes out of this catalepsy, he appears to have no knowledge of the lapse of time, or of circumstances taking place while he sleeps. The fit comes upon him instantly, without so far as is known, any warning. His eyes close, his jaws are set, his muscles contract, and his whole frame is rigid, so that if standing, he continues in that altitude partly bent over; and it is not easy to pull him down. He has continued in this condition for months together, unable to speak or move. Various experiments have seen tried to restore him to consciousness, without effect. The men sleeps on, lives, eats, retains perfect health, with a pulse at 80, and without variation. When sleep, he may be placed upon his feet, and he will stand for three days and nights in succession. In order to feed him, it is necessary to pry open his firmly set jaw; and in that manner that little food is introduced into his stomach. He is not, however, much emaciated, keeps his natural color, and appears entirely without disease, excepting that which produces his strange sleep. When he wakes, he comes out of his trance suddenly, his rigid muscles relax at once, he asks for meat or drink, and eats voraciously. If asked why he sleeps so much, he appears to regard it as an imposition, just as in the active man would receive an intimation that he was considered sluggish.

Executors' Notice. Notice is here by given, that on the 21st inst. (June) Letters, Testamentary on the estate of Clairborne Myers, deceased, were granted to the undersigned by the Judge of Probate of the County of Autauga. All persons having claims against said Clairborne Myers, or against his the state, are requested to present them within the time allotted by law, or they will be barred; and all persons indebted are requested to make payment to the undersigned. R.C. Myers, W.L. Yancey

The State of Alabama, Autauga county, Special Court of Probate, June 28, 1853. This day came Francis F. DeBardelaban and John A. Houser, executors of the last will and testament of Henry DeBardelaban, deceased, and filed their accounts and vouchers for the annual settlement of the estate of said deceased. It is therefore ordered that notice be given for forty days, by publication for three successive weeks in the Autauga Citizen, a newspaper published in said county, notifying all persons interested to be and appear at a court to be held on the 9th day of August next, to show cause why said account should not be stated and allowed, and said settlement be made. Henly Brown, Judge of Probate

The State of Alabama, Autauga county, Special Court of Probate, June 28, 1853.
This day came Thomas W. Hutchinson, one of the administrators of the estate of Adam Fralick, deceased, and filed his account and vouchers for the annual settlement of the estate of said deceased, which was examined and ordered to be filed for the inspection of all concerned. It is therefore ordered, that notice be given for forty days, by publication for three successive weeks in the Autauga Citizen, notifying all persons interested to be and appear at a Court to be held on the 9th day of August next, to show cause why said account should not be stated and allowed, and said settlement be made. Henly Brown, Judge of Probate

The State of Alabama, Autauga county, Special Court of Probate, June 28, 1853.
This day came Thomas W. Hutchinson, one of the administrators of the estate of Jacob H. Fralick, deceased, and filed his account and vouchers for the annual settlement of the estate of said deceased, which was examined and ordered to be filed for the inspection of all concerned. It is therefore ordered, that notice be given for forty days, by publication for three successive weeks in the Autauga Citizen, notifying all persons interested to be and appear at a Court to be held on the 9th day of August next, to show cause why said account should not be stated and allowed, and said settlement be made. Henly Brown, Judge of Probate

Vol. 1, Thursday, July 7, 1853, No. 23

We are authorized to announce Eli J. Duramus as a candidate for Tax Collector of Autauga county at the ensuing August election.

The announcement of Eli J. Duramus as a candidate for Tax Collector, will be found in its proper place. It is been reported at Mr. Duramus had declined running for that office, but he says it is not so-and he ought to know.

The Dallas *Gazette* has, we perceive, changed hands, and will be conducted hereafter by A.J. Campbell, Esq. Mr. Brewer withdrawals from the editorial department.

The Celebration. The anniversary of American Independence, as we anticipated, was celebrated in this place with all the "pomp and splendor" incident to such occasions. The loud thunder of cannon was heard at the dawn of day, startling our peaceful citizens from their quiet slumbers, and announcing to them the propriety of quitting their couches, and to prepare for the proper observance of the day. At the hour of nine, our streets were dotted with groups of men, women and children, and patiently waiting for the commencement of the days' amusements. At ten o'clock the Autauga Guards met by appointment, and after going through various "military tactics," took up "the line of march" for "headquarters"-a beautiful spot selected by a committee of young men, where was prepared an excellent dinner, and plenty of it. Arriving there, refreshing themselves, the declaration of Independence was read by Dr. J.D. O'Bannon-after which, Wm. H. Northington, John C. Reid, James T. DeJarnette, Esq's., all others, were called upon for speeches, all of whom responded in short but appropriate addresses. After the speaking, the target shooting commenced, which he ended by the plume being awarded to James T. DeJarnette, Esq., he having made the three best shots...

Editorial Brevities.
The White House. The repairs of the White House have been commenced under the superintendence of Col. Lee, of the Civil Engineers. The interior of the building is to be painted throughout, the walls repapered, and the ceiling frescoed. And apparatus for warming the house by steam is also to be introduced, and new furniture will be provided. These and other contemplated improvements will require about three months, and will doubtless render it necessary for the President and his family to remove to some other residence.

Women of Kentucky. The Bowling Green (Ky.) *Standard* says that difficulty occurred in that county on the third inst. between Mrs. Marion Bunch and Miss Brown, in which the latter was killed. The particulars which led to this horrid tragedy are unknown, or the means by which it was effected. A sister of Miss Brown, in attempting to appease the affray, received several severe wounds which it is feared will prove fatal.

Rail Road Meeting. In accordance with a call in the Autauga Citizen and the Autauga Mercury, a goodly number of the citizens of Autauga County met in Autaugaville on Saturday, June 25th. On motion, E. Shackelford was called to the Chair, and T.J. Motley requested to act as Secretary. The meeting being called to order, its object was briefly set forth by J.R. Jones, Esq., on whose motion the Chairman appointed a Committee of five to draft a series of resolutions, and report immediately. The Chair appointed the following gentlemen: J.R. Jones, Esq., L. Howard, A.K. McWilliams, John Lamar, and L.M. Whetstone. On motion, Wm. H. Northington, T. Nunn, C. Moncrief, Saml. Stoudemier and John H. Barlow were added to the Committee-who retired and made the following report:... Which, on motion, was adopted. After which, there were several animated addresses by J.R. Jones, Dr.

C.M. Howard, L. Howard, Wm. H. Northington, and John P. Hobarts, in support of the preamble and resolutions. It was *Resolved*, that the proceedings of this meeting be published in the county papers, with the request that all papers friendly to the enterprise will please copy. On motion, the meeting adjourned. E. Shackelford, Ch'm, T.J. Motley, Sec'y.

The Crim. Con. Case in Washington. The Washington correspondent of the Baltimore Sun, who signs himself "Mercury," gives the following account of the shooting of young Hester by Morrison, which lately took place in that city: The unfortunate shooting case of last evening, in which A.J. Morrison shot his own wife, and the young man, A.J. Hester, in her company, engrosses a large portion of the public mind today. It is generally supposed a young Hester will recover. All the particulars of this tragedy can only be adduced by a careful judicial investigation. The shooting took place in the parlor in Mr. Berkeley's boarding house, where Morrison and wife boarded, and a lady and Hester were sitting on the sofa at the time, when Morrison suddenly came in. In Hester's statement of the matter, he acknowledges being on very intimate terms with M. And his wife, as if the latter were his sister. As a young man, he said, "he had not placed his hand on Mrs. Morrison, and never had any intentions towards her, having always thought too much of her. *He had no recollection how his pantaloons came off."* When officers when into Mr. Berkeley's for the purpose of arresting Mr. Morrison, they found him at the bedside of his wife engaged and affection in attentions, and expressing his belief in her conjugal fidelity by a design to force her.

Miss Martha M. Henry, M. D., of Providence, R.I., has been elected Professor of Obstetrics and Diseases of Women and Children, in the Female Medical College of Pennsylvania.

Vol. 1, Thursday, July 14, 1853, No. 24

Wm. N. Thompson has consented that his friends may use his name in the present canvass as they think proper. We therefore announce him as a Candidate for a seat in the next Legislative Assembly of the State. A host of friends, without distinction of Party.

The Methodist Church in Prattville will be dedicated on the 24th inst. (4th Sabbath.) The dedication sermon will be preached by Rev. J. Hamilton, D. D., at 11 o'clock, A. M. The Rev. P.P. Neely, D. D., will preach in the afternoon.

The California Duel. No news has yet been received from San Francisco, later than the 1st of June. Consequently we are without any information with regard to the result of the duel between Dr. Gwin and Mr. McCorkle, who had gone out to fight that day. The second of Gwin was Mr. Dameron, formally of Mobile; McCorkle, Mr. Marshall, late member of Congress. The following item in the New York express contains fuller information as to the facts, and we have hitherto seen: "Dr. Gwin, the United States Senator, and Mr. McCorkle, late member of Congress, we have announced as going out from San Francisco, June 1st, to fight a duel with rifles, at thirty paces. Their quarrel originated in politics-McCorkle charging Gwin with being corrupt and being connected with certain Banking Houses in California, and receiving large favors from the government. Gwin challenged McCorkle who accepted fixing rifles as the weapons, and the distance at thirty yards. The officers went in pursuit, but they had passed to some adjoining county. Mrs. Gwin with their daughter was almost distracted. The fight was to take place June 1st, at ten o'clock. McCorkle is a young unmarried man, of great coolness and self possession. Bets were freely made that McCorkle would kill the doctor.

Serious Difficulty. A recontre took place in this city last Tuesday, between two brothers, named Sweet, and a Mr. Rodifer. It seems one of the Sweets and Rodifer had a fist fight in the cars going to Montevallo, the day before. Tuesday morning, the Sweets went round to the boarding house of Rodifer, and called him out. One of them struck him, and whilst he and Rodifer were engaged in a fight, the other brother stabbed him with a sharp instrument, supposed it to be a saddler's awl. Whilst Rodifer turned to assail him, the one who attacked him first drew out a pistol and shot him. These are the facts as we learned them. The one that stabbed has been apprehended, and sent to jail, the other has made his escape. It is supposed that Rodifer will not live. They all recently moved here. Our city has heretofore been noted for quiet and good order, but with the large influx of strangers amongst us, we can not look here after for such "piping times of peace." - *Selma Reporter*

Editorial Brevities.
The dispatch from Washington of the 28th ult., says: the resolution of the first proximo for the classification of clerks is the absorbing theme this week in Washington. The law reduces the permanent clerical force in the Executive Departments from upwards of 1,000 to 750-the reduction being principally in the Treasury, Interior and Navy Departments. It reclassifies the whole except the Clerks in the State Department, dividing them in four classes with the salaries of $9,000.00, $1,500.00 and $1,800.00. The departments are busy examining and black balling, and the Whigs are generally alarmed. The principal changes will be made about the 1st of the month. Hon. John A. Morison has been appointed Inspector of Drugs of Philadelphia. The marriage of W.C. Johnson, of Utica, to a grand niece of John Quincy, today, caused quite a sensation in fashionable circles.

The Philadelphia papers announced the death of the distinguished Dr. N. Chapman, on Friday week. He was born in Virginia, graduated Edinburg, Scotland, and in early life settled in Philadelphia. He occupied a Professor's chair in the Pennsylvania University from 1811 to 1850, when age and failing strength caused his resignation. The Trustees then conferred on him the honorary distinction of Emeritus Professor. As a professional man he was talented, learned and eminently successful, whilst in private life his convivial disposition, strong affections, and brilliant wit, made him the favorite of all whom he was brought into association. Among the numerous positions and all parts of the country, no man was better known, or more beloved.

The Thehuanterec Grant. In the supreme court of New York, in the matter of Francisco P. Falconet against Albert G. Sloo, to recover $600,000.00 against 15,000 interest, an attachment was granted on the 30th ult., against the property of the defendant in New York. It appears that Falconet, who resides in Mexico, at the instance of the agent of the defendant paid that government $300,000.00 for Mr. Sloo, on account of the Tehuantepec grant, and bound himself to pay $300,000.00 more, in two drafts, during July and August. Since then, is alleged, Mr. Sloo has refused to honor the drafts of the plaintiff, upon him, for the money advanced, and hence the attachment.

Dr. Reid, a traveler through the islands of Peru, is said to have found lately, in the Desert of Alacama, the dried remains of an assemblage of beings, five or six hundred in number, men, women, and children, seated in a semi circle, as when alive, staring into the burning waste before them. They had not been buried: life had not departed before they thus sat around, but hope was gone, the Spanish invaders were at hand, and no escape being left, they had come hither to die. They still sat immovable in that dreary desert, dried like mummies by the effect of the hot air; they still kept their position sitting up as in solemn council, while over that dread Aropagus silence broods everlastingly.

Late and Interesting from Mexico. Advices from Mexico to the 18th ult. have been received. Santa Anna's birthday was celebrated with great pomp at the Capitol. Lots for the conscription of the regular army are to be drawn on the 15th of July, and for the militia on the 25th of August. The standing army used to consist of 26,553 men, and the militia of 64,946. Indians are ravaging Coahuila. Senor Aguilar has taken charge of the portfolio of the Ministry of State. The telegraph has been completed to Jalapa, and dispatches received over it from the city of Mexico. The introduction of arms in Mexico has been prohibited. Don Fedrico Fulquez has been appointed Minister to New Grenada, and it was said that he would also visit Venezuela and Ecuador in his official character. The *Odren* proposes that he shall be authorized to invite these and all other Hispano-American States to a general Congress like that which Bolivar called together at Panama in 1823 to sustain the rights of Spain, threatens to absorb the sovereignty of the content and to destroy the Hispano-American race. It states that two such an alliance the old mother country would unite. The *Universal* also contends that Mexico will be aided by European nations in case of another war with the United States. It is announced officially that, the expedition of Raousset de Boulbon against Sonora has been broken up.

Large Milk Dealer. It is stated that Mr. Joseph Brown, of Concord, in this county, who runs a daily car over the Fitchburg road, for the purpose of supplying a large number of dealers in Boston, carries down in a year about 218,000 gallons of milk, and that which is set in other ways must swell the amount to 250,000 gallons. He also carries large quantities from other towns, his connections extending as far as Harvard, in Worcester county. He pays about 10

1/2 cents per gallon, and sells into the Boston dealers at 14 cents, who retail it at five and six cents per quart. His entire sales, including what he takes from Harvard, Groton, Littleton and Lincoln, cannot be much short, of 350,000 gallons, worth some $49,000.00, of which amount $30,000.00 goes to Concord. - [*Lowell* Journal.]

Mr. Nathan Munro died at Newport, R.I., on the 28th ult., in the 100th year of his age. The deceased has had 7 children, 17 grandchildren, 140 great-grand-children, and 25 great-great-grand-children.

Mr. O'Reailly, the great telegraph man, rights in regard to the Pacific Telegraph, to Dr. James Suram, that "a company is now organized for carrying out my proposed Atlantic and Pacific line-the directors of which include the Presidents of seven Telegraph lines-of which I am elected President. The interest of Professor Morse, between the Mississippi and California, are secured to the company by Mr. Kendall. Thus old Adversaries are brought together for a great purpose."

Convention of the Craft. We take the following account of the proceedings had by the "Printers' Convention," from the Baton Roge *Comet*, of the 5th instant: *Printers State Convention.* - at twelve o'clock Monday the 4th inst., they assembled in the Judiciary Committee Room at the Capitol, and organized by selecting Geo. A. Pike, Chairman, and Jas. F. Blackman Secretary. The Chairman briefly stated the object of the meeting-to establish a union of the press in Louisiana-to encourage good fellowship, and to unite the craft in an association for mutual protection and benefit. To accomplish this object, it was, on motion of W.R. Adams, Esq., *Resolved*, "That this Association will be called the Louisiana press Union, with annual meetings, to take place on the 22d of February, at the State Capitol." George A. Pike was elected President, and J.F. Blackman and P.M. Hatch were elected Corresponding Secretaries, and A.P. Converse, Treasurer. On motion of Mr. Blackman, it was resolved, at the editorial corps of East and West Baton Rogue constitute a Joint Committee to prepare an address to the Editors and Printers in the State of Louisiana, on the subject of the Press Union, and also to prepare resolutions to be submitted in circular form for the approval of the brethren, which resolutions, is sanctioned by a majority of the Editors and Printers in the State, shall govern the fraternity until the next annual meeting. On motion of T.B.R. Hatch, the meeting adjourned. Geo. A. Pike, President, J.F. Blackman, Secretary.

Married. On Sunday morning last, by L. Spigener, Esq., Mr. Thomas L. Prewitt to Miss Luisa Durden, all of this town.

The State of Alabama, Autauga county. Taken up, by James M. Baggett, and posted before A.T. Love, a justice of the Peace in and for said county, a grey mare, about ten years old, fifteen hands high, a small saddle mark on the right side of her back, a small knot on the inside of her left fore-leg, and small black specks on the flank and behind the shoulders and under the jaw. Appraised at sixty five dollars, by James M. Parish and Elijah Mims, Sr. Henly Brown, Judge of Probate.

Election Notice. An election will be held at the several election precincts in the County of Autauga, *On the First Monday of August Next*, For Governor of the State of Alabama; For a member to Congress for the third congressional district of Alabama; For a State Senator for the senatorial district of the counties of Autauga and Montgomery; For a member to the Legislature for Autauga county; and For Tax Collector for Autauga county. The following named persons are appointed Managers and Returning Officers and their respective pre-

cincts:
Precinct No. 1. - Green Barber, Jas. Popwell, Kenon Wells, managers. Isaac W. Cox, returning officer.
Precinct No. 2-Joseph B. Rogers, James L. Johnson, John Smith, managers. Alex R. Dennison, returning officer.
Precinct No. 3. - D.C. Neal, Jesse Gray, M.E. Norris, managers. J.B. Hart, returning officer.
Precinct No. 4. - Evans A. Long, Duncan McKeithen, Milton Goree, managers. Isaac Beatsell, returning officer.
Precinct No. 5. - Mills Rogers, John Merrett, George Rogers, managers. Jas. I. Alexander, returning officer.
Precinct No. 6. - John A. Houser, Lewis R. Davis, Samuel Faulkner, managers. Frank Hicks, returning officer.
Precinct No. 7. - Wm. Limbrick, Wiley Ross, Wm. Jones, managers. Wm. Wiley, returning officer.
Precinct No. 8. - Wm. L. Taylor, Alex Sample, Jesse A. Ricks, managers. Jas. Walker, returning officer.
Precinct No. 9. - John H. Pool, L. Caver, Lewis Jones, managers. Andrew Jackson, returning officer.
Precinct No. 10. - John W. Goodson, Patrick McDonnell, James M. Cook, managers.
The polls must be opened at each place of voting, in each precinct, between the hours of 9 and 10 in the morning, and kept open without intermission or adjournment until the hour of 5 in the afternoon, and no longer. - [*New Code, page 96, section 204.* James A. Lawler, Shff. Autauga Co.

Vol. 1, Thursday, July 21, 1853, No. 25

Reminiscences of Autauga county. [*Written for the Autauga Citizen.*] I promised, in my last communication, to introduce you and your readers to the Dutch Bend neighborhood, and if I should linger here longer than is interesting, please excuse me, for with these people were my earliest associations in this county, and they, too, of a very pleasant character. In my mind, at the moment, I am visiting from house to house, inquiring for the sires and the mothers of their old homestead. The answer comes back, go to yonder graveyard-there lie my father and mother-true, it is, the old folks have passed away-gone to that "bourne from whence no traveler returns." Since they are gone, how pleasant the thought to me that whilst in life they were as fathers and mothers to me, in the days of my orphanage boyhood. Shall I bid them a final adieu? No! A brighter thought ahead-in the resurrection morn, we shall meet again, that under far different circumstances. Indulge me in this retrospect-although mornful, yet not without a cup of joy. Taking the whole scope of county from Autaugaville, including Col. Pickett's down to the river, tracing the whole of the Dutch Bend, there is but one family circle but what has lost in most instances both father and mother. I allude to uncle Louis Houser and wife. They still survive; but the old man is hovering between life and death, ready and willing, I trust, to depart at a moments warning. What a striking comment this fact of the mutability of all things beneath the circle of the sun. I now turn to the living. This whole section of country is occupied by the descendants of a people doing honor to their fathers and mothers, who, before them, were tillers of the soil; industrious, honest, frugal and punctual in all things-the "bone and sinew" of the country-and more than this, their example and morals and religion not surpassed, if equaled, in any neighborhood of all my acquaintance, almost to a man and a woman they are a pious church-going people and had ever been, since my earliest acquaintance with them. They have regularly kept up a Sabbath school for more than thirty years, and whether they had a minister to preach or not they met for Sabbath school and social devotion. They have prospered it in there worldly affairs-many of them come to this country poor. By dint of hard labor, and by economy, they acquired an easy competency, which is all anyone needs or dare have, unless at his own peril. None of them have made overgrown fortunes-what they have, they have made as much by saving as any other way-their lands are fine and productive, but not rich. They have made pretty much their own provisions, and lived on what they made; they have rarely failed in raising abundant crops of wheat and rice for their own use. One error of this neighborhood has ever been and still exists, they have not had all the time a school of as high grade is they should. Every neighborhood should secure a good school at any reasonable sacrifice of money, in order to have intelligence generally diffused amongst their children. Many of these people have given their children liberal educations at a much greater expense than they could have done at home after all the parade of high schools abroad. They are not the schools for a wide an extended intelligence amongst the mass of people-good and well conducted neighborhood schools are best for her country's good. I would not entirely dispense with high schools, they have a good influence, when properly conducted, but there should be fewer of them, and those few better endowed. This neighborhood was settled at an early period in this state's history, mostly by persons from Orangeburg District, S.C., of German descent, as their names plainly indicate, viz.: Stoudemier, Houser, Murph, and Whetstone,-these men, are the original heads of families, in what has been easily termed the Dutch Bend. There are some two or three families, from Georgia, in the same neighborhood. Lewis C. Davis, Mark Howard and Dr. James Mitchel. This intermingling from different States use of mutual advantage in forming settlements in a new country. The Georgians are better cotton planters than the Carolinians, whilst the Carolinians succeed better in rice and wheat. Both parties must be stubborn, indeed, if they cannot learn something from each other to profit. I will bring this to a close, which perhaps is already too long, by introducing new and your readers to the Taylor and Tyus neighborhood. An Old Citizen.

T.H. Watts candidate for the State Senate, will address the citizens of Prattville on Monday next.

A Southern Lady in Europe. The people on the continent of Europe have been affirming for the past twenty years that the character of the English people has become completely changed, that her travelers are vulgar, domineering and upstart. We admit a great deal of this to be true, but it is not from any change in the national character, but in the very different class of travelers who have been racing through the continental tour. Travelers on the continent were formally persons of elegant leisure, refinement and education; now, opulent vulgarity, which seeks in eclat of travel weight could not claim by nature or education, is found alike in France, Germany, Switzerland and Italy, misrepresenting and depreciating the character of their country and countrymen. We are very particular in the choice of a suitable person to represent us in the Courts of Europe, and although we cannot, of course, select those who shall represent us socially, we have the privilege of rejoicing in one we hear that any one of our gifted country women, cordially welcome to the best society of Europe, will have the opportunity of showing that in no essential element of true refinement of the educated classes of our people in any way deficient. Madam Octavio Le Vert, of Mobile, in order to satisfy a lifelong desire to visit Europe and to gratify her friend, Lady Emeline Wortley, by accepting a cordial and pressing invitation to visit her at her home, some weeks ago sailed for England, and is doubtless at this moment enjoying the hospitality of her numerous friends in that country. A lady possessed of the high accomplishments and fascinating conversational powers of Madam Le Vert would, as soon as known, become a welcome and delightful member of any society she chose, but it is a pleasant thing that the proverbial coldness of the English character toward strangers will be dissipated by the warm and glowing reception and she will receive from Lady Wortley-a passport at once to the social circles of elegant, educated and refined. Madam Le Vert is eminently qualified to produce on her return a most acceptable book of travels, for she will have an opportunity which few travelers possess, of giving us a true and reliable picture of the manners and habits of a class of people we have all a curiosity to know and understand, and we trust she will be sufficiently regardful of those she has left behind her to give us the benefit of her observations. It is the intention of Madam Le Vert to visit Miss Frederika Bremer at her residence in Stockholm, where she was sojourn for some time. Are accomplished and interesting daughter, Miss Octavio Le Vert, is the companion of her rambles. Most seriously we do hope that her visit to Europe will realize all her expectations. -N. O. Delta.

Editorial Brevities.
The death of Mr. Maurice O'Connell, M. P. (The eldest son of the great Daniel), is announced by the Herman's news. Mr. O'Connell died suddenly, on the 17th of June, at his apartments in Loudon. After having represented the county of Clare from 1826 to 1832, he was returned for the borough of Tralee, in the latter year, and has continued to represent it for the last twenty years. He will probably be succeeded as a member for Tralee by a member of his family. His oldest son, a very fine boy, is a new midshipman in the Royal Navy, not long returned from the West Indies.

Buchanan, it is believed, threw up his office of envoy to England because he and Marcy, the Secretary of State, could not agree on the fishery question. It was stated when Buchanan was appointed that he accepted the office for the purpose of settling his fish business. But he wanted plenary powers, and Marcy wouldn't give them. We trust they may patch up the difficulty. Buchanan is a fit man for the office.

Gen. Rusk and Texas Railroads. The able and patriotic Senator is making use of his Senatorial vacation, by stirring up the of the people of his State, and urging them to a development of its immense resources by constructing railroads. The General is well acquainted with his subject, and for his zealous advocacy of an untiring devotion to this noble cause, his constituents have bestowed upon him the honored title of the DeWitt Clinton of Texas. In a late speech he made to his countrymen, he expressed his confidence in the passage of a bill by the next Congress authorizing the construction of the road to the Pacific; and perhaps make liberal appropriations to aid in its construction. He is equally positive that the location of the route, depends in and a great measure, upon the action of the Legislature of Texas, and contends that, by adopting a liberal and enlightened policy, the route through Texas can be secured.

Executor's Sale. Will be sold to the highest bidder, at the late residence of the Henry DeBardelaben, deceased, on Tuesday, the 23d day of August next, 1853, on a credit until the 1st day of March, 1854, a portion of the personal and a perishable property of said deceased, consisting in part, of horses, hogs, cows, sheep, carriage and harness, household and kitchen furniture, &c. &c. Terms-The purchasers will be required to give small notes, with at least two approved securities. John A. Houser, F.F. DeBardelaben, Executors.

Vol. 1, Thursday, July 28, 1853, No. 26

On Monday last, according to appointment, the several candidates for office, with one or two exceptions, met at this place and engaged in discussing the principal topics that are now agitating the country. Judge Moore, the Southern Rights candidate for Congress, opened the discussion, which, we regret, we did not hear. Thos. Watts, Esq., the candidate for the Senate, followed in a very appropriate speech. Maj. Bolling Hall, the candidate for the House, made a very pretty speech, which done credit to himself, and gave entire satisfaction to his party. Everything went off quietly and pleasantly.

Death of S. A. Godman, Esq. We learn, with regret, the death of S.A. Godman, Esq., Editor of the Family Friend, published in Columbia, S.C., and the writer of several sketches which have had a wide spread popularity. Mr. Godman had earned for himself an enviable reputation, but this man of talent, and of high and generous impulses too; and his early and unexpected death is a just cause of a deep and general regret.

Dedication of the M. E. Church. The dedication of the elegant room for the use of the Methodist church, in Prattville, took place on last Sunday, the 24th inst. The dedication sermon was preached by Dr. J. Hamilton, and will long be remembered by his large and attentive audience as a chaste and eloquent production. His dedicatory remarks were impressive and beautiful-in fact, the whole surface prepared by the venerable devine gave evidence as much study and care, and was strikingly appropriate to the occasion. His great personal popularity as a minister drew many from a distance, none of whom, we have reason to believe, were disappointed in him. The choir, though smaller in number than usual, performed their part well, so that the entire services were made very interesting to visitors, and truly gratifying to our own citizens. We learned that a copy of Dr. Hamilton's sermon has been solicited for publication. It is eminently worth of preservation, and we trust that it may be obtained. It was expected that Dr. Neely, of Marion, would preach in the afternoon, and the Rev. Mr. Gillespie, of Tuskegee, at night. From some cause unknown neither of those gentlemen were present, which occasioned much disappointment to many. The afternoon services, however, was well performed by the pastor of the church, Rev. S.O. Capers. At night Dr. Hamilton favored us with another excellent discourse. We shall here give a brief description of the church. It is seventy five by sixty feet. The walls and ceiling are painted in Frescoe by Mr. Charles Potthoff, of New Orleans. The work is admirably designed and executed-the cornice, pilasters, pannelling, &c., stand out so naturally that the eye can scarcely detect the deception. The curtain behind the pulpit is so skillfully painted that many of the strangers to have visited the church would not believe that it was part of the wall until they had satisfied themselves by touching it. The pulpit is painted plain white and polished. The book board and cushion are of rich maroon velvet. The altar is of a semi circle form-the furniture is very rich, and consists of a sofa and two chairs-the chairs stand in front of the pulpit, and on either side of a richly covered table. There are three double rows of seats, besides the slips to the right and left the pulpit, capable of seating seven hundred persons comfortably. There are four main aisles-two in the center at one on each side next to the walls, which extend all round from the entrance to the pulpit. This is well thought of-our most beautiful churches are often stained and disfigured by persons leaning their heads against the walls. The church has been handsomely carpeted by the exertions of a few young ladies. It is also indebted to them for the beautiful cover for the table and the fine rug in the pulpit. The slips are bountifully supplied with hymn books, and are also provided with the racks for hats, &c. Crickets for the comfort of the ladies, and last, not least, an abundant supply of spittoons for gentleman, who cannot refrain (?) from using tobacco in churches. It is hoped that all such will take the hint-use the spittoons and be careful to spare the floor. In every particular the comfort of church goers has been carefully studied, and excellent taste displayed throughout. It meets the admiration of all who have seen it, and many visitors pronounced it the handsomest room in the State. Our citizens, therefore, may well be proud of it.

Editorial Brevities.
Casualty by Lightning. On Monday last, Mr. Thomas McGehee, youngest son of Mr. Abner McGehee, of this county, while returning to his plantation about ten miles below this city, in a violent storm, was instantly killed by a stroke of lightning. His horse was killed. His companion who was riding with him escaped with a slight shock. The deceased was a young gentleman about the age of twenty years, and was highly esteemed by his friends. The affliction falls with crushing weight on his venerable surviving parent. - *Journal*.

Reminiscences of Autauga County. [*Written for the Autauga Citizen*] Messrs. editors: In order to redeem the pledge given in my last communication, I continue my Reminiscences of the Taylor and Tyus neighborhood, that with this shall close my communications at the present,-supporting that both you and your readers are tired of them. [No, not at all. -Eds.] To me it has been rather an agreeable pastime than otherwise, as I love to think of olden times, and old associates and associations. Although many with whom I was appointed in by-gone days are now in the spirit land yet their memory is pleasant. They were my friends, and I love to think of them; the time is not far distant when I show mingle with them again. The neighborhood above alluded to was settled by Benjamin Taylor and his sons and sons-in-law, mostly. They moved from Cahaba valley, in this State. The old man was a good farmer, and excellent neighbor, and a pious member of the church. He raised up his family in this way, and, I trust, are all following in his footsteps. He died many years since. His widowed still lives, though far advanced in life. Near Mr. Taylor resides Lewis Tyus, who, with his excellent lady, still live to enjoy the fruits of their labor, on the same farm that they cleared up. This is as it should be. Old folks have no business pulling up stakes and removing to new countries, where they have to start in the world afresh; let this be for their children. Still, it seems a little hard that the old folks should be deserted when they most need the helping hand of their children. But the good of society seems to demand that children should separate from their parents, and set up for themselves, and mix and mingle with other society different from that they were raised with. In the same neighborhood lived three bachelor brothers, who originally moved from Maryland. They occupied an area of country on Swift Creek six miles in length and two miles in width. These men were model farmers, and so far as industry, economy and frugality don't go to constitute good neighborship, they were certainly good neighbors; nay, more-they were steady, sober quiet, peaceable citizens, and, withall, honest; that they were, of course, of no advantage to the neighborhood in the way of aiding in the keeping up a good school-an important item, in my opinion, in constituting good citizenship. These men died several years since, at a much earlier period of life than usual for men of their temperate habits. The question arises in my mind-might not at least two of out of the three been now living, had they followed the dictates of nature, and taking unto themselves help-meets? There is no question they would have far happier and more useful. This is what men should live for-to be happy and useful; and their greatest happiness should consist, too, in *making others happy and useful*. Before I close this communication, indulge me in a few reflections on the neighborhood west of the one just spoken of. When I first came to this county, Ezell and Gordon had a country store where near the spot where Leonidas Howard now lives. The population of this neighborhood has changed more than any other of my acquaintance-I allude to the first settlers. I cannot, at this moment, call to my mind one of the old settlers. And why this change more here than any other?

It has always been looked upon has healthy, and the lands on about equality with the last mentioned. The cause, in my opinion, is, when the neighborhood was first settled, a miserable *grog-shop* was located there, and still exists,-though more than one church has been discontinued. The principal part of the citizens have to travel some eight or ten miles to worship. My observation through life goes to teach me that no people can be happy or prosperous without churches and good schools. It requires of all the restraints of religion and intelligence to subdue the unruly passions of men-indeed, in many instances, prove too feeble. I challenge any individual-I care not if he himself indulges in the use of liquor-to trace carefully the history of every family in the neighborhoods, where a grog-shop is kept up, for the last thirty years, to bear any other testimony and that already borne, to the inconstancy and instability of population. I must bring this to a close. There are other sections of our county equally interesting, which should I resume my reminiscences, will be recollected. An Old Citizen.

Death of Judge Wallace. Judge James B. Wallace, of Tuscaloosa, died of apoplexy the 8th inst. The deceased was one of the most prominent and useful men of this county and was, at the time of his death, a candidate to represent Tuscaloosa county in the lower branch of the Legislature.

Jenny Lind Goldschmidt is said to be a happy mother of a fine daughter.

Obituary. Died, in Prattville, Ala., on the 23d inst., Mr. J.P. Temple, aged about 28 years. The subject of this notice had been recently removed to this place but by his urbane and gentlemanly deportment he had succeeded in commanding the esteem and the confidence of all who knew him. In his intercourse with his fellows he manifested that integrity of purpose and individuality of action which every where bespeak the man of talent and worth, and that he was appreciated, the large number that attended his funeral amply testifies. Too soon, alas, did the all-wise disposer of events see fit to remove him from our midst, for we loved his society; but our loss is undoubtedly his gain, for he has gone to that God "who doeth all things well." During his protracted sickness the kind of family at whose house he was and the neighbors generally, watched over him with anxious care and fond solicitude, and on that day following his death, (Sunday) just as the last rays of the departing sun were shedding their refulgence o'er the earth, we deposited his remains in the last resting place of mortality. A fitting time, it was, to lay to pulseless body of that true and noble brother quietly down to its long repose. And as a faithful band of brothers of the "mystic tie," joined their hands around his consecrated grave, and quietly deposited on his cold bosom the *ever-green*, a sacred memento of their order-Those waging themselves to the dead that, *ever-living* as was this emblem, should his memory be in their hearts. Many bosoms swelled with emotion, and tears started from many eyes as she, who had been so devoted in her attachment and watchfulness, stooped down and deposited the first portion of cold earth upon the bosom of him whose joys she had shared, and who sorrow she had assuaged. This was a novel and a strange sight to me; but, on reflection, I can view it as none other than the seal of her ardent and undying love for her dear departed husband. The "mystic brothers" had deposited their emblem in the silent tomb, and why should not the stricken widow silently express her confidence in God, and her hope in Heaven, by also depositing, not an emblem, but a portion of that common element which council the common mother of all the living. A Friend.

Again in Slavery. Several weeks since, says the Cincinnati *Gazette*, of the 28th ult., we published a statement that a couple of slaves were manumitted by Mr. Orville Thomas, of Louisiana. Recent occurrence induce us to state again the following facts: Mr. Thomas was on his way to the East, when he arrived here he was told that he would lose his slaves. He then resolved that he would anticipate their designs, if they had in the ideas of leaving him, and on the morning he left, he called them before him, and told them they were free, and that he would have their papers made out on his return. They were taken by surprise and did not seem to express any great degree of joy upon the announcement which they were so much interested being made. On Tuesday morning Mr. Thomas returned, and as he was about entering the Burnet House, he was met by his boys, who requested the privilege to be taken back again. They present and if they would prefer returning with their master to Louisiana, than to remain in Cincinnati and have their freedom. We afterward learned that the result was just what Mr. Thomas expected, for he did not believe they could take care of themselves. He received them, and Wednesday morning the party left on the Tishamingo for Louisville, en route for home.

Vol. 1, Thursday, August 4, 1853, No. 27

The Election. We are not able to furnish our readers with the official returns of the election in this number of our paper, but will endeavor to do so next week. Maj. Bolling Hall has been elected as representative from this country twenty-two votes over his opponent, Wm. N. Thompson. We call that pretty close work. John W. Clarke is elected tax collector for the county. Thos. H. Watts has been elected senator, as a matter of course. Maj. S.W. Harris, it is supposed, is elected by a large majority over his opponent, Judge Moore. Col. Winston is no doubt elected for governor. From all we can learn, the election passed off quietly and pleasantly at every box in the county.

The Election Yesterday. The following are all the returns we have received up to the time we go to press:
For Congress. Montgomery City-Clopton 397, Abercrombie 295-112
For Governor. Montgomery City-Winston 240, Ernest 409
The regular Whig county ticket is doubtless elected by a considerable majority. - *Advertiser*

Hard to Believe. The San Francisco Herald gives the following history of a pine tree in California, call the Fremont Pine. It is hard to credit: in circumference, two feet from the ground, it measured twenty-nine feet, or nine feet in diameter. At the commencement of the rainy season last autumn, Levin Payne and T.A. Eimit determined on cutting it down, for the purpose of working in into shingles. It was chopped off two feet from the ground, and there was no diminution in size for forty feet upward. As many men as could work around it chopped it off in two days. Seven men commenced operations upon it, and have continued, but with a little interruption, the entire winter and spring. The first eight feet, though perfectly sound, was not worked in consequence of it being a little ealy, or cross-grained. About this, eight cuts were taken, or seventy-five feet from the stump, it was seven feet eight inches in diameter. From these eight cuts, five hundred shakes, four feet long by six inches wide, and two hundred and twenty-five thousand sixteen inch shingles has been made by riving and shaving and without the loss of timber. Three more eight feet cuts will easily make forty thousand shingles more, but with some little loss of timber, there being a few small dry limbs in the last cut. This will make in all two hundred and sixty-five thousand shingles, at twelve dollars per thousand, the price they brought at the stump, and we have no less a some than $3,180 for shingles alone, besides shakes, rails, and fence posts. The entire length of the tree was two hundred and thirty feet. It may be asked by the "old folks at home," how we manage to saw into blocks a tree that, when lying upon the ground, is two feet higher than most men's heads? We answer, that it is chopped into on both sides about twenty inches, and then sawed off into cuts eight feet long; these are then split with powder and quartered, and then sawed into sixteen inch single blocks. It may seem to some like another California story, and so it is; but it is, nevertheless, true. We have seen and measured it, and can test to the fact as regards its size.

Late from California.
A duel took place at Marysville between Col. Rust, of the Express, and Judge Stidger, of the Herald. The Judge was wounded in the coat tail, and the affair was settled.

Mr. Wm. O'Donahue, one of the Irish patriots and exiles in Australia, has escaped and arrived in San Francisco on the 22d of June. He has published an account of his escape.

A shocking murder, fracticide and suicide took place in Sacramento on the 28th of June. A man named Joseph M. Strible having taken offense against his brother, Henry E. Strible, entered his room last night for the purpose of killing him. The wife being awake, he struck her with the axe, then attacked and mortally wounded the brother, then turned upon the wife and cut her throat and went out and cut his own. He did not succeed in killing himself immediately, but died a day or two afterwards. The brother, it is thought will recover. The wife's name was Agnes Strible and represented as a beautiful woman about twenty-three years of age.

Gen. Lane has been elected delegate to Congress by about 1000 majority over Skinner.

Editorial Brevities.
False Roulette Tables. The New York Day Book says: "Among the articles from the gambling place of Jeremiah Donovan, the other day, was a roulette table, so constructed that the party betting was wholly at the mercy of those having charge of the game, and if they elected that he should not win, it was impossible for him to do so. This fact should operate as a warning to those tempted to stake their money: and such may be assured that nearly all instruments used by professed gamblers are of the same character."

The "Black Warrior" is the name of the war horse which President Pierce rode at the review of the military on the Battery, New York, and up Broadway to the Palace. This animal is said to be upwards of twenty-one years of age and is owned by Major Merrill, of the United States Dragoons. The Black Warrior participated in the Florida war, where he received two wounds, and is the only survivor of a battle with the Indians. The President rode this veteran charger during the Mexican war.

The Freesoldier Dix. It is reported here, says a dispatch from Washington, under date of the 25th ult., to the N. O. *Delta*, that John A. Dix has been appointed Minister to France, but the fact is to be kept secret until the August elections are over.

Fred Douglas is about to become editor of the Boston Commonwealth, a freesoil and abolition paper.

A fortnight ago a grand swimming contest at Hartford, Connecticut, took place. Seventeen swimmers entered the list-nine Americans and eight Germans. Upwards of two thousand persons, men and women, were present. The competitors swam from the railroad bridge to a point opposite the bathing establishment, distant nearly a mile. W. Moll, a German, came in ahead.

A Valuable Discovery. Each succeeding year discloses more and more fully the surprising and varied resources of the Northwestern section of Georgia. Gold, Iron and Plumbago have been long known to be abundant. Silver and Copper, the latter in immense quantities, have been more recently added to the list of minerals; and quite recently an inexhaustible quarry of superior Hydraulic Limestone has been discovered on the estate of Rev. C.W. Howard of Cass County. Specimens of the cement formed from this lime have been shown us which or equal to any which can be obtained elsewhere. Hydraulic Lime is selling at six dollars per barrel in this market; Mr. Howard informs us that he can furnish it at one dollar and a half.

Brevet Major Francis C. Hall, U.S. Marine Corps, commanding at Gosport, died at Norfolk on the 12th instant. He was a native of Maryland, and entered the service July 5, 1852.

The California papers intimate that Lola Montez is about to be married. Her betrothed must be a bold man.

Good Hit. In the course of a discussion in the Massachusetts Convention a good deal was said about the licentiousness of the press, whereupon Col. Schouler, of Boston, made a fair retort: "A great deal has been said about the licentiousness of the public press. Now, sir, I happen to have had a great deal to do with the public press, and I must say that the most licentious part of my experience with the public press has been in the defense of men in public stations. [Great Laughter.] I trust, Mr. President, I am not out of order." [Laughter.]

It is reported from Washington that Mr. John M. Daniel, editor of the Richmond *Examiner*, has been appointed Charge of Affairs to Sardinia, in the place of Hon. R.K. Meade, declined.

Reminiscences of Autauga County. [*Written for the Autauga Citizen*] Messrs. Editors: at your request, I continue my reminiscences-hoping, at the same time, your readers will be interested. The next neighborhood I shall touch upon is Independence. This, in the early settlement of the country, was not thought to be a desirable location, in consequence of the poorness of the soil. But how often do the first settlers commit errors in this way by all pressing to the most desirable parts, and running the lands up to a price far above its value. James Jackson, Esq., a far-seeing and sagacious gentleman, settled the one mile north of where Independence now stands,-or, rather, where it once claimed its location. He bought up a considerable portion of this land, and afterwards realized a handsome profit. He formed around him a settlement, consisting of his son-in-law, Capt. L. Long, now of this county, his father in law, R.-. Motley, and his sons. None of the old settlers, does not recollect the "old man Motley," with palsied hands and faltering voice, always with snuff box in hand, and cracking his good-humored jokes upon his friends? But he, together with his sons, have all passed away. Oddly two of his daughters are now living-Mrs. Jackson, widow of James Jackson, and mother of A. Jackson, Esq., and Gen. C. Jackson, near Coosada; and of Mrs. James Howard, of Macon county. Those were amongst the most intimate acquaintances. I know of no section of our county that has more generally succeeded in the planting interest than this-though always considered poor. But observation teaches me that rich lands are not the surest road to wealth. Industry and energy on poor lands will more than equalize the advantages of a rich soil; necessity often drives men to do what they would not do under other circumstances. Independence, at one time, did considerable business for an inland village; but it had a short career. David Newton, a young man raised on a farm in this county, set up with a small lot of goods, but soon extended his business, (perhaps, beyond his means.) He died at an early age, and his estate proved insolvent. He possessed rare business qualities for one who had no experience, and had he lived, no doubt would have acquired a large fortune. He had several brothers, all of whom have succeeded; they are mostly farmers. Here let me drop another hint on the subject. In passing through the several villages of my acquaintance of this county, and recollecting how few have succeeded in every coming out whole-footed in the mercantile business, it is astonishing to see how many young men are seeking situations as clerks. Tis' very true, a good knowledge of human nature may be obtained behind the counter, with an invaluable amount of business tact; yet it is running too great a risk for those acquirements-too much precious time is squandered in youth. The great fault of the present age is, our young men are into great a hurry to get rich: they must do in a few years (or at least attempt it) what should require a whole life-time. The population of this section has greatly changed; in fact, almost entirely the first settlers have either died or moved off. It, too, has been infested with one of those accursed grog-shops-the bane of every section of every country where they are located. When will men learn to consider their own interests? There has been several attempts to establish a Methodist church in this place, that all ways without success. There has, however, been a Baptist church for many years within a mile of it and a respectable neighborhood school, for many years taught by Mrs. Livinis Waugh, a lady of deep piety and inestimable worth-highly qualified, both by nature and experience, to manage a school to advantage. This lady died a few years back, deeply lamented by all who had the pleasure of her acquaintance. It is difficult to estimate the worth of such a woman in a neighborhood. In recounting the many acquaintances of my early youth, one man of this neighborhood, (though not one of its first settlers) comes to my recollection. He still lives; I mean John G. Herman, a German by birth, who came to this country more than thirty years back. He landed in Vernon pennyless-a stranger in a strange land, worn down with disease, and not knowing a word of English. He worked his way up from Mobile on a pole boat, as cook and washer. He met with sympathizing friends, who encouraged him in business. And now, where do we find him? On a comfortable farm near Independence, with some twenty-five or thirty servants, and out of debt; the father of some four or five children, whom he has raised and educated respectably. Two of his daughter's married respectable men of this county, Dr. Sullens and L.M. Whetstone. Who, after witnessing such an example of this, will say that a poor man cannot rise in this country? Mr. Herman was successful by dint of hard labor and strict economy. He married a girl poorer than himself; that she proved a help-meet indeed-working late and early. I can see no impediments to a poor man marrying, if he can meet with just such a wife. But take care young men in this matter, where you will scratch a poor man's head all your life. And now, Messrs. Editors, I shall make no more promises for or against continuing my reminiscences. If the spirit moves me, you may have another paper; if not, you must supply its place with something else. Old Citizen.

Repetition in Sermons. Old Father Bushnell, of Vermont, used to say that the best criticism that he ever received on his preaching was a little boy who sat right at his foot, looking up into his face, as he was preaching in a crowded room of a private house. As he was going on very earnestly, though little fellow spoke out, *"You said that afore."*

Ladies' Masonry. We have long felt the want of some good work a exemplifying those degrees, which are more particularly designed for ladies, and we find this desideratum Langley filled in a little book now before us entitled "Ladies Masonry," by Past Grand Master Leigh, of Ala. Perhaps of all the degrees of the kind, which are now conferred in our lodges and chapters, the Heroine of Jericho and Holy Virgin are most beautiful and instructive. We would therefore most cordially commend this work of our excellent and reverend companion to all those masons, who deserve to place the advantages of our time honored institution within the reach of those for whom it's great privileges were designed-the widow and the orphan. - *Grenada (Miss.) Republican.* The above books, diplomas, &c, are for sale by Dr. John A. Whetstone, Robinson Springs, to whom all communications, prepaid, must be addressed. Price-book and two diplomas, $2.50. Book and one diploma, $2.00.

Dissolution. The copartnership heretofore existing, under the name and style of W.C. Allen & Co., is this day dissolved by mutual consent. The unsettled business will be attended to by both of the partners. W.C. Allen, B.F. Miles

W.C. Allen will continue the business at the same place, and would say to the friends and customers of the old concern, that he expects to keep a GOOD STOCK OF GOOD GOODS, and will sell them on as good terms as will be given in town. He would be happy to show his goods to all who may favor him with a call, and hopes that by strict attention to business, and fair liberal dealing, to merit a fair share of his former patronage.

For sale. The subscriber offers for sale his house and lot, situated on one of the principal streets in the town of Prattville. The lot is about two acres in size, and contains all the necessary out-buildings, nearly new. The garden spot is the best in town. He also offers his Office and lot for sale-(opposite the drug store). The lot faces on the main street, 36 feet front, and runs back to the creek. It is well finished, new, and sufficiently large for a small mercantile business of any kind. My health demands a change of residence, and good bargains may be had. For terms, apply to Wm. H. Northington, Esq., who will act as my agent during my temporary absence from the State. J.D. O'Bannon, M.D.

Vol. 1, Thursday, August 11, 1853, No. 28

Mr. William Smith will accept our thanks for the fine water melon he presented us last week. It weighed forty pounds! Who can beat that?

Kentucky Election. An election was held in Kentucky on the 1st inst. for members of Congress and State Legislature. Mr. Preston, Whig candidate for Congress, had 800 majority over English, democrat, at noon, and is certainly elected in the Louisville District.

Reward of Fidelity. A faithful body servant of the late Vice President King, it is said, is now living in Washington. He was set free by Mr. King, who also gave him $2,000 in money, and his gold watch, for the faithful manner in which he served him.

Shocking Affair in Virginia. We learn from the Petersburg Express, Mr. Henry Birdsong, of Sussex county, Va., and his little son, while lying in bed on Friday night, were both shot through one of the windows of their chamber. The shooting was done with a double barrel gun, heavily loaded with the buckshot. The load entered the leg of Mr. B.'s son at the thigh, passed entirely through, and terribly lacerated the other. Mr. B. Also received an entire load in his abdomen, which proves that both barrels of the gun were discharged. Their wounds are considered mortal. Suspicion rest upon two of his slaves.

Death of Judge Wallace. The Tuscaloosa Monitor announces the death of Judge (D. or B.?) Wallace. It occurred on Monday week. He was apparently in perfect health until an hour before his decease, which is attributed to apoplexy. At the time of his death he was a candidate of the Legislature in Tuscaloosa. He was born in Edgefield District, S.C., was subsequently a printer and in office in Nashville; then studied law, and finally removed to this State, where he held many important offices.

A Mail Robber Arrested. The *Observer*, published at Fayetteville, North Carolina, states that a young man named William Tinnin was arrested in that place on the 23d ultimo, on the charge of robbing the mail. He was arrested whilst endeavoring to cash a check on the Cape Fear Bank, which had been stolen from a letter taken from the mail. He had been employed as a clerk in the post office at Green Springs, and is supposed to be the perpetrator of a number of robberies of the mail which have recently occurred in that vicinity. He was fully committed for trial.

Editorial Brevities.
The Pittsburgh Post says it is rumored at Col. McCanales, of that city, has been tendered the mission to Venezuela.

Alabama Legislature.
SENATE. The newly elected senators, as far as heard from, are, for the Senatorial Districts of
1. Mobile-T.B. Bethea
5. Barbour-*Peterson*
6. Pike-Harrel Hobdy
7. Russell-*B.H. Baker*
8. Macon-*N.H. Clanton*
9. Montgomery and Autauga-*T.H. Watts*
10. Dallas and Wilcox-S.R. Blake

11. Sumter, Choctaw and Washington-Woodward
12. Green and Marengo-*J.D. Webb*
13. Perry and Bibb-*Cocke*
14. Lowndes and Butler-*Crenshaw*
15. Coosa-J.R. Powell
16. Tallapoosa-*Kimbal*
17. Chambers-*Chas. McLemore*
21. Jefferson and Shelby-Moses Kelly
22. Tuscaloosa-*Robt. Jemison, Jr.*
23. Henry and Dale-*Searcy*
24. Conecuh, Covington and Coffee-*Ashly*
25. Pickens-*Lee*
36. Madison-Acklen
27. Benton-Wm. B. Martin

HOUSE OF REPRESENTATIVES.
Autauga-Hall
Benton-Wills, Davis and Whatley
Baldwin-*Wilkins*
Barbour-*McCall*, +*Comer*, +*Cochran*
Bibb-Davis
Butler-Burnett, Yeldell
Chambers-*Hall, Todd, Robertson* *
Dale-*Ward*
Dallas-*Hatcher, Phillis*
Green-*Benners, Inge*
Henry-*Odum*
Lowndes-Cook, *Webb*
Madison-Humphries, Laughinhouse
Marengo- *Greagh*, Foscue
Macon-*Abercrombie, Rutherford, Paine*
Mobile-Walker, Owen, Meek, Bell
Montgomery- *Belser, Judge*
Pike- McBryde, *Horne*, Faraior
Perry-Cole, *Talbert*
Russell-*Calhoun*,++ *Nelson*
St. Clair- Whitsett, Portis
Talladega-*Shelley*, Curry, Bishop
Tuscaloosa-Martin, Brown
Tallapoosa-*Gibson, Holly, Gillam*
Wilcox-Fox, Irwin
*=Whigs, Southern Rights Men marked thus+; and Union men thus ++.

Carrying out the Inaugural. The late fall issue gives copious accounts of the arrest of Costa, the Hungarian, at Smyrna: It has been a long since that locality has been so thoroughly waked up, as it has been by the energy of Captain Stringham, of the St. Louis. The most straightforward statement to hand, says that Martin Kossta, had been but a few days in Smyrna, although another account says he had been eight months concealed in this city. At all events, on the evening of the 22d ult., he was quietly smoking in a Greek coffee house on the wharf, (not the private dwelling of a Sardinian, as was at first reported,) when a band of ten men came to the spot, and arrested him as a Hungarian, who was permitted to go to

America on pledging his word never to return to Turkish territory. Costa struggled with his assailants, and knocked one or two of them into the water, and at length leaped into the stream, and swam towards a ship. He was then overtaken, dragged into a boat, and take an onboard the Austrian brig-of-war Hussar, where he was heavily ironed. It was observed that six of his captors remained on board the brig, and the rest returned ashore. The affair would appear to have blown over for that night, that next morning it was generally talked of, and the most intense excitement arose. Mr. Brown, the United States Consul, learning that Costa was last from America, waited on the consul-general of Austria, saying that he understood that a native of Hungary, who had become an American citizen, had been taken by force on board the Austrian brig-of-war, and he wished to see the man, and ask him for explanations. The Austrian consul denied all knowledge of the fact! Mr. Brown then proceeded to the brig, and requested an interview with the prisoner, which was refused, and meantime the vessel was preparing to depart. Just at that moment, the Cervette St. Louis, Captain Stringham commanding, sailed into the harbor, and the consul lost no time in communicating the circumstances. Our accounts clash here. It would seem a captain Stringham, having gone abroad the Austrian, was told by the lieutenant that he had no prisoner in the ship! Returning on board a second time accompanied by Mr. Brown, they found Commander Schartz, captain of the brig, whom Captain Stringham thus addressed: "Your lieutenant, sir, has lied! The meanest cabin-boy in the American service would not be guilty of such cowardice!" Demanding then to see the prisoner, Costa was brought on deck in irons. Captain Stringham asked: "Are you an American?" "No I am a Hungarian." "Have you an American passport?" To which (like a blockhead) he replied: *"No I am a Hungarian and I will die a Hungarian!"* The Americans could do no more, and left the brig. Learning however soon after, that Costa had taken the oath of citizenship, and seeing the Austrian brig preparing to depart, Captain Stringham sent a message that "as they had on board a prisoner carried off by force from a foreign independent territory, and who had sworn allegiance to the government of the United States, he should feel it to his duty to insist upon the brig remaining under his guns until he recovered instructions from Constantinople; and if any attempt were made to depart, he would at once fire into the brig."

A New Rose. M. Delhommeau, a gardener at Le Mans, France, has at the present moment a rose tree in full bloom which is the admiration of all amateurs. It is a hybrid, and bears a flower of a bluish lilac color, a tinge which has never before been obtained. The flowers produced are most abundant, very strong and regular, and measure nearly four inches in diameter. It has flowered this year for the first time.

The Lowell Courier says it is currently reported and believed to be quite authentic, that the mother of the celebrated French patriot, Lamartine, was a Massachusetts girl named Waitsill Brigham. She married the father of the present eminent statesman Lamartine, when quite young, in Boston, and then went to France, where she remained during her life.

An instance says the Memphis Appeal, has recently occurred in Cincinnati in which an lady was a maid, a wife and a widow, all in one day. Mrs. Connell wife of the man who was so cruelly murdered on Front street; the other evening of the day on which the fatal affray occurred. At morn a maid, at noon a wife, at evening a widow.

For Sale. The subscriber offers for sale his plantation and residence situated midway between Prattville and Robinson Springs, containing over two hundred acres, more than half in woodland and has a fine Spring, excellent Orchard, flower-garden &c. A good bargain may be had, by early application. Terms easy. Also for sale, thirty cows and calves, a yoke of oxen, corn, fodder, peas, &c. Dr. John A. Whetstone

Administrator's Sale. Will be sold on the 3d day of September next, at the late residence of William C. Wyatt, deceased, all the personal property belonging to the estate of said deceased, viz.: household furniture, plantation and blacksmith tools, two wagons one buggy, and six head of cattle, &c., on a credit until the first day of January next. Daniel H. Wyatt, Administrator

Sheriff's Sale. Will be sold to the highest bidder, for cash, at the Courthouse door, in the town of Kingston, on the first Monday of September next, within the legal hours of sale, CHARLOTTE, a Negro woman, and her child named Harrison, and DICK, a Negro man. Levied on the property of Henry Dennis, to satisfy an execution in my office from the Circuit Court of Autauga county, in favor of James R. Dennis and against the said Henry Dennis. James A. Lawler, Shff. Autauga Co.

The State of Alabama, Autauga county, Special Court of Probate, July 20, 1853.
This day came John F. Horton, administrator of the estate of Andrew S. Harris, deceased, and filed his petition, setting forth that said deceased died ceased of subdivision lots Nos. 1, 2, 3, 4, 5, 6, 7 and 8, of original lot No. 187, and the balance of said lot, except about half an acre in the south-east corner, and praise in order to sell said lots of land and buildings, situated in West Wetumpka, to make and equitable distribution among the heirs of said deceased. It is therefore ordered, that notice of said petition be given by publication in the Autauga Citizen for three successive weeks, to Mary (H.?) Harris, widow of said deceased, and Louisa and Mary Ann Harris, minors, who reside beyond the limits of the State, to appear at a Court to be held on the 19th day of September next, to show cause why said lots of land should not be sold. Henly Brown, Judge of Probate

Vol. 1, Thursday, August 18, 1853, No. 29

A communication in reply to "Justice" signed by those who gave their signatures to the petition for the appointment of Benj. Durden as postmaster at this place, has been unavoidably crowded out, in consequence of its being handed in too late.

Grapes. A bunch of the largest and most delicious grapes we have ever tasted, was presented to us a few days since by Miss Fanny Witter, Sarah Vilcent and Maria Witter. The bunch weighed two pounds and two ounces, which, we do not hesitate to say, cannot be beat in these *diggings*. The young ladies will please accept our thanks for their fine present, and, moreover, they may rest assured that we would be pleased to hear from them again.

Railroad Convention. Pursuant to adjournment of a meeting held in Autaugaville on the 25th day of June, a railroad convention met at this place on Saturday, the 13th inst. It was organized by appointing Daniel Pratt, President, John P. Figh, Vice President, and John Hardy and W.T. Hatchet, Secretaries. The President explained the object of the convention in a few appropriate remarks, when, upon motion of Jesse R. Jones, Esq., a committee of nine was appointed, to which the President was afterwards added, to draft resolutions for the convention. The committee consisted of Messrs. Chas. T. Pollard, Thos. H. Watts and James E. Belser, of Montgomery; John Hardy, of Selma; B. Trimble, of Wetumpka; Dr. Thos. P. Frith, D.B. Smedley, Bolling Hall, Jesse R. Jones and Daniel Pratt, of Autauga. The committee retired, and after a short absence returned and reported through Mr. Pollard, their chairman, the following resolutions:

1st. *Resolved*, That in the opinion of this convention a railroad from the city of Montgomery by the most direct and practicable route to Selma through the county of Autauga, extending from thence to the Mississippi line in the direction of Jackson, Miss., will form an indispensable linking in the chain of railroads, which are soon to connect the Atlantic and Pacific oceans.

2d. *Resolved*, further, that a railroad running on the most direct practicable route from the city of Montgomery through the counties of Autauga and Shelby, and from thence through the northwestern counties of the State to some points on the Tennessee river, is of the utmost importance in effecting a development of the mineral resources of the State of Alabama.

3d. *Resolved*, further, that we cordially approve of both of these enterprises, and that we will use our best exertions to have them completed at the earliest possible time.

4th. *Resolved*, that a committee of fourteen be appointed by the President of this convention, (of which he shall be one) selected along the line of the proposed great central road, and that he be requested to notify them of their appointment, and urge upon their meeting in Montgomery as early as the second Monday in November to prepare a charter for it, and to furnish such views to the committees of the Legislature, as may promote the success of this work.

5th. *Resolved*, that the President of this convention appoint a committee of nine, (of which he shall be one) who shall take all necessary steps to procure a charter, and do everything which may be requisite to promote the building of the road, under the second resolution.

6th. *Resolved*, that the President at his convenience appoint nine persons (of which he shall be one) to represent this meeting in the railroad convention to be held at Elyton on the 24th inst.

Committee appointed under the first resolution:

Col. Chas. T. Pollard, Montgomery
Hon. Geo. Goldwaite, Montgomery
Col. J.W. Lapsley, Selma
Col. W.S. Philips, Selma

Col. J.L. Price, Uniontown
Joseph R. Johns, Esq., Uniontown
Hon. F.S. Lyon, Demopolis
Daniel Pratt, Esq., Prattville
Dr. C.M. Howard, Mulberry
Gen. Patton, Livingston
Hon. T. Rearis, Gainesville
W.E. Clarke, Esq., Linden
Col. S.P. Storrs, Wetumpka
N.S. Graham, Esq., Wetumpka
Committee appointed under the second resolution:
Col. Chas. T. Pollard, Montgomery
Col. S.P. Storrs, Wetumpka
N.S. Graham, Esq., Wetumpka
John S. Storrs, Esq., Montevallo
Wm. S. Mudd, Elyton
Maj. Wm. Montgomery, Prattville
Daniel Pratt, Esq., Prattville
Jesse R. Jones, Esq., Kingston
Absalom Jackson, Esq., R. Springs
Committee appointed to attend the railroad convention at Elyton on the 24th inst.:
Col. S.P. Storrs, Wetumpka
Col. L.P. Saxon, Wetumpka
Gen. Crawford M. Jackson, R. Springs
Gen. E. Shackleford, Independence
Wm. H. Northington, Esq., Prattville
Dr. C.M. Howard, Mulberry
Jesse R. Jones, Esq., Kingston
Wm. N. Thompson, Esq., Kingston
Caleb Moncreif, Esq., Prattville
Daniel Pratt, Esq., Prattville
Montgomery, Selma, Wetumpka and various points in this county were represented. Judging from the number who attended on the occasion, and the harmony and unanimity which prevailed throughout the proceedings, we set down the establishment and early completion of these two roads as a fixed fact. Speeches in support of the resolutions were made by Col. Chas. T. Pollard, Thos. H. Watts, Esq., Jas. E. Belser, Esq. and John Hardy, Esq., and they were passed unanimously.

Editorial Brevities.
The European papers states that recently R. Hobbs, the Yankee lockmaker, within three minutes picked the premium lock which had been awarded a prize of L10 from the Society of Arts, Mr. Chubb, the celebrated locksmith, presiding. Hobbs opened it in the presence of the society, with a needle and a thin strip of steel. That Hobbs will be a death of Chubb.

A duel was fought in the vicinity of this city, early yesterday morning, says the Charleston *Courier*, between John Donovant, Esq., of Chester, and J.D. Legare, Esq., of this city, in which, we regret to state, the latter was killed at the first fire.

Very Gallant. Rev. A.D. Eddy, of Newark, New Jersey, in the discussion upon slavery in the Presbyterian Assembly, at Buffalo, defended himself from the charge that he had married a slave holder. It was untrue. She never had but one slave, and that *was the one she married*. He had no wish to escape from her bondage.

U S Senator. Robert S. Johnson, late representative in Congress from Arkansas, has been appointed by Governor Conway, of that State, to fill the vacancy in the United States Senate, occasioned by the resignation of Mr. Borland.

The Richmond Enquirer says that Governor Johnson tendered the office of Treasurer of the Commonwealth of Virginia to the Hon. Henry A. Wise, of Accomac county, who declined the appointment. The office has been since tendered to J.B. Stovall Esq., who has not been heard from in response.

We notice by the last news from California that Tod Robinson formerly of this state, has been nominated by the recent Whig State Convention for Justice of the Supreme court.

New Cotton. The first bale of new cotton was received in this place yesterday morning, by Waller & Terrell, from J.H. Cogburn, Esq. and was raised on the plantation of the estate of J.R. Conyers, by Wm. G. Rudder-the quality classed middling. The cotton was offered at auction by M. Harwell, Esq., and bid off by L.B. Pope agent, at 11 1/4 cents. - *Advertiser.*

The New Orleans *Crescent* announces the death on the 2d inst. of N.J.C. Crenshaw, one of the editors of that paper after an illness of five days, of yellow fever. The deceased was a native of Nashville, Tenn., and had only been resident in New Orleans for a few months. The Crescent speaks in high terms of his agreeable manners and propriety of deportment.

Mr. Editor-Herewith I hand you at a letter from Col. Charles T. Pollard, which I desire you to publish. It is well known that Col. Pollard's connection with railroads for many years past, has given him better opportunities of judging correctly on this subject than most other persons in our own State. His views appear to be sound and practical, and I hope that every man I know in Alabama will read them. If twenty men could be found in Alabama, of the same enterprise, experienced and practical judgment, in railroad matters, we would have nothing to fear. All that is necessary to Alabama's success in railroads, is to have them set forth in their true light by such men as the people have confidence in. This would induce them to examine into the subject themselves, or in other words, the people want to be properly awakened on the subject. In relation to the Pensacola and Montgomery, and Mobile and Girard railroads, I may hereafter express my views. I hope you will insert this letter and much oblige, Yours, &c, Daniel Pratt.

Died. Near Centerville, Bibb County, Alabama, Richard A. Dansby, of typhoid fever, after an illness of 23 days, aged 21 years and four months. A young man, both and industrious an enterprising character, with many friends, and no enemies. His parents mourn not as those without hope, for he died, with faith, firm and fixed in his redemption, through our Lord and Savior Jesus Christ.

The State of Alabama, Autauga County, Special Court of Probate, August 12, 1853.
This day came William H. Northington, Administrator of the Estate of John Brogan, deceased, and filed his accounts and vouchers for the annual settlement of the Estate of said deceased, which was examined, and ordered to be filed for the inspection of all concerned. It is therefore ordered, that notice be given for forty days, by publication for three successive weeks in the Autauga Citizen, a newspaper published in said County, notifying all persons

interested to be and appear at a Court to be held on the 12th day of September next, to show cause why said Account should not be stated and allowed, and said settlement be made. Henly Brown, Judge of Probate.

Vol. 1, Thursday, August 25, 1853, No. 30

We are indebted to Hon. Benj. Fitzpatrick for valuable congressional documents.

Mr. Morrill, the skillful daguerrean artist who has recently been among us, is now located at Robinson's Springs, where he is prepared to take likenesses in a superior manner. We would advise the good people in that neighborhood to give him a call, by all means.

Fearful Death. About four weeks since, a Mr. Beyington, of Oberlin, Ohio, was killed by a stallion. The horse was seized with a fit of madness, caught the man in his mouth and threw him into the air. When he struck the ground, the horse jumped upon him with his forefeet, seized him by the head, and broke his neck short off, severing the jugular vein with his teeth.

The Frankfort, (Ky.) Yeoman nominates Mr. Breckenridge, M. C. Elect from the Ashland district, for Speaker of the House of Representatives. The Yeoman says: "he is destined at some future day to fill the office of President of the U. States." One noble Representative of Ashland district was Speaker of the House, but he never gained the Presidential chair.

Editorial Brevities.
Vote for Governor. We are not yet in possession of the full vote for Governor. In forty counties it stands as follows:
Winston, 30,862
Earnest, 9,509
Walker, 1,068
Nix, 7,046

Cotton Tree. Gen. John Wilson, who now resides in San Francisco, has written to Governor Foote, of Mississippi, about a group of Islands in the Pacific known as the Navigator Islands. With the letter Gen. Wilson sends to Gov. Foote some pickings of cotton taken from one of the cotton trees which grow on those islands. This tree attains the extraordinary height of thirty feet, with a diameter of one foot, and branches spreading thirty feet. The boll is about the size of a goose egg. When the cotton tree is in full bloom, it presents a superb appearance, looking like an immense snowball tree, of the kind that adorns so many of our gardens.

Excitement at Baltimore. Quite an excitement has prevailed at Baltimore, growing out of street preaching. An indignation meeting was held in Monument Square on the 27th, and Mayor Hollins was denounced for ordering the police to put a stop to the preaching of an old market house and street corner declaimer, who, under the plea of preaching morality, was in the habit of uttering the most violent harangues against sects and persons, and had become more bitter than ever, to the danger of the peace of the city. The Mayor has published an address in which he expresses his determination not to be intimidated, and calls on the friends of order to aid him in checking mob violence. Another meeting was to be held on the evening of the 29th.

It is said that Madame Achille Murat, who recently returned from France, whither she went on a visit to her relative, the Emperor, has arrived at her plantation near Tallahassee.

First Bale of the Season. A bale of New Cotton from the plantation of Major Richard A. Ward, was sold in this city yesterday, to Messrs. Benton & Whitaker at 13 7/8 cents per pound. The price bespeaks the quality. - *Tallahassee Sentinel, 2d.*

A Singular Case. A Miss Read, of West Boylston, took cloroform a few days ago, for the purpose of having a tooth extracted, she was attacked with severe pains in her head, became unconscious, and apparently died. Her friends, supposing her dead, laid her out for burial, and began to prepare for the funeral ceremonies; but their grief was unexpectedly turned to joy and astonishment, on finding that the supposed dead began to revive. She eventually recovered the full possession of her faculties; but what is still more singular in her case, we are told she suffers violent pains in the head as regularly as evening approaches, and at length, and about the same hour each night, falls into a swoon very similar to that which in the first instance was supposed to have been the sleep of death. This case certainly presents a most remarkable escape from premature burial. - *Worcester Times.*

A Mr. Isaac F. Shepard, of Boston, in letters addressed to the Hon. Abbott Lawrence and Hon. Edward Everett, proposes a plan by which Mount Vernon may be secured to the people of the United States forever as their common property. He estimates the cost of purchase, improving and repairing, salary of superintendent, and labor, including a six per cent fund of $100,000, would amount to a cash capital of $350,000. This sum, he proposes, should be raised by voluntary subscription among the people and the estate held by a board of trustees composed of the President of the United States, and Governor of Virginia, *ex officio*, and one person to be elected by the Legislature of each State. Messrs. Everett and Lawrence fully concur in the opinion that Mount Vernon ought to become public property.

Fugitive Slave. A fugitive slave arrived, at Cincinnati from Piqua, Miami county, Ohio, and was brought before Judge McLean, who on hearing the evidence, remanded him to his master, who had come from Kentucky in search of him. Judge McLean delivered an elaborate opinion on the case, sustaining the rights of the South and the constitutionality of the fugitive slave law.

Alabama Penitentiary. Mr. Moore, leasee of the Penitentiary at Wetumpka, has furnished a committee of temperance men with the following statement: Agreeably to your request, I interrogated the convicts in this Institution as to their habits in the use of intoxicating drinks, previous to their incarceration, and the following is the result of my inquiries:
No. who have abstained entirely-3
No. of moderate drinkers, but who were never intoxicated-27
No. of moderate drinkers occasionally intoxicated-90
No. of moderate drinkers, but who were never intoxicated-65
No. who have abstained for two years-2
No. who have abstained for three years-1
No. who have abstained for five years-1
No. who have abstained for seven years-1
No. who have abstained for fifteen years-2
Total-192
Of the above number, 74 admit that the crimes for which they were convicted, were committed while under the influence of intoxicating drinks.

Dr. McFarlane publishes in the True Delta another article on his filth theory in relation to epidemics. He takes up the condition of New Orleans within the period between 1823 and 1833. The contrast of the city then and now is interesting, if it does not establish the conclusion he draws from it. We extract the following: To speak in plain and comprehensive language, the city was one widespread morase. Canal street was a bog, and there was not a square yard of paving from that street to Carrollton. There were no paved sidewalks, that in their stead flatboat gunwales constituted the only mode of progress for pedestrians, and these rotted and had to be replaced every few years. I have seen a horse perish in the mud in Camp street, opposite Lafayette Square, and, when Lafayette himself visited the city the four splendid horses which were provided to convey his carriage from place to place, stalled opposite the Arcade in Magazine street, and were unable to flounder any further through the mud: it became necessary to provide planks so as to extricate "the nation's guest" from what was considered rather a perilous situation, and to remove him from the wooden sidewalk, which formed the margin of the street. The levee from Canal street upward was one wide display of desolation. No wharves, covered with rich produce, lined the Mississippi banks. No steamboat or shipping gave animation to the scene, and in the summer nothing but a wide extended batture, conveyed with rotting and offensive vegetable decomposition, was presented to eye. In the rear, Gravier's Canal, the Goose Pond, so-called, extended up to the corner of Barrone street occupying all the space on which the Poydras Market now stands, until it terminated at Carroll street, in what had been intended as a future basin, and filled with carrion and impurity. If a cart in those days stalled in the streets, there being no terra firma by which to extricate it, it had to remain in the mud until the next dry spell, when it was dug out. Planks were laid along the streets, on which cotton and tobacco were rolled in the warehouses, by hand, at a dollar a bale or hogshead. There was no police, and at night a few sleepy gens d'armas crept at a snail's space along the streets. There was not they scavenger's cart in the whole city above Canal street, and a few below, and if there had been they could not have got along through the streets. As may readily be supposed there was no thought of cleaning the streets. If a horse or cow died, it lay undisturbed until an outcry from the neighboring inhabitants, when the chain gang dragged it, by the aid of horse power, to the lower end of the Goose Pond, and either threw it in, were covered it with a few inches of mud. And what was the condition of New Orleans during all this period, in point of health? Infinitely better than it is at present. About once in three or five years-for the old French, Spanish and Creole, population declared that it always came odd years, and that rule seems to hold good even now-about once in three or five years we have been visited with epidemic yellow fever, which rarely commences before September, and terminated in October. Could filth, or offal, or decomposition have had anything to do with the triennial visitation of epidemic yellow fever, where all was filth, offal and vegetable decomposition, at all times, and during all seasons? Or was there more filth, or offal decomposition during the odd years, than the ones? The idea of is preposterous. Now look at the city of New Orleans, paved from one end to the other, blended sidewalks of bricks and granite, magnificent wharves lining almost the whole extent of the city, splendid edifices of undecomposible substance, a vigilant hyglenistic police and a Board of Health, nuisance boats to receive it and remove the offal of the city at the earliest moment, and hundreds of carts and laborers to prevent offensive collections in the streets. At what is the result of all of this? A desolating epidemic yellow fever commences its ravages in July, unprecedentedly early in the whole history of N. Orleans, and ravages our recent inhabitants, without distinction.

The State of Alabama, Autauga county, Special Court of Probate, August 17, 1853.
This day came Nancy Slaton, guardian of Caroline E. Slaton and Martha J. Slaton, minors, and filed her accounts and vouchers for the annual settlements of said wards estates, which was examined an ordered to be filed for the inspection of all concerned. It is therefore ordered, that notice be given for forty days, by publication for three successive weeks in the Autauga Citizen, a newspaper published in said county, notifying all persons interested to be and appear at a court to be held on the 27th day of September next, to show cause, if any, why said account should not be stated and allowed, and said settlement to be made. Henly

Brown, Judge of Probate.

The State of Alabama, Autauga county, Special Court of Probate, August 18, 1853.
This day Malcolm Smith, Administrator of estate of George Laycock, deceased, and made the application to sell two negroes, Sam and Wilson, for the purpose of paying the debts of said deceased and to make a distribution among the heirs of said deceased. It is therefore ordered that notice of said application be given by publication in the Autauga Citizen for three successive weeks, to all persons interested to be and appear at a court to be held on the 8th day of September next, to show cause why said negroes should not be sold. Henly Brown, Judge of Probate.

Vol. 1, Thursday, September 1, 1853, No. 31

Editorial Brevities.
The telegram states that Mr. Cobb, of Georgia, will be sent as minister to France.

The opposition, at the last mail accounts, to the appointment of Mr. Dix, had not ceased. Mr. Dix might release the President by withdrawing; but, we suppose, he thinks that it is a question of slavery or anti slavery, and therefore, like his freesoil brethren, is not likely to take any steps from courtesy.

The Washington Republic says that a delegation from New York was in the capital pressing the President to appoint Mr. Bancroft, the historian of the United States; but this proposition was not received with favor.

Caleb Cushing is also recommended for the post.

Mr. Editor-it is not my wish to perpetuate the controversy between "Justice," and "Justice vs. Justice," but as the latter gentleman found it necessary to pay me a double faced compliment, I ask an insertion in your columns of my own signature. I do not like the idea wasting powder and shot at a mark behind a tree, and would not, in this instance, if the identity of "Justice vs. Justice," was not so easily guessed at. My object is not to abuse and villify the author of that communication, but merely to place myself, and this Post Office matter in a proper light before our public, and let them judge whether I am "pandering to the jealouses of a particular few," by wishing to retain the Post Office in this place. In the summer of 1851, a respectable portion of the citizens of this place, of both political parties, waited on me in my office, desiring to know if I would accept the office of Postmaster, if they would recommend me, to which of replied affirmatively if I could get a suitable and responsible deputy to take charge of the business. I was accordingly recommended and received my appointment in August, 1851, and Messrs. W.C. Allen & Co. took upon themselves the obligation to have the business of the Office attended to. Mr. James Allen was sworn in as deputy Postmaster, and received a part of the emoluments of the Office until January, 1852, and he and I at our own expense fitted up a temporary apartment for the Office in Morgan and Tickner's brick building, being the most suitable place for the Office at that time. After the first of January, 1852, the Office being moved into the building now occupied, because of its greater security, and that better arrangements could be made to have the Office attended to, the emoluments of the Office went to the firm of W. C. Allen & Co., Mr. B.F. Miles coming in as one of that firm. Since the dessolution of that firm, I have made arrangement for Mr. Miles to act as my deputy, and he has been sworn in accordingly. I never knew that the people was dissatisfied with this arrangement until a few weeks since, and then, the reasons given were not such as to impress me very strongly in favor of yielding my position. Mr. Benjamin Durden came to me then and asked if I received the emoluments of the Post Office, to which I answered no, not even the postage of my letters. Mr. Durden being told me that some of his friends in the county, (not his relatives either) wished him to apply for the Post Office; he further mentioned that he was no longer the mover in this matter, but it was done by his friends in the county, and that it was on *party grounds;* these friends thought that Mr. Pratt's motive in fitting up the Post Office in the Brick Building was to control the Office, and that they thought it ought to be moved. I never told Mr. Durden that I did not want this Office nor that I wanted to get rid of it-would as soon as he would have it as anyone else; but, on the contrary, plainly intimated to him that I did not think *him* qualified to discharge its duties, and advised him to have nothing to do with it. The above is a fair statement of the substance of the conversation I had with Mr. Durden on the subject. I never mentioned this conversation (a part of which are now regret to bring to light) until since the communication of "Justice vs. Justice," made its appearance, and my object now in making this statement is to present to the public my true position in this matter, and my wish is that this may be the last of it. My sole object, in consenting to accept and hold the Office was to contribute to its permanency, and good management. It is well known that previous to the time the Office had been frequently changed, and no one seemed to desire it, the cause the emoluments did not compensate for the necessary attention. It is true, that in my acceptance of it, I had an interested motive, as agent of the Prattville Manufacturing Company, but I hope I was not influenced altogether by self interest, and in this respect I may say that in now retaining it I have a double interest-being agent for two establishments, for both of which I am daily receiving and forwarding letters of importance. And though this is the case, I am persuaded that a more liberal view than that taken by "Justice vs. Justice" will decide that I have not been influenced solely by interested motives, nor to " pander to the jealouses of that particular few." S. Mims

Reminiscences of Autauga County. [*Written for the Autauga Citizen*]
Mr. Editor-After one or two weeks respite, I again take up my reminiscences, and will introduce you and your readers to the Rocky Mount neighborhood, remarkable for its healthiness and the substantial character at its citizens, who were mostly from Georgia and South Carolina, whose names are still perpetuated in the same vicinity that their descendants. Messrs. Bolling Hall, Aley Pollard, Maj. Abner Hill and Mr. Pierce were all from Georgia. Jacob Whetstone, Col. Arthur Hayne and Col. Cragon from South Carolina. Dr. Z. Pope and Littleton Rice from Georgia. These men were all substantial citizens, who succeeded well in farming-men who have commanded respect in any age or country, that they have all passed away and left their earthly inheritance to be enjoyed by their children. Col. Hayne, at an early period, sold out his land and negroes to Dr. Z. Pope on long time-light gray energy and perseverance the Doctor found himself owner of a fine farm and negroes to cultivate it, at the expiration of the credit-one instance at least, when the credit system proved advantageous to the purchaser. To say the least of it, such trades are hazardous, and particularly so, one all depends upon the price of cotton, which fluctuates so often. The Doctor was remarkable for his untiring energy, perseverance and judicious management in farming, and when a practicing physician, was said to be successful. Col. Cragon died at an early period and was succeeded by his son-in-law, Capt. John Duncan, who was bred and born an Irishman. He was remarkable for his fine tastes for gardening, gentlemanly and urbane manners, and fine conversational powers. Another gentleman whose name I have left out, deserves a place in my humble reminiscence. Who does not remember Gen. Elmore, who lived at Mortar creek? Tall, erect and manly at the age of seventy. In looking back upon these old men whose names I have introduced, it is with pride that I think of them. The question very naturally arises in my mind, will their sons fill their places in every respect, with perhaps far superior advantages? - this is a matter for their consideration. In my youth they were before me as patterns-have I profited by their example of good citizenship? I trust I have, but in view of such responsibilities, who is able to look them full in the face without fearful misgivings of a failure-yet, many now acting out their parts on life's theater, as they did, what will be the record made of us by those who want to follow us? I know the age we live in is called a progressive one, and so it ought to be, and really, in many respects, is, but I doubt very much whether the present generation will turn out anything superior to those characters just mentioned. I mean for real solid worth and energy of character, and I am not afraid to place the whites of those men side by side of any of their daughters, who have been raised the under far more advantageous circumstances, so far is that facilities of a literary education is con-

cerned. I mean in regard to filling up that beautiful picture of the housewife, which Solomon sketches in. But, Mr. Editor, if I go on this strain much longer your readers will call me an old Fogy-be it so. I won't deny and I am an admirer of olden time folks, I like to see and converse with them-they appear to me to be better models of real substantial worth, made of finer and better materials, if not so finely polished. Adieu for the present. An Old Citizen.

Obituary. Death, the leveler of all mankind, has again been in our midst-again has another warm hearted, noble friend fallen in the his resistless stroke-a fond affectionate wife and children made a widow and orphans and numerous bereaved friends left with them to morn his untimely death. Col. John P. DeJarnette was born in Anson county, North Carolina, in October, 1800, aged nearly fifty three years. He was educated in that State, but at an early age moved to the State of Alabama, county of Autauga, where he continue to reside up to the day of his death, which occurred at his residence, after a long and painful illness, on the 19th ult. Col. DeJarnette was a very popular man, and frequently represented this county in the lower branch of the Legislature, with the entire satisfaction to his constituents, and honor to himself. He was a zealous and unswerving democrat, and had the unbounded confidence of his party. Col. DeJarnette, as soon as he became of age, attached himself to the Masonic fraternity, and assisted in organizing the first lodge ever formed in this county. (Autauga Lodge No. 31,) and continued an officer and member up to the day of his death. His heart, hand and purse were ever opened to aid the poor, the widow and the orphan, and though he never attached himself to any Church, he was always ready to give liberally to the support of preachers, the Missionary, Sabbath schools, and the Bible cause. In the various relations of life, he sustained an enviable position-as a husband, affectionate-as a father, kind and tender-as a friend, true and confiding. But he has gone-let us imitate his many virtues, fondly remember him, and let his bereaved family and friends consult themselves with the reflection, that "Jesus hath done all things well." J.A. W. North Carolina papers will please copy.

The State of Alabama, Autauga county, Special Court of Probate, August 22, 1853.
Ordered that notice be given to the creditors of the estate of Alfred Parker, deceased, by publication in the Autauga Citizen, a newspaper published at Prattville, in said county, once a week for six successive weeks, that James A. Lawler, sheriff and ex-officio administrator of the estate of said estate, and filed his report and statements setting forth that said estate is insolvent, and that the 17th day of October next, has been appointed to hear and determine the same at the Probate court room in Kingston, in said county. Henly Brown, Judge of Probate.

The State of Alabama, Autauga county.
Taken up by John C. Lassiter, and posted before A. Samples, a Justice of the Peace, in an for said county, a Sorrel horse, fourteen hands high, nine years old, roan spots on his right shoulder, left hind foot and half the leg white, star in his face and scar on his back from the saddle, and appraised at forty dollars, by Leroy Flanagan and Wm. Presley, 22d day of August, 1853. Henly Brown, Judge of Probate.

For Sale. A tract of land, known as the Joe May land, containing three hundred and fifty acres three hundred of which is in cultivation, and fifty in woodland. Also, one dwelling house in Washington, all of which is lying near the Alabama river, which I will sell low for cash. M.B. Pollard

Vol. 1, Thursday, September 8, 1853, No. 32

Mr. Editor-In your paper of the 1st inst., I perceive an article over the signature of S. Mims, purporting to be a reply to "Justice vs. Justice," and in order to place himself right before "the public," he seems to have deemed it necessary to introduce what *he* terms a *"fair statement of the substance of a conversation"* he had with me in relation to the Post Office in this place, and his versions of that conversation is of such a character as to render it necessary that I should ask a place in your columns, in order that I may make known to "the public" my "true position" in reference to the Post Office difficulty, for I am persuaded that, notwithstanding I am not very expert at writing "Reminiscences," and have not the good fortune to be the agent of "two wealthy establishments," and though I am not so vain, presumptious and arrogant as to think that I am the only man about Prattville who can give permanency to the Post Office, yet, the public feel quite as much interest in my "position" as they do in that of S. Mims, Esquire, "agent of the Prattville Manufacturing Company." As Mr. Mims has condescended to stoop from his lofty "position" to inform the public why he *most graciously* consented to accept the Post Office in the first instance, and now desires to retain it, I will give moral reasons for seeking and desiring to obtain it. He says that his reason for accepting it, was, that he was solicited by a respectable portion of both parties, and that he desired to "contribute to its permanency and good management," and he clearly intimates that his desire to retain it arises chiefly from the fact that he is "the agent of two wealthy companies," but I am not prepared to believe that they will find much favor among the plain republicans of old Autauga. He seems to attach some importance to the fact that he was solicited to accept the office by members of both parties. This will be easily accounted for by those who are acquainted with his equivocal position in politics, for "He wires in and wires out, and leaves the people still in doubt, whether the snake that make the track, was going in or coming out." Gentleman occupying such a "position" as this may sometimes obtain the support of both parties for a brief period, and this support is not on unfrequently prolonged by a system of duplicity and political dodging-shunning the ballot box in important and trying political contests, but such devices are generally short lived, and when those who resort to them are weighed in the balance, they are found wanting in all the elements which constitute the honest and upright politician, and they have once become objects of distrust and suspicion to all *parties*. But a sufficient, and, I suppose, in his estimation, a satisfactory reply to all this would be that he is an agent of "two establishments," whose interest or feelings demands neutrality on his part. I have applied for the office, and am endeavoring to obtain it, simply from the fact that I am poor, and the profits arising therefrom would aid me in the support of a large and dependent family, (the most of whom have been and are yet, humble, but honest and faithful laborers in one of the "establishments" for which my friend M. is agent.) My claims to the office are set forth in a petition which is now deposited in the Post Office department in Washington city, signed by between thirty and forty of the most respectable and substantial citizens in this community, and, if I were as destitute of modesty as Mr. M. has shown himself to be, I might here set forth those claims, but I forbear, but Mr. M. insists that I am not qualified to discharge the duties of the office; were I as egotistical as he is, I might settle this question by simply asserting that my attachments were superior to his, but I feel proud that I am not driven to a "position" so humiliating to my sense of propriety, therefore, in reply to this grave objection, I will simply state, the gentleman above alluded to, as the signers of my petition, (all of whom would compare favorably in point of intellect and attainments, with the *gifted agent*,) have, over their own signatures, certified that I *am qualified*. I will now briefly advert to the conversation alluded by Mr. M., and, in doing so, I shall simply notice those points about which we differ. Mr. M. says that he did not say to me that he "would as soon I have the office as any person, quotation more in reply to which I have simply to say that my recollection on this point is distinct and clear, and that if he denies positively using such language in substance, he denies the truth, for he certainly used it. He says that I told him" that my political friends were of opinion that Mr. Pratt's motive in fitting up the Post Office in the brick building was to control the office, and that they thought it ought to be moved. "The only reply I have to make to this, is, that it is false, an utterly false, without even the semblance of truth to redeem it-there is an inprobability stamped upon the very face of it. And now, Mr. Editor, I hope that this whole matter has assumed such a form as to render it unnecessary that Mr. M. or myself should trouble you or the public any longer in relation to it. As the lawyers would say, we have " arrived at an issue of fact, "which cannot be determined by a newspaper controversy. Respectfully, Benj. Durden

We regret to chronicle the death of Mr. M. Fitzpatrick, son of Gov. Benj. Fitzpatrick, who fell a victim to the prevailing epidemic in New Orleans, on the 22d inst., aged about 22 years. Mr. F. had been engaged in business in New Orleans some two or three years; and supposing his long residence there would protect him from the fever, he refused to leave his post, though urged to do so by his father and friends. *Advertiser & Gazette.*

Governor Collier has appointed Turner Reavis, Esq., of Gainesville, Judge of the 7th Judicial Circuit, to supply the vacancy occasioned by the resignation of the Honorable B.W. Huntington.

Married-Near Kingston, on the 1st inst., by J.R. Jones, Esq., Dr. John B. Moodie, to Miss Edna Rollison, all of this county.

Vol. 1, Thursday, September 15, 1853, No. 33

Elyton Railroad Convention. In pursuance to a call made by the citizens of Jefferson county upon the friends of Internal Improvements throughout the State to hold a Convention at Elyton, on Wednesday, the 24th of August, the following gentleman appeared as delegates from their respective counties:

Blount--David Hendrix, A. Jones, H. Huffstuller, J. Jones, W. Byrd, W.H. Edwards, W. Reed, A. Allgoo, W.A. Croump, G.W. Montgomery, W.L. Lewis, J.P. Cowden, W.H. Stoke, John Buckler, P. Palmer, T.W. Hendrix, J. Hill, Lewis Cole, L. Huffstuller, J. Hudson, W. Huffstuller, H.D. Harbin, J. Anderson, R. Tidwell, J.T. Oozby, A.P. Gillespid, R.D. Cowden, K. Gamble, Geo. Carnes, W.L. Wilson, J.B. Cooker, W. Graves, A. Murphree, A.J. Hood, A.M. Gibson, P.M. Musgrove, J.M. McRae, J. Hendrix, G.L. Brindley, W. Hudson, J. Thompson, M.H. Hannah, R.C. Mason, W.D. Wilson, B.H. Sapp, M. Ward, J.R. Glasscock, W. Byars, J. Calvert, M. Glasscock, E.G. Musgrove, H.M. Tidmore.

Coosa-N.S. Graham, W.T. Hatchett, R. Smoot.

Dallas-W.S. Phillips, T.B. Goolsby, J.W. Lapsley, W.B. King, C.C. Pegues, A. White, R.A. Baker, B.I. Harrison, J. Weedon, Jas. Adams, J.M. Lapsley, J.E. Prestridge, Col. W.S. Burr, T.W. Street, G. Hewitt, S.R. Shelton, John Hardy.

Green-J.W. Taylor, S.W. Cockrell, Moses Hubbard.

Jefferson-M. Kelley, M.T. Porter, G.W. Clark, O.S. Bunsell, W. Hawkies, L.F. Green, S.A. Tarrant, J.H. Hewitt, B.E. Green, W.M. Adkins, L.G. McMillion, J. Camp, D. Hanby, M. Massey, J.H. Baker, W.A. Walker, Z. Hagood, O.M. Smith, R. Baire, S.S. Earle, J. Harris, A.J. Waldrop, E. Wood, J. Nenes, P. Bagly, P. Downs, R.H. Greene, James Tarrent, W.J. Rocket, M.L. McMillion, J.W. McWilliams, W.S. Mudd.

Marshall-Frank Gilbreath, R. Parker, J.S. Ditto, F. Dillon, C. Farris, B.B. Ramsey, W.M. Griffin, R.S. Pierce, Tom Barclay.

Morgan-H.F. Scruggs, H.V. Philpot.

Montgomery-Thos. J. Judge, Gen. R. Elmore, J.P. Figh.

Perry-John D. Phelan, Andrew B. Moore, J.P. Perham.

Shelby-D.E. Watrous, J.S. Storrs, John Sumner, J.P. Morgan, J.H. Oakes, H.R. Lyman, Jas. Gregory, William McConaughoy, J.M. Norment, W.B. Harrington, S.G. Brown.

Sumter-J.L. Childress, G.B. Mobly, R. Craig.

Talladega-W.W. Mattison.

Tuscaloosa-Prof. L.C. Garland, Prof. F.A.P. Bennard, Thomas Maxwell, J.S. Hayes, E. McMath, J.C. Spencer, W.A. Battle, M. Finley, S.J. Leach, James Fitts, A.P. Walker.

Walker-E.G. Musgrove, A. Stephens, A. Cain, W.B. Drendon, T.M. Gobbert, W.B. Taylor, Jas. Savage, F.A. Musgrove, J. Crear, W.N. Gibson, Martin Wood, John Irwin, M. Camak.

On motion of Col. W.S. Earnest, of Jefferson county, Col. W.S. Phillips, of Dallas, was called to the Chair, for the purpose of organizing the Convention. The following delegates were then proposed as officers of the Convention, by a committee of one from each county represented, who were appointed for that purpose, through their Chairman, Gen. R. Elmore, of Montgomery, and the selection ratified by the Convention:

For President-Hon. John D. Phelan, of Perry

For Vice President-R.A. Baker, of Dallas; A.M. Gibson, of Blount; M. Hubbard, of Greene; Moses Kelley, of Jefferson; W.M. Griffin, of Marshall; H.V. Philpot, of Morgan; D.E. Watrous, of Shelby; B. Craig, of Sumter; W.W. Mattison, of Talladega; F.A.P. Bernard, of Tuscaloosa; J.P. Figh, of Montgomery; N.S. Graham, of Coosa; J.P. Perham, of Perry.

For Secretaries-J.M. Morment, of Shelby; John Hardy, of Dallas; Thos. C. Barclay, of Marshall; A.P. Walker, of Tuscaloosa.

A committee of three, composed of W.S. Earnest, Dr. J.E. Prestridge and R. Elmore, were appointed to inform the gentlemen of their selection, and to conduct them to their seats. The President, on taking the Chair, made a short address, explaining the object of the Convention, and urging the great importance of effecting a Railroad connection between North and South Alabama. On Motion of Col. W.S. Earnest, the following delegates were appointed a committee to draft and report suitable resolutions for the consideration of the Convention: Prof. Garland, of Tuscaloosa, Chairman; A.B. Moore, of Perry; J.W. Lapsley, of Dallas; T.J. Judge, of Montgomery; Wm. S. Mudd, of Jefferson; Jos. W. Taylor, of Greene; Wm. T. Hatchett, of Coosa; John S. Storrs, of Shelby; James Hendrix, of Blount; Jas. L. Childress, of Sumter; H.F. Scruggs, of Morgan; T.C. Barclay, of Marshall; W.W. Mattison, of Talladega; E.G. Musgroe, of Walker.

The order of the day was then announced by Col. Earnest, when the large assembly was addressed by Prof. F.A.B. Bernard, of Tuscaloosa, in an able speech, abounding in interesting details respecting Railroads. Gen. Philpot, of Morgan, was then introduced to the audience, and delivered a good address in support of the general objects in view. Dinner was then announced as being ready, when the large assembly repaired to the long the lines of tables, prepared to accommodate three thousand persons a, most bountifully supplied with an excellent dinner, provided by the good citizens of Jefferson county, of which all partook with good cheer. After dinner, the Rev. J.P. Perham, of Perry, entertained the large assembly for over two hours, on the great importance of Railroads generally, and the paramount importance of a connection between North and South Alabama by Railroad. The convention then adjourned until tomorrow morning, at 9 o'clock.

Thursday morning, 9 o'clock. The convention assembled according to adjournment. After the minutes of the preceding day had been read, Gen. Elmore, of Montgomery, offered the following resolutions which were adopted:

Resolved, that the ordinary Parliamentary Laws as laid down in Jefferson's manual; shall govern this Convention.

Resolved, that when the ayes and noes are called on voting, on all propositions, resolutions or otherwise, that the vote shall be controlled and governed by the number of the representatives of the State Legislature, and that when one or more counties are entitled to the Senator, that the county represented in the convention shall cast the senatorial vote.

J.P. Figh, of Montgomery, offered the following which was adopted:

Resolved, that no member shall address the meeting any longer than 30 minutes on any one question.

The committee on resolutions, through their chairman, Prof. L.C. Garland, made the following report, and on presenting it, addressed the Convention in a clear and happy style, in support of the policy therein recommended:

RESOLUTIONS.

Resolved, 1st, As the sense of this Convention that it is the duty of the State of Alabama to aid, by appropriate means, in the construction of works of Internal Improvements within its limits.

2. That as the most eligible plan for accomplishing that object, in the present condition of the State, we recommend the construction, by its aid, of a railroad of the first-class, connecting the waters of the Tennessee river with the waters of the Mobile Bay, so as to connect north and south Alabama.

3. That the said road when constructed shall be held under the control of the State for the common benefit of all its citizens, and that roads built by private enterprize or in any other mode from any section of the State, shall be allowed to connect with the said road which is to be a common central system.

4. That with the view of locating the said central road to the greatest advantage, we recommend a thorough and immediate typographical and geological survey by the State of all

practibable routes likely to accomplish that object.

5. That we recommend to the Legislature of the State to make provision at its next session, for the immediate, thorough and general geological survey of the State, and for its vigorous prosecution to completion at the earliest practicable period.

Col. W.S. Earnest, and Wm. S. Mudd, Esq., of Jefferson, addressed the Convention in favor, and Mr. Gibson of Blount, and Mr. Greene of Jefferson, against the adoption of the resolutions.

In pursuance of a unanimous wish of the Convention, evinced by a motion put and carried to that effect, the President of the Convention here addressed that body giving his views upon the resolutions reported by the committee, in the course of which he admitted that his original views had been modified to some extent by the action of the committee, and warmly urged the adoption of the report as it stood. His address was elaborate and listened to with great attention, and elicited at its close a hearty cheer from the whole body of the Convention.

The vote upon the resolution was then taken by counties, and they were unanimously carried, the vote being as follows:

County	Yeas	Nays
Blount	3	
Coosa	3	
Dallas	3	
Greene	3	
Jefferson	2	
Marshall	3	
Morgan	2	
Montgomery	3	
Perry	3	
Shelby	2	
Sumter	3	
Talladega	4	
Tuskaloosa		3
Walker	2	

Col. Phillips, of Dallas, then offered the following which was unanimously adopted:

Resolved, That our Senators and Representatives in Congress be and they hereby requested to use their efforts to secure a donation from the General Government, of a competent quantity of public lands to aid in the construction of the railroad contemplated in the proceedings of this Convention, as well as other railroads in Alabama now in progress of construction, or which may be hereafter contemplated.

J.W. Taylor, of Greene, then offered the following resolution, which was unanimously adopted:

Resolved, That a committee of — be appointed by the President of the Convention to prepare and transmit to the Legislature of Alabama, at its next session, a memorial in behalf of the trunk line of railroad recommended by this Convention. Said memorial to conform in substance and spirit with the resolutions adopted.

On motion the blank was filled by *five*.

The President appointed the following gentlemen said committee:

J.W. Taylor, of Greene, Chairman; Daniel E. Watrous, Shelby; J.W. Lapsley, Dallas; Gen. R. Elmore, Montgomery; A.M. Gibson, Blount; R.A. Baker, of Dallas, offered the following resolution, which was adopted:

Resolved, That this Convention request a copy for publication of the addresses of Prof. Garland and the Hon. J.D. Phelan.

Hon. Thos. J. Judge, of Montgomery, offered the following resolutions, which were adopted:

Resolved, That the thanks of this Convention be, and the same are hereby tendered to the Hon. John D. Phelan, for the dignified and impartial manner in which he has presided over its deliberations; and for the able address delivered by a him to the Convention, pursuant to its request.

Resolved, That the thanks of this convention be also tendered to the Secretaries of the same, for the satisfactory manner in which they have discharge their duty.

J.S. Storrs, of Shelby, offered the following which was adopted:

Resolved, That the thanks of this convention be tendered to the citizens of Elyton, for the kindness and hospitality with which its members have been received and entertained during its session.

On motion of Col. J.W. Lapsley, of Dallas, it was adopted:

Resolved, That all the papers in the State friendly to the objects of this convention, be requested to publish its proceedings.

The President addressed the Convention, returning his thanks, and congratulating the body upon the harmonious and concilliatary spirit that had characterized its deliberations. On motion of Gen. Elmore, of Montgomery, the Convention adjourned *sine die*. Jno. D. Phelan, President; J.M. Norment, John Hardy, Thos. C. Barclay, A.P. Walker, Secretaries

Editorial Brevities.

Death of a Faithful Public Servant. Capt. Chas. A. Beck, for twenty eight years keeper of the light on Long Island Head near Boston, died Friday week. The deceased was a native of Sweden; served many years in the United States navy; was in the frigate Constitution, and was appointed prize master of one of the vessels she took. At New Orleans, in 1815, he presented himself to General Jackson, and worked a gun aboard the schooner Caroline on the day of the battle.

Two Printers Gone. It is our painful duty, this morning, to announce the demise of two members of the typographical corps of this city. The first, a very worthy young man, who arrived at our city a few months ago, and has been ever since employed in our office as a compositor. He yesterday fell a victim to the relentless scourge now disseminating our city. His name was Octavius G. Cantley, aged about 20 years, born in Tuscaloosa, Alabama, where he has left and aged mother to morn her loss. He had a very delicate constitution, and death gained an easy victory. The Tuscaloosa papers will confer a favor by conveying the mournful intelligence to his relatives. The other was that of Thomas McElroy, one of the compositors on the Crescent, who also died yesterday, of yellow fever. He was born in Pennsylvania, about thirty years ago, and has been for a long period in this city. Poor Tom! May the earth rest lightly upon thee! These are the first deaths among the craft we have been called upon to record, and we need scarcely say that we sincerely hope they may be the last. Many of them are now sick, some have recovered, and are about again. The sick among them are well cared for, and their brethren spare no pains to comfort them and assuage their sufferings. *N.O. Delta, Saturday.*

Obituary. Departed this life, at her residence in Shreveport, on Wednesday the 10th ult., at 3 o'clock, a. m. Elizabeth Hall, wife of Col. Dixon Hall, late of Alabama, and daughter of Henry Harris, of Georgia, aged 44 years. She and her husband were born and brought in the same neighborhood, in Hancock county, Georgia, and having attended the same school, and participated in the same amusements, they formad for each other, and children, and attachment that "grew with their growth, and strengthened with their strength," and which manifested itself, during her late illness, in all the vigor and ardor of which the affection of mankind is susceptible. To portray all the lovely attributes, peculiar to this lamented lady, were a task for which the writer feels wholly incompetent. Suffer it, therefore, to recount, without any attempt at eloquence, some of the most prominent of those amiable qualities, that gave birth and nourishment to that ardent affection, which cost her death to elicit from the aching bosom of her bereaved consort, those mournful groans, and sighs, and tears, of inconsolable sorrow-that caused her affectionate children, as they stood around the board upon which her body lay, to heave those heart-rending lamentations, and to ejaculate, in sorrow's most pathetic accent, "O my poor mother!" And that caused all who knew her, ("for to know her was to love her") to lament her death, and regard the loss as irreparable, not only to her husband and children, but also to the community in which she had lived. To her husband she was affectionate and submissive, almost to a fault. He was the object of her first and only love-and she knew he loved *her* with a devotion that approached idolatry-and that he was never so happy as when contributing to *her* happiness, or administering to *her* wants, and therefore nothing was enjoyment without his participation-no place desirable without his presence-his trouble was hers-his joys hers-and his friends hers, in short, they were, emphatically, "one flesh." As he approached home, after an absence, however long or short, and under whatever circumstances, he had no fear of meeting a frown, or hearing a reproachful complaint. To her children, she was to "bring them up the way they should go," and to inculcate in their minds the importance of piety morality, benevolence, generosity, industry and economy. To a friend, she was candid, sincere and generous and ever ready and willing to incommode herself to render them assistance, or to do them a benefit. To the stranger, she was a true Samaritan, ever ready to relieve the afflicted, and comfort the distressed. She bore her late illness with patient resignation, and passed calmly from life, in the full belief of the Christian religion, and with, administrator firm reliance on the promises of Christ. She often remarked, while sick, that death had no fears for her, and that her solitude to live, grew out of her affection for her husband and children.

Committed. To the jail of Autauga county, by Jesse R. Jones, Esq., September 8th, 1853, a Negro boy who says that his name is Wilson and that he belongs to Miles G. Harris, of Hancock county, Georgia. Said boy is of mulatto complexion, about 25 or 26 years of age, five feet five inches high, will weigh about 140 or 145 pounds, a large bushy head of hair, and grows rather low on the forehead, (no scars.) The owner is required to come forward, prove property, pay charges and take him away, or he will be dealt with at the law directs in such cases. Jas. A. Lawler, Shff Autauga Co.

The State of Alabama, Autauga county, Special Court of Probate, September 13th, 1853.
This day came Harriett L. Ticknor, Administratrix of the estate of Simon B. Ticknor, and filed her accounts and vouchers for the annual settlement of the estate of said deceased, which was examined, and ordered to be filed for the inspection of all concerned. It is therefore ordered that notice be given for forty days, by publication for three successive weeks in the Autauga Citizen, a newspaper published in said county, notifying all persons interested to be and appear at a court to be held on the 24th day of October next, to show cause why said account should not be stated and allowed, and said settlement be made. Henly Brown, Judge of Probate

The State of Alabama, Autauga county, Special Court of Probate, September 7, 1853.
This day came F.E.L. Morgan, administrator of the estate the William S. Morgan, deceased, and filed his accounts and vouchers for the annual settlement of the estate of said deceased, which was examined and ordered to be filed for the inspection of all concerned. It is therefore ordered, than notice be given for forty days, by publication for three successive weeks in

the Autauga Citizen, a newspaper published in said county, notifying all persons interested to be and appear at a Court to be held on the 18th day of October next, to show cause, if any, why said account should not be stated and allowed, and said settlement be made. Henly Brown, Judge of Probate.

Vol. 1, Thursday, September 22, 1853, No. 34

A special Washington correspondent of the New York Herald, writing on the 9th inst., says that the rumor that General Cass has been offered the mission to France is destitute of foundation. Up to the present time no person has been selected for the post, nor is it now probable the appointment will be made for several days.

Death of Admiral Cockburn. Among the items of foreign news brought by the steamer, is a notice of the death of Admiral Sir George Cockburn, of the British Navy. He died at Leamington on the 19th of August, at the advanced age of eighty two. Those who remember the late invasion of this country by Great Britain, (says the Baltimore *American*,) will not fail to recollect the outrages-outrages which reflected the deepest disgrace on the British Nation-committed under the authority, and even in many cases under the supervision of this British Naval commander. He was styled, during the time he remained in the waters of Maryland and Virginia, the "Scourge of Chesapeake," as it was during this period that the Commodore burned the houses and robbed the henroosts of all who lived near enough to the shore to be visited by the marauding parties dispatched by him. At Washington, among the other unpardonable atrocities to the memory of those gallant men who stormed Tripoli and Algiers, and reduced to submission the pirates of the Mediterranean-a feet from which British commerce derived even more benefit than that of this country.

Editorial Brevities.
The freesoilers at Boston have nominated Henry Wilson as their candidate for Governor.

The National Intelligencer publishes from stenographic notes taken at this time by the veteran Gales, a speech on the war of 1812, covering several columns of that paper, delivered by John Randolph in the House of Representatives on the 12th January, 1813, on the bill for raising an additional army of 20,000 men, giving to the President the appointment of all the officers under field offices. This speech, with an immence mass of the other reminiscences, will form a portion of the work now preparing by Messrs. Gales & Seaton, under the sanction of the Government, which is to embody and preserve the already perishing history of the earlier Congresses.

Mr. James Hobb, of New Orleans, who visited Europe some weeks since for the purpose of negotiating a loan on account of the New Orleans Jackson and Great Northern railroad company, it is stated, is now on his mission.

C.K. Gardiner, Esq., of Washington, appointed Survey General of Oregon, will sail for that territory on the 20th of the present month. Capt. Gardiner, of the army, son of the former gentleman, who participated in most of the former battles of the Mexican war, and was a Hon. E mentioned in the dispatches of the Commander-in-chief, will resign his commission and settle in Oregon. It is expected that Oregon will become a state of the Union in 1855, and that Gen. Lane, present Delegate will be one of the first Senators.

The Washington *Union* learns by letter, from Mr. Maberly, the director of the London Post Office, that the average weight of the British mailbag for Australia is twelve and half tons. The letters and newspapers sent from this country to San Francisco by each mail average in weight two and a half tons.

There is a sycophantic paragraph going the rounds of the papers about Gov. Bigler setting type the other day in a printing office, as if it was a wonderful thing or there was any great condescension in it. We doubt not there are a great many smarter men than Gov. Bigler setting type, and guess that he was rather a poor type-sticker, or he would not have been turned out to other pursuits, to bring up finally in the office of a mere Governor of a State, which in these days the most ordinary man can fill! It takes something more than an ordinary to shine a type setter. *Richmond Dispatch.*

The Next President. A writer in the Newark Daily Mercury nominates for the next President Commander Duncan W. Ingraham, of South Carolina, who distinguished himself in the rescue of the Hungarian Koszta, before Smyrna.

Estimates of the Cotton Crop. Joseph Macbeth won the purse made up in April last at the Charleston Courier office, for the nearest estimate of the cotton crop. His estimate was 3,253,679 bales. There were sixty competitors.

Mr. Greely has formally and finally taken leave of the Whig party, and declares that henceforth the New York Tribune shall "have no ticket for State or other officers under its head."

We find in the Montgomery papers the following from our kind-hearted Governor: Executive Chamber. Montgomery, September 12, 1853. The prevalence of Yellow Fever in Mobile to an extent hitherto exualled, has occasioned sorrow and grief in every circle. Among the poor of the city the suffering has been most severely felt. Many of our often found in the same, and several in the same room without the means of obtaining the necessaries of life, to say nothing of the comforts so essential to the sick. This state of things should not be permitted to continue. We had ample means at command to supply the destitution and want. I do most respectfully suggest that contributions be made by the benevolent throughout the country; and that the Clergy and Ministers of every religious denomination in the State having the charge of Churches, take up collections in their several congregations, without delay, for the relief of the suffering poor of Mobile. All contributions and collections may be transmitted to the Benevolent Associations of the city, to Gen. T.L. Toulmin, or to Col. T. Sanford of the Custom House, with the confidence that the monies will be judiciously and faithfully applied. *Whenever it's done should be done quickly.* H.W. Collier.

Mr. Marsh, the American Minister at Constantinople, on his return to that city from Greece, where he went about a year ago on the affairs of Dr. King, was handsomely received by the Sultan. Mr. Marsh was accompanied by the commander and officers of the Levant, and by Captain Walker, of the United States army, and made the Sultan a proper address, in which he gave him an assurance of the entire sympathies of the President and people of the United States into position of which he is placed at the demands of Russia. The Sultan, in reply, expressed his satisfaction with the good feeling which exists in the United States towards himself and his cause, and assured Mr. Marsh that it should be his constant endeavor to cultivate and strengthen them.

Rev. P.P. Neely, D. D. This distinguished gentleman, says the Columbia (Tenn.) Intelligencer, who, with his family has been spending a few weeks in our town, left this morning for his home in the south. During his stay in our midst, he preached several times at the Methodist Church to large and delighted audiences. Although yet a young man, Dr. Neely enjoys the enviable reputation of being one of the most eloquent pulpit orators in the South West; and the title he has nobly won justly wears. His mein in the pulpit is to replete with grace and dignity; his voice is clear and musical; his language is all ways forcible and faultless; his language is always forcible faultlessly elegant; his enunciation is perfection itself, and his every gesticulation is strikingly expressive and he has ever at his command, all that is grand in nature, useful in all art, sublime in philosophy, entertaining in history, charming in classic literature, winning in rhetoric, and all that is bright and beautiful in poetry and fancy. His is that eloquence which charms all ears, captivates all hearts-that never woos but to win. The career that is now before him beckons him onward, is destined to be as brilliant as his own exuberant fancy. Dr. Neely is now a member of the Alabama Conference, and was also last year, at Marion in the southern part of the State. - *Marion Commonwealth.*

Restitution. The Union says the Treasurer of the United States on the 8th instant, received from the Rev. John F. Hickey one thousand dollars, as a restoration to the Treasury of the United States by some person whose name is not given.

Jenny Lind Goldsmith, on the 15th of August presented a son to Otto in the city of Dresden.

Vol. 1, Thursday, September 29, 1853, No. 35

Large Apples. We are presented, a few days since, by Dr. S.P. Smith, with five of the largest apples we remember ever having seen, which were plucked from his orchard. The five weighed three pounds and 13 1/2 ounces-the largest measured thirteen inches round, and weighed thirteen ounces they are a species of the Russet and Royal George. Several editors, of late, have been making their brags about their okra stalks, melons, gourd vines, &c., but we defy them to beat our apples. Many thanks to the Doctor for his fine present.

Editorial Brevities.
From Mexico. The U S minister to Mexico, it is said, has renewed a proposition made by Mr. Webster to Signor Larrainzar, touching the Boundary line between the two countries. This Government proposes to buy, it is said, a strip of territory south of the Gila, sufficient for a line of settlement. The price named which this government is prepared to pay for the cession and for a release of claims on account of preceding Indian depredation, said to be $10,000,000. Mr. Webster's correspondence with the Mexican Minister was in connection with the Mesilla dispute, and as the basis, of the instructions to Gen. Gadsden.

A duel was fought on the 3d of August between Lieut. Wm. H. Scott, late of the United States Army, and Lieut. Porter Smith, a gentleman who served with credit in the Mississippi regiment during the Mexican war, and afterwards a Maj. in the Cuba expedition under Lopez. Smith was mortally wounded at the second fire, and died on the 17th August. He was the challenging party, and the cause of the quarrel is said to have been of a trifling nature. He was about twenty four years of age, and the son of Judge Pinckney Smith, of Mississippi.

Mr. Crazel, of Davidson county, Tenn., in attempting to shoot a Mr. Bagby, shot himself in the thigh and has since died.

Jasper J. Quillen was killed in Lauderdale county on the 10th inst, by Thornton Corum, who was committed.

A daughter of Col. Wilson at South Carrollton, Kentucky, recently shot a young man with a revolver for slandering her. The ball took effect in his throat, inflicting a fatal wound.

Reminiscences of Autauga County. Mr. Editor-Ill health has prevented my reminiscences for several issues past. It has been my wish to give one more besides the present if circumstances would permit. In my last I discovered that you omitted several names that I had associated with those you brought out. I hope you and your readers will not think it out of place if I here introduce them. I mean the names of Messrs. Dixon and William Hall, Col. Peyton Bibb and Robert J. Glenn, who were early settlers of the Rocky Mount neighborhood. These gentlemen have all passed away. They were worthy citizens and model planters, originally from the state of Georgia. Their descendants are still amongst us. May they imitate their many excellent qualities. This neighborhood, too, furnished Alabama with her first Governor, the Hon.— Bibb, a man of precious memory, who died shortly after his election, greatly mourned and missed by the councillors of State. I do not remember ever having seen Governor Bibb, but his praises were upon the lips of all who knew him. I propose, in this communication, to speak of this neighborhood, a few of the first settlers remaining amongst to the present day. Among them is the widow of Thomas Hill, father of the late Major Abner Hill, mentioned in a former communication. This lady still lives at an advanced age, enjoying her mental faculties to an almost unparalleled degree of perfection.

At her residence was the first court held in this county-also an election precinct, at which was elected a member to frame our State constitution. The name of this gentleman was James Jackson, from the State of Georgia, whose name was mentioned as one of the first settlers of the Independence neighborhood. (He first settled in this neighborhood and afterwards removed to the Independence neighborhood.) Near this place was the first corn mill erected in this county by Thomas Smith, who still lives amongst us in the enjoyment of find health at the age of seventy years. This gentleman has raised a goodly number of sons and daughters, the most or all of whom are still living amongst us. Another man I would also mentioned in connection with this, is that of Col. Organ Tatum, who, at the age of sixty still lives amongst us, they find specimen of health and comfort. The Colonel's children have all left him and gone to the west, save one daughter, who is sole heir to her father's and mother's visits and little presents. I wonder if the children out west don't envy her such happiness. No matter, they had no business leaving. Another old settler is Thomas Coleman, who, together with two sons, still live amongst us. The old gentleman enjoys fine health and follows up his business closely, and has lately married a young wife to cheer him through the remainder of life. Here let me drop a reflection on old age. How peacefully must glide along grey hairs over life's closing scenes when one can look back at a life spent in virtuous thoughts and deeds, who can count over a goodly number of children well settled in life, without a blush upon their character. I envy no man for his wealth or his fame, that I do covet that father's pride of heart who can look out upon his children filling up their destinies when life with honor and credit to themselves and their parents. Deny me not this boon, oh, my God-what ever else, save heaven, thou mayest deny me, deny me not this one thing, and I shall praise thee with my latest breath. As to this place, Prattville, I shall speak but little. It speaks for its self. Little did Mr. Smith and others, who reared the first mill one mile below this, think at this day there would be such a village on such an unsightly site as this. Perhaps we now have as little idea of what may be here and in other places in this county equally improbable twenty five years to come. We lived in an age of improvement-our march is onward and upward. There are other names that could be associated in this communication-Berry, Tatum and Malcolm Smith, who, I think, was an early settler, but removed to Coosa and afterwards can back to his old neighborhood. Many others, whose names have escaped my recollection. One whose name was early associated with Washington has recently died in Montgomery, Lot Porter, who was well known to all the old settlers of this county. None who had dealings with Lot Porter as a merchant gave him any other name and character but that of an honest man. Thus we are swiftly passing away-happy for us if we are but prepared for that eventful moment. Old Citizen.

The State of Alabama, Autauga county, Special Court of Probate, September 24, 1853. This day came James M. Cook, and Cader Rogers, administrators of the estate of James Cook deceased, and filed their accounts and vouchers for the final settlement of the estate of said deceased, which was examined, and ordered to be filed for the inspection of all concerned. It is therefore ordered that notice be given for forty days, by publication for three successive weeks in the Autauga Citizen, a newspaper published in said county, notifying all persons interested to be and appear at a court to be held on the 8th day of November next, to show cause why said account should not be stated and allowed and said settlement be made. Henly Brown, Judge of Probate.

The State of Alabama, Autauga county, Special Court of Probate, September 18, 1853. This day came John Merritt, guardian of Henry P. Hamilton, a minor, and filed his accounts and vouchers for the annual settlement of said wards estate, which was examined and ordered to be filed for the inspection of all concerned. It is therefore ordered, that notice be giving for forty days by publication for three successive weeks in the Autauga Citizen, a newspaper published in said county, notifying all persons interested to be and appear at a court to be held on the 8th day of November next, to show cause why said account should not be stated and allowed, and said settlement be made. Henly Brown, Judge of Probate

Vol. 1, Thursday, October 6, 1853, No. 36

Editorial Brevities.

The Camden and Amboy Railroad have compromised with the Rev. James Purviance, of Mississippi, (formerly of Baltimore,) who, with his wife and child, were injured in the fearful collision of cars on their road on 8th of August, by paying him ten hundred damages. Mr. Purviance's foot was slightly hurt, his daughter's thigh broke, and his lady badly hurt in the hips. They are still detained in New York, but have all nearly recovered.

Rev. Henry Ward Beecher, of Brooklyn, brother of Mrs. Harriett Beecher Stowe, has been presented, by a few of the wealthy members of his congregation, with some $15,000, for the purchase of a country seat for a summer residence.

Notice. Will be sold, on the premises to the highest bidder, on the 7th day of November next, in 80 acre lots, the 16th Section in township 18, Range 15. Purchasers will be required to give notes with two good securities payable with interest from date in four equal annual installments. The above described section is one of the very best timbered sections of land in the country, and has running through it a stream three fine Mill seats, and water amply sufficient to run a saw mill that will do a profitable business. Elias B. Goodson, Britan Boon, D.N. Smith, Trustees.

Vol. 1, Thursday, October 13, 1853, No. 37

The Whig Convention met at Syracuse on Wednesday, the 5th inst., Washington Hunt presiding. J.M. Cook was nominated for Comptroller, and Ogden Hoffman for Attorney General.

List of Letters. Remaining in the Post Office at Autauga County, Ala., for the quarter ending September 30th, 1853, J.H. Alford, S. Adams, E.F. Betts, E.S. Buyck, Mrs. J. Buyr, N. Butler, R. Brown, Mrs. D. Chambliss, Miss E. Chapson, J. Clark, C. Chitwood, T.J. Camp, B.J. Drummond, S.C. Dirden, J.B. Dicken, S.J. Guy, L.M. Grant, J.J. Hunt, Miss S.E. Hilmes, J. Hearlth, Mrs. R. Hays, P. Heoely, M. Hawkins, A. Hoston, J.A. Johnson, Johnson & Allen, J. Johnson, Wm. W. Kinny, F. Kilough, D. Leacock, Wm. L. Moon, D. Muse, Mrs. S. Mabery, E.L. Magreder, Miss M. McKeetheren, Miss M. McDuffer, B.F. Marten, Rev. M. Marsh, G. Stoutamire, C. Scott, J. Sewot, F. Spencer, J.G. Ulrick, Miss P. Vick. Persons calling for the above letters will please say they are advertised. S. Mims, P.M., Per H. Miles, Dp'ty.

Vol. 1, Thursday, October 20, 1853, No. 38

A Remarkable Water Drinker. The Boston Medical Journal has an account of a man who is supposed to be the greatest drinker among men in America, if not on the globe. He is living, in excellent health at the age of fifty eight years, and in a state of perpetual thirst. The individual alluded to is Mr. James Webb, of Fairhaven, Mass. Under every aspect in which the case may be examined is remarkable, and perhaps unparalleled in the annals of the physiology. In early infancy the quantity of water he consumed was so large as to astonish those who witnessed it. A development in size and weight of the body required a corresponding increase in the quantity of his aquatic potations. Under ordinary circumstances three gallons of water is rather a short daily allowance for him and it would be impossible for him to live through the night with less than a pailful. With this immense amount of cold water daily poured into the stomach, Mr. Webb has been in good health and spirits.

The Hon. Jere. Clemens will please accept our thanks for valuable congressional documents.

Gen. German, the new governor of Minnesota, has issued an order, in which he says the liquor traffic among the Indians "must and shall be stopped." The agent is ordered to (?) up and destroy all liquor offered for sale (?) them.

Editorial Brevities. Manila
The Washington *Star* states positively that Mr. Cushing is not going to China, and asserts that the Mission has been tendered to the Hon. George M. Dallas who will probably accept.

A match race for ten thousand dollars is to come off in Nashville on the 3d of December next between William Cheatham's celebrated racer *Compromise* and A. & O. Towle's mare *Cordelia Reed.*

Washington Items. The President has appointed John W. Underwood, of Georgia, Associate Justice of the U.S. territory at Utah.

Attorney General Cushing's opinion on the Texas five million matter, has been fully approved by President Pierce. The opinion recommends a retention of the five millions by the Treasurer until other Legislation on the part of Congress; into the main points, fully sustains the course of the Filmore Administration in relation to the subject.

Professor Agassiz. Contrary to former records, we learn that this eminent naturalist has not resigned his professorship in the Medical College of South Carolina. He will remain at the north during the winter for his health.

The Salem Register says that Abbott Lawrence has announced his intention of bestowing $50,000 on the Lawrence Scientific School, at Cambridge, in addition to the same amount given by him to an institution some eight years ago.

Another Tragedy! Another murder took place yesterday afternoon on George, between Race and Elm street. A few months since a man named John Ellis Murray succeeded in enticing a young female, named Elizabeth Clay, to elope with him to the city, promising to marry her after they arrived here. By misrepresentations, it is alleged, he postponed the marriage from day to day, and then from week to week, and a few days since began to taunther as not being a true woman. Again promising silently to marry her the next day, he managed to seduced her, and returned to his boarding house. For several days she did not see nor hear from him, and began to make inquiries as to his whereabouts. She yesterday learned that on Friday night last he had married to a female named Mary Brandon, and that they were residing in a house on George, between Elm and Race streets. Procurring a pistol she proceeded to the house, and knocking at the door, was admitted by Murray's wife. Murray, who was seated in one corner of the room, rose much agitated and demanded what she wanted in his house. She inquired the cause of his desertion and marriage to another female. He replied that he had a right to do as he pleased, and wished her to leave his presence. Just as he was approaching her, evidently to compel her to leave the house, she drew her pistol and fired; the ball injured his head, and he fell a corpse at her feet. She then went out and told some citizens of what she had done and requested them to show her to the watch house, that she might give up. The citizens went with her to the watch house, where she gave her self up and was lodged in one of the cells. Her examination will probably take place today. The corner held an inquest and returned a verdict in accordance with the above facts. - [Cincinnati Gazette.]

Death of an Outlaw. The Galveston Civilian has a letter dated Montgomery, Texas, October 1st, in which the writer says: A sad occurrence took place in our between seven and eight o'clock. A man, well known in this section of the country, if not in others, named Eg Oliver, was shot from his horse on the public square. He had been arrested by the sheriff of which was for an assault with intent to kill a fellow named Lang in this county. It being the greatest charge on which the sheriff was authorized to arrest him, he brought him to our town and delivered him to our sheriff, who committed him to jail in default of bail. About a week before court began here he broke out, and was then supposed left. But during court he was seen several times in this vicinity, and one night went to the house of our sheriff and called him up, but would not let him approach near enough to arrest him. Yesterday, while most of our citizens were at dinner, he rode into the square, galloped about it, and then rode off again, in defiance to all. He was pursued by the sheriff and several citizens but eluded the pursuit, and last night just at dark come into town again, threatening, as I am informed, to burn the jail. In attempting to arrest him for the purpose of recommitting him, he refused to surrender, and while in the act, as was supposed from his action (it was dark) of shooting upon those gathering around him, he was shot down, fell from his horse and died immediately. Who committed the deed, can never be known, as there were several shots fired at the same time. Thus perished a man, who, by his reckless and lawless course of life has been a terror to some, and respected but by few. May the memory of his many errors be buried with him. He has left a wife and two young children who have been compelled to flee from him, and seek protection under the roof of strangers.

Agricultural Fair. The second Annual Fair of the Robinson Springs Agricultural Association will be held on the 2d, 3d and 4th days of November next, at their grounds in Autauga county. The Society have prepared stalls for all stock offered for exhibition, and shelter in safe houses for articles as require protection from the weather. One or more addresses will be delivered on suitable subjects by distinguished agriculturists. The agricultural world is cordially invited to attend. Jos. H. Hall, Sec'ty.

COMMITTEES OF THE AUTAUGA COUNTY AGRICULTURAL FAIR
FIELD CROPS William Graham, Chairman-D.C. Neal, Or Tatum, L. Parker, L. Tyus, Hon. Henly Brown
THOROUGH BRED CATTLE. A.J. Pickett, Chairman.-Geo. Reives, Jas. O. Long, Benj. Saxon, C. Bellinger, J.G. Winter
NATIVE OR GRADE CATTLE. R.M. Cherry, Chairman.-S. McWhorter, Wm. Wiglesworth,

A.W. DeBardelaben, A. McKeithen, H. Gardner.
HORSES. Hon Benj. Fitzpatrick, Chairman.-B.C. Owen, W. Callaway, James Powell, W.A. Morgan, J.L. Chambers.
JACKS, JENNETTS AND MULES. Malcom Smith, Chairman.-Dr. Penick, Ramond Robinson, Wm. Montgomery, Dr. Thos. Frith.
HOGS. R. Myers, Chairman.-Patrick Norris, Howell Rose, A. Baker, B.S. Griffin.
SHEEP AND GOATS. John Steele, Chairman.-L.G. Robinson, Henry Holmes, Wm. DeJarnette, Geo. Spigners, Jos. Sandiford.
POULTRY. Gen. E.Y. Fair, Chairman.-Gen. Rush Elmore, T.D. Hall, Wm. H. Rives, G.A. Edwards, Dr. Jos. Vincent.
HOUSEHOLD DEPARTMENT. Wm. L. Yancey, Chairman.-L.P. Saxon, Mrs. Ann Elmore, Mrs. E.A. Rives, Mrs. Eliza Brown, Mrs. W.S. Hadnot, Mrs. Susan Lewis.
DAIRY. Chas. T. Pollard, Chairman.-Jas. M. Smith, Mrs. John Steele, Mrs. Harriet Goodwyn, Mrs. Malcom Smith, Mrs. S. Mims.
DOMESTIC MANUFACTURES. John Nickels, Chairman. -John A. Elmore, Mrs. Nancy Slaton, Mrs. Nancy Long, Mrs. Emily Jackson, Mrs. Sarah Bibb, Mrs. Mary B. Hall, Mrs. Emma Reese.
NEEDLE AND FANCY WORK. Dr. Wilson, chairman.-Elmore Fitzpatrick, Mrs. Sarah Pickett, Mrs. A. Fitzpatrick, Miss E.A. Rives, Miss Sallie Taylor, Mrs. Daniel Pratt, Mrs. W.H. Rives.
MISCELLANEOUS. S.W. Maris, Chairman.-Evans Presley, W.T. Hall, Dr. H. Smith, Nat. Reese, W. Zeigler.
LEATHER. Mr. Comstock, Chairman.-A. Crumpler, J. Gue, P. Bibb, J. Zeigler, J.D. Graves, Maj. B. Easterling, Dr. Shelton.
FRUITS. Abram Martin, Chairman.-A.M. Baldwin, Dr. Jos. Chapman, Peter Cooper, Dr. S.P. Smith, Dr. Mason, F. Fay.
MECHANICAL DEPARTMENT. D.B. Smedley, Chairman.-L. Howard, E.S. Morgan, N. Ivey, Wm. Walker, R. Divany, Col. L. Spigener.
VEGETABLES. L. Long, Chairman.-A.Y. Smith, Mills Rogers, Mrs. Matilda Pope, Mrs. Louisa Hall, Mrs. C. Myers, Mrs. Susan Elmore.
FINE ARTS. Hon. Goe. Goldwhaithe, Chairman.-J.T. Moore, Lewis Owen, S. Swan, Mrs. Laura Holt, Mrs. Laura Elmore
MARSHALLS. Capt. Joseph S. Reese, Col. W.B. Hall, E.A. Long, D. McKeithen, B.R. Hall, F. Pope, Col. C. Shelton.
Premiums will be awarded in articles of Plates, Medals, &c. By order of the Executive committee. Special Committee composed of members of Executive Committee. No article offered for exhibition can be removed during the Fair without special permission from the Executive Committee. The premiums will be awarded on the last day of the exhibition. Bolling Hall, Daniel Pratt, G.W. Hails, R.J. Glenn, Jos H. Hall, Executive Committee.

The State of Alabama, Autauga county.
The Judge of Probate for said county having granted to me letters of administration on the estate of Marietta P. Richardson dated the 12th day of July, 1853, all persons holding claims against said estate are requested to present them as required by the statute, or they will be barred. Seth P. Stoors, Administrator.

Vol. 1, Thursday, October 27, 1853, No. 39

Route to California. Col. Benton furnished the National Intelligencer with an account of Lieutenant Beal's exploration of the route to California. The party were only 43 traveling days in going through from the Missouri fountain. They found the route good for any sort of a wagon and well supplied with grass, water, &c. The account is one of great interest, but too long for our columns. Col. B. is delighted with the prospect.

Editorial Brevities.
The eastern papers announced the death on the 5th inst. of Mahlon Dickerson, of New Jersey. He was in his 80th year and was somewhat notable in his lifetime. He was a native of New Jersey, and was elected Governor of that State in 1815. In 1817 he was elected United States Senator, and was continued in that office sixteen years. In 1834 he became Secretary of the Navy, in the Cabinet of President Jackson, and retained that office until 1838, more than a year after the accession of President Van Buren.

The mother of John Mitchell, one of the Irish patriots, who is reported to have escaped from Australia, with two of his sister's and a brother, reside in New York. Mrs. Mitchell has received letters from her son, announcing his speedy arrival in the United States.

Slave at Boston. A slave belonging to Col. Clenatham, of New Orleans, has been taken before the U.S. District Court at Boston by the abolitionists, on the ground that she was detained against her will. The charge, however, was just proved and the case consequently dismissed.

Assistant Surgeon Steiner, USA, recently acquitted by civil courts in Texas for the murder of the late Major Arnold, of the 2d Dragoons, is to be tried by an army court martial for the same offense. Orders to that end were sent out on the receipt of official information of the homicide, at the War Department. If, on being acquitted by the civil authorities, he left the post, prior to the receipt of the military order above referred to, he will be arrested under it where ever he can be found.

Bronson vs. Guthrie. The reply of collector Bronson, of New York, to Secretary Guthrie has been published. It is severe. Mr. Bronson regards the attempt to interfere with his appointments of the subordinates in his office as unwarrantable, and refuses to resign.

Mr. O'Connor, the U.S. District Attorney, has also written a letter assailing the Washington *Union*.

Homicide. At a late hour on Saturday night, says the Augusta *Chronicle & Sentinel*, an altercation occurred in the street, between Peter Feagan, one of the City Watchmen and Augustus Cartledge shot him with a pistol, of which he died in a few minutes. A Corner's Jury found a verdict accordingly.

"Potomac," the Washington correspondent of the Baltimore *Patriot*, says that a strong and systematic effort will be made to place Col. Benton in the Speaker's Chair of the next House of Representatives.

The Paris correspondent of the National Intelligencer states that M. Kossuth from his retreat in England, has been making overtures to the Porte, with a view to his return to the Turkish dominions during the present conjecture. These overtures are said to have been coldly met by the Sultan.

Reminiscences of Autauga County. Mr. Editor-according to promise, this is to be my last article. No doubt many of your readers have wished for such an event some time past. I regret that the want of time and space has cause me to leave it out many names and events, which should have had a place. In the outset my object was two-fold: first, to amuse myself as a recreation: second, to aid in giving some interest, is possible, to our village paper, being the first ever established in our county. How far I have accomplished the latter is for your readers to determine. I believe such a subject from some writers might bring much interest to your columns, and I do hope some one will follow the suggestion. My old friend, Col. A.J. Pickett, is peculiarly fitted for such a work, as his thoughts have for many years been directed in such a channel, possessing, at the same time, a talent peculiar for such a work. One event I passed over, which I will here relate. Capt. J.P. House, who has long resided in our county, raised the first crop of corn ever planted in the county. This was near the forks of Coosa and Tallapoosa, whilst the Indians yet lived here. The Captain still lives, and at no great distance from this spot. He long lived a bachelor, but at last married a wife and has redeemed his time, by presenting a specimen of fine, healthy looking children, one of which he has recently given in marriage to the son of an old school mate of mine, as I have just learned from the Rev. S.O. Capers, who had the honor of tying the knot. Prosperity attend my old friend, and success to the young couple. Another gentleman whose name I then leave to introduce, is the Hon. Henly Brown, who is an old citizen and is favorably known to everybody in the county as a faithful public servant. He still lives and is at his post. Indulge me, gentle reader, now, in retracing my footsteps to a spot which I hastily glanced at in my second article. That spot he is Vernon-and pray, sir, what is there in this place to interest? much, very much to me. It was the place where first I pitched my tent in Alabama and called my home. The place where I passed the two last years of my school days-the place where I first started in business and make what little I now have to support a large and rising family of children-the place where my character and habits were mostly formed-the place where I formed my strongest attachments amongst friends, and near where many of them still live, and whom, I hope, to retain the latest period of my life's existence, and whom I hope to meet in another and better mode of existence. Poor and forsaken as she now appears, all these associations crowd upon me and cause my affections to still linger there. Well do I remember my feelings on reaching a spot where I was to make my future home, though but a few rudely constructed log huts then was to my young heart as much in the scenery to interest me, particularly the bold and beautiful Alabama, majestically winding its way to the ocean of waters, bearing on its bosom the many heavily laden water crafts, though rudely constructed, and dependent all together in going downstream upon the current for their motive power, yet, answering all the purposes of navigation. This to a Georgian or South Carolinian was a great consideration, especially to those who were in the habit of wagoning some 125 to 180 miles. But how changed the scene for the better, when our astonished citizens heard the wild snort of the steamer moving up our bold, beautiful Alabama, like a thing of life. Oh, I shall never forget the almost wild delight which I felt when the Harriett first hove in sight of our Vernon wharf. Old and young, big and little, white and black, crowded to the banks to look, to gaze upon the wonder of the world. Reader, which you believe it, if I were to tell you now that such an insignificant would scarcely attract the notice of old Sambo, whilst hoeing his master's cotton. 'Tis true, there is no more comparison between that boat and the magnificent steamers that now ply up and down our river, than between the Harriett and the pole boats then in vogue, which required from 60 to 90 days to make a trip. Thus the world wags on. Our country owes much to the energy and enterprise of one man who did more than any other to improve the navigation of our rivers and adapting boats suitable for the stream. I mean the lamented Capt. W.W. Frye, who, after all his toil and exposure, died in the prime of life fortuneless. The example of that man has had a sound influence upon the captains who have succeeded. The most of them are laboring men, who can be found at their post at all hours of the night. To this alone may be attributed the success on our river, and the freedom from accident. May the memory of such a man coexist with the State. I turned now to the recollection of one individual connected with this place. I allude to my old preceptor Daniel McLeod. Who it is it that does not remember, with gratitude, his old Domine, though he may have had his foibles and faults-the man who, for years, patiently and preservingly labored to teach the "young the ideal how to shoot," who bore with our many childish and youthful follies. I am not that man, reader. I still cherish a fondness for the name of that man. Though often vexed enough with him to have choked him, had I dared to do it, still, all is forgotten, and I love to dwell upon his memory. Long since he passed away, and his name almost forgotten, save by his pupils. My old preceptor was of Scotch descent, born in North Carolina, and educated at Chappel Hill. He was a fine scholar, particularly excelling in the Latin and Greek. The latter he read with great fluency, assisted by his having learned the Gaulic language in his youth. He was a man of great excentricacy of character, scarcely ever observing a medium in anything. In stature he was below the median size, thin visage, of a light elastic step as nimble as a cat, performed elegantly on the violin, his favorite tunes Scottish airs-one in particular I remember to have heard him play, which he called "Muckle Sandy." This was all music and life, and was calculated to make the foot flutter. Many other things could I write about this man, but I have already extended this article beyond my usual limits. Perhaps, before I close, I ought to ask pardon of the reader for trespassing upon his patience, and for submitting to the public articles so hastily and carelessly gotten up; but they were never intended for the eye of the critic, but for plain men like the writer. I hope someone more competent than myself will take up the subject. In this matter of writing I am inclined to think there is a good deal of false pride. It does not follow, as a matter of course, that a man should be thoroughly educated in order to entertain the public mind-hence, much talent is buried that might be usefully employed. Respectfully, Old Citizen.

New Mexico. At the latest dates, a spirited contest was going on in New Mexico preliminary to the choice of a delegate from that territory to the U.S. House of Representatives. There were two candidates up, both warmly supported. One was William Carr Lane, the late Whig governor, who started up the Mesilla difficulty, and the other was Gallegos, a discarded Mexican priest, who does not speak a word of English. The latter is supported by many of the New Mexicans. It seemed very doubtful who would be chosen, that the odds were in favor of Galegos. He was lately a member of the Legislature of the territory, or, rather, was elected as such, but never took his seat.

Died, after a protracted illness, in the 26th year of her age, M. A., consort of the late Bolling Mitchell, of Texas. The deceased, from her youth, had a pensive cast of mind, full of reflection and pious emotions, which enabled her to meet with great composer the gloomy changes which, for the last few years, encompassed her life, and it may be truly said she lived as long as life had any charms for her. The partner of her youth has been entombed in less than twelve months-her beloved mother in a most feeble and languishing condition, that for the five little children she has left, death would have been a welcome messenger. Oh! May be orphans, early in life, have pious examples presented for their guidance in years to come, and the gospel truth indelibly impressed upon their hearts. In addition to mother and children, she has left to mourn her loss a sister and two brothers, and many relatives and friends. A few years before her death she felt the warming influences of God's holy love pervade her heart too strongly to be repressed by the cold formalities of some, and gave it vent in shouts to his praise. Why she did not attached herself to some church was known, perhaps, only to herself; but on the evening of her death, in conversation with brother McKever, gave most ample testimony that all was well in relation to the future, and greatly desired that her strength might soon return, in order to be baptised. She met the last struggle of death and with the same calmness and serenity so characteristic of her life. Death has sundered the warm ties of affection, which united many hearts-but she goes to a heavenly land to have those ties healed, which were broken by a father's and a husband's death-both of whom relied on God's promises and felt the influences of his spirit resting upon and cheering them in the last hour. How expressive of such things are the words of a poet, "The eyes that shuts in a dieing hour, opens the next in bliss, the welcome sounds in a heavenly land, e're the parting's hushed in this." A Friend.

A large, faint nebulous comet resembling a star-cluster, was detected near the forward paw of the Great Bear, on the night of September 11, by Mr. C. Bruhns, in Berlin.

The Hon. Tristam Burgess for many years U S Senator from Rhode Island, died in Providence in the 84th year of his age.

The State of Alabama, Autauga County, Special Court of Probate, October 11, 1853.
This day came A. Sample, executor of the last will and testament of Margarette Sample, and filed his accounts and vouchers for the annual settlement of the estate of said deceased, which was examined and ordered to be filed for the inspection of all concerned. It is therefore ordered, that notice be given for forty days, by publication for three successive weeks in the Autauga Citizen, a newspaper published in said county, notifying all persons interested to be and appear at a court to be held on the 26th day of November next, to show cause, if any, why said account should not be stated and allowed, and said settlement be made. Henly Brown, Judge of Probate

This State of Alabama, Autauga County, Special Court of Probate, October 24, 1853.
This day can James H. Burnes, guardian of Robert F. Burnes, a minor, and filed his accounts and vouchers for the annual settlement of said ward's estate, which was examined, and ordered to be filed for the inspection of all concerned. It is there for ordered that notice be given for forty days, by publication for three successive weeks in the Autauga Citizen, a newspaper published in said county, notifying all persons interested to be and appear at a court to be held on the fifth day of October next, to show cause why said account should not be stated and allowed, and said settlement be made. Henly Brown, Judge of Probate

Vol. 1, Thursday, November 3, 1853, No. 40

The lecture announced by Rev S.O. Capers, for to-night, is postponed till the evening of the 8th inst., in consequence of the Fair.

Editorial Brevities.
Capt. Jernigan, of Orange county, advertises in the Ocala Mirror that he is about to raise a company for the forcible removal of the Indians. The Mirror deprecates any war by the State, as the editor believes it would as effectually destroy its prosperity.

An important arbitration case was to have been argued before Mr. Petigru, of Mobile, and Daniel Lord, of New York, on the 13th inst., at Philadelphia, to settle certain charges against Amos Kendal and associates, of improper and secret appropriation to their own use of some $50,000 of funds belonging to the Washington and New Orleans Telegraph company. A report by Messrs. Cuyler, McCrary and Mowry, asserts the facts alleged against Kendal to be true. The charges were preferred by a New York stockholder.

The Late Prize Fight. The Albany Register of the 18th inst. is "gratify to learn that Governor Seymour has taken energetic measures to bring all the parties and accessories in the late brutal price fight at Boston Corners to justice, and to cause such punishment to be administered to them as the violated laws and outraged decencies of life require. As it is a matter of some doubt as to which State has jurisdiction over the place where the outrage was committed, Governor Seymour we understand has corresponded with and secured the cooperation of the authorities of Massachusetts and Connecticut in enforcing the law against the offenders. "

Almost a Duel. A challenge was recently passed between Judge Gholson and Judge Rogers, of Aberdeen, to settle a difference growing out of the political canvass now going on in Mississippi, by a hostile meeting on the Alabama side of the line. The parties, with their seconds, started for the place of meeting, and proceeded as far as Columbus, when Judge Rogers was taken ill, and the meeting consequently postponed. Subsequently their friends interposed and the matter was amicably adjusted.

Omar Pacha, Commander-in-chief of the Turkish Troops on the lower Danube, is by birth a native of Austrian Crotia. Sometime since he fled to Turkey and after being run successfully demanded by Austria as a refuge, he entered the Turkish Army and by force of merit has raised himself to his present commanding position. He has had considerable military experience, as in addition to his service, in an inferior capacity. He commanded the Turkish troops in their operations against Posnia and Montenegro. He is represented to be at present in command of a fine Army, nearly one hundred thousand strong, well prepared and anxious for an encounter with the deadly foes of their religion and country.

Two More Prize Fights. John Hall and Patrick Manly were arrested in New York, on Sunday, just as they were about to commence a prize fight for $100, in the rear of a house on Mulberry street. The two other pugilist, named Clare and Queen, it is reported, had a prize fight on Sunday, on Staten island-these fights grew out of the disgrace one between Sullivan and Morrissy.

The third balloting to place in the Tennessee Legislature on the 20th instant for U S Senator. Cave Johnson had 40 votes, John Bell 29, Henry 14, and Nelson 12. Johnson was withdrawn.

Curious Statistics. Mr. Saml. Brown of London, who appears to have devoted much of his time and attention to the peculiarities of the progress of population in reference to sexes, has given us the following very curious information: "the proportion of males and females born in any given period of time bears a constant relation to the respective ages of the parents, it seems that, where the father is older than the mother, the production of male offspring is greater than that of females, and vice versa. In other words, where the father is some years older than the mother, which is more often the case, the chances are that there will issue more male children; and in cases where the lady is the oldest, more females will be produced. The statistic has not resulted from the inquiries in one country alone, but all over Europe. It seems to depend on a general law in the animal economy, and to be a provision of nature for guarding against a too large population of existing females in any state of society, since a thousand accidents happened to men for which women are exempt, independently of wars which from the belligerent character of the human organization, are in every age calculated to carry off a large proportion of mankind." In connection with these facts, says the New York Herald there is another, is covered by late Mr. Sadler of England, which shows that early marriage is do not lead to redundancy of population, but on the contrary, that marriages rather later in life produce a larger amount of children who arrive at a healthy maturity.

European Legion. The New York Journal of Commerce Lawrence act on the arrival of the reason war news from Europe, a private meeting of some exiles, of different countries, took place in that city, and that, by their unanimous decision, Major Leonard P. Terzucanowski, formerly sidecamp of General Murowslaski, and afterwards Commander in Chief of the French legion in Sicily, was appointed to form in this country a volunteer legion intended to sail for Constantinople; they chose him as their chief, and swore to render him respect and obedience.

Washington Items.
The appointment of Robert M. McLane, of Maryland, as commissioner to China, and Levi K. Bowen, of Maryland, as Consul to Bordeaux, are officially announced.

The special correspondent of a New York paper telegraphs that the Cabinet is about to break up and that Gen. Cushing seeks the Premiership.

On the 20th instant the gin house of Major Jas. L. O'Neil, Perry county, was destroyed by fire. About fifty five bales of cotton were consumed.

Married. On the 20th of October, by the Rev. S.O. Capers, at the residence of Capt. Jacob House, Benjamin B. Alexander, of Lowndes county, to Miss Martha House, of Autauga county, Alabama.

Vol. 1, Thursday, November 10, 1853, No. 41

Editorial Brevities.
The University of Alabama, at Tuscaloosa, has resumed its session for the winter under most favorable auspices. There were over a hundred students present the first week. A new instructor in the Modern Languages, Prof. Deloffree, has entered on his duties. The town and vicinity are perfectly healthy.

A Fast Printing Press. The New York *Tribune* states that a Frenchman named Victor Beaumont, residing in that city, has invented a printing press combining the principles of the Napier and Hoe presses, which will produce sixty thousand impressions per hour, or print thirty thousand sheets on both side. It has been purchased by the Messrs. Hoe, a strong intimation that the invention is a valuable one.

It is stated that a lawsuit is now pending in Philadelphia before the United States Circuit Court, in which Mrs. Harriet Beecher Stowe and her husband are the plaintiffs, and F.W. Thomas, of Philadelphia, the publisher of a German translation of Uncle Tom's Cabin, the defendant. The question at issue is, whether a copyright holds in any other language than that in which the work is entered. It has never been raised before, and there is no precedent bearing on it either in England or this country. The question was argued during the past week.

Secretary Marcy writes to Josia Foster, of Sandwhich, whose son, a seaman on board the "Lenox," was badly injured in the affair at the Chincha Islands, that "the government of the United States is by no means insensible to the wrong inflicted upon its citizens in the attack upon them by an armed force of Peru, on board the United States merchant ship Defiance. Ample reparation will be demanded for the acts of violence which have been perpetrated at the Chincha Islands."

The Washington *Star* states that there is on the files of the State Department a written application for the French Mission on behalf of James Gorden Bennett. The *Star* says it will have this interesting document brought to light when Congress meets. Bennett has a characteristic article on the subject in his paper on Saturday, in which he does not deny the statement of the *Star* but urges his qualifications for the post, and intimates that he will anticipate the Star in the publication of the documents.

The notorious Dr. Hines, said the Mobile Tribune, has been arrested in New Orleans for swindling. We trust that the next Penitentiary which gets the scamp, will hold him without intervention of Governor's pardons.

Valuable Discovery. Professor Strobel, of the American Female Institute, has made the discovery that the Sweet Potato Vine may be saved during the winter and use the following spring in propagating in a new crop. He has tried this experiment to his entire satisfaction, and publishes the result for the benefit of the public. His method of saving is thus stated: "in the Fall (any time before frost) the vines may be cut in any convenient length, and placed in layers, on the surface of the earth, to the depth of twelve or eighteen inches; cover the vines, whilst damp, with partially rotted straw, (either pine for wheat will answer) to the depth of six inches, and cover the whole with a light soil about four inches deep. In this way the vines will keep during the winter and in the Spring they will put out sprouts as abundantly as the potato itself when bedded. The draws or sprouts can be planted first, and the vine itself can be subsequently cut and used as we generally plant slips. This experiment is worthy big consideration of farmers, as it will save a great many seed potatoes, (particularly on large plantations,) which can be used for feeding. Let every farmer, however, make the experiment for himself, and be governed by the result."

The State of Alabama, Autauga county.
The Judge of Probate of said county has granted to me letters of administration on the estate of James Townsend, dates the 5th day of November, 1853, all persons holding claims against said estate are requested to present them as required by the statute, where they will be barred. James A. Lawler, Shff. and Admr. Ex-officio.

Vol. 1, Thursday, November 17, 1853, No. 42

The Legislature. On Monday last both houses of the Legislature met in the Capitol, Montgomery, at 12 M. Nearly all the members were present, and none, we believe, evinced any fear from the recent yellow fever in that place. We were glad to see (as we were present,) so much harmony and good feeling existing among the members, and sincerely hope their future action will be based upon the same. In the Senate, Mr. McLemore was called to the Chair, for the purpose of organization. Mr. Wm. B. Martin, of Benton, was elected President over Gen. Frazier, of Jackson. Joseph H. Phelan, of Coosa, (d) was elected Secretary, W.L. Nicholson, (d) of Marshall, assistant Secretary, and J.C. Austin, (d) of Jackson, Doorkeeper. A resolution was passed instructing the Senate to inform the House that it was organized, and ready to proceed to business. Mr. Kelly presented a bill to exempt 100 bushels of corn from execution, which, on motion, was read three times, and passed, under a suspicion of the rule. Mr. Cocke presented that a deal to repeal the law requiring Administrators to sell slaves at the Courthouse. On motion, the Senate adjourned until Tuesday, at ten o'clock. In the House, Mr. Walker, from Lauderdale, was called to the Chair for the purpose of organization. Mr. Garret, of Coosa, was elected Speaker, without opposition,-having received the nomination of a Democratic caucus, over Mr. Hall of Autauga. Mr. Graham, (d) of Coosa, was elected Clerk, Mr. Elmore, (d) of Montgomery, Assistant Clerk, Mr. J.A. Hagan, (w) of Talladega, Engrossing Clerk, and James Brundridge, Doorkeeper. Mr. Davis, of Benton, introduced a bill to exempt a hundred bushels of corn from sale under execution, which was read one time and ordered for a second reading. Mr. Foscue introduced a resolution to admit Editors and Reporters to seats on the floor of the House, which was adopted. On motion, the House adjourned until Tuesday morning, ten o'clock.

The Henry Clay Case. The trial of Mr. Collyer, one of the owners, and Captain Tallman, and other officers of the steamer Henry Clay, for manslaughter, in reference to the loss of life by the burning of that vessel, which has been going on in the United States Circuit Court of New York for nearly two weeks, was concluded on Wednesday. The parties indicted were declared *not guilty*, the jury returning a verdict of acquittal after a consultation of only twenty minutes.

A Speck of War. A Washington correspondent of the New York Mirror writes: "From dispatches received from Mr. Gadson, Minister to Mexico, there can be very little doubt that, in relation to the Mesilla Valley, we shall have war."

Editorial Brevities.
The English government proposes to present Mr. Hargreaves, the first discoverer of gold in Australia, with $25,000, which that gentleman declines to receive, on the ground of its insufficiency.

There is a journal called the *Charivari* published daily in Paris, which has attained great popularity. Mr. Scoville, of the *Pick*, has started a similar enterprise in New York and he intends to give a big caricature of the leading events and people. The first number was to have appeared on Monday last.

Kentucky will soon have to elect a United States Senator to the seat now occupied by Mr. Dixon, whose term expires. That gentleman being been very ill health, announces that he will not be a candidate for re-election; and the Kentucky papers say that the joys of his successor will lie between Mr. Crittenden and Mr. Robertson.

Ex-Collector Bronson has been nominated for the United States Senate, to secede Mr. Seward whose term expires in 1855, by the Democratic Convention of Orange county, New York.

A woman named Adelia Butler and her daughter Janet, were arrested in New York lately, for inducing children to steal. Janet the daughter and a little girl picked the pockets of a lady in the cars in 3rd Avenue by direction of the mother.

Twenty one slaves, all young and valuable, freed by the will of their late master, James Wardlaw, of Fayette county, Ky., have left Lexington for Baltimore, in charge of an agent of the Colonization Society, to fulfill the condition of their liberator by embarking for Liberia at that port. Their master left the ample provisions for sending them, as well as means to begin life within Liberia.

Escape of A.J. Collins. The Pensacola *Democrat* of the 3d inst., says: "On Monday morning last, at the dawn of day, nowwithstanding the most unremitted vigilance of the Sheriff and his assistants, the Jail in this city was broken open, and the prisoner A.J. Collins made his escape. And reward to of $300 is offered for his apprehension."

Reports of Committees. Of the 2d Agricultural Fair held on the 2d, 3d, and 4th days of November, 1853. Report of the committee on Field Crops, Judge Wm. Graham, Chairman, D.C. Neal, Richard Smooth. F.W. Jordan, Daniel Pratt and C.J. Pollard. The Committee on Field crops beg leave to make the following report:
To Joel Zeigler for the best bale of cotton, first premium, being a superior article and highly creditable to the producer, $5.00
To Robert J. Glenn for the greatest production on one acre of low-ground corn, being 82 7/8 bushels. First premium $5.00
To Daniel Pratt, for the best bale of native grass hay, first premium, $3.00
To R.J. Glenn best bale of pea vine hay, first premium $3.00
To William Walker for the best lot of sweet potatoes first premium, $2.00
Under a modified regulation of the Society, we award,
To R.J. Glenn for the best specimen of oats, $2.00
To R.J. Glenn for the best specimen of rye, $2.00
R.J. Glenn exhibited a very superior specimen of ground peas, also a large variety of superior field peas. The Committee regret that the required certificates did not accompany the same, and consequently do not feel authorized to award a premium. The Committee also regret that there was no proper exhibit of the produce of an acre of upland corn. They feel constrained to notice the very respectable field of corn by Mr. Joel Zeigler and would remind the successful competitor that Mr. Zeigler treads very close upon him and would advise him to be mindful of the future. Mr. Zeigler's yield was 81 bushels to the acre. We cannot omit to mention a very superior yield and a very superior article of corn by Mr. Abram Keener, being a yield of 71 bushels per acre of fourteen acres. Mr. James W. Wigglesworth also exhibited a fine specimen of corn, yielding per acre 41 1/2 bushels, without certificate or statement on what kind of land raised. Decidedly the largest sweet potatoes were exhibited by Col. B.S. Griffin, of Coosa, but did not receive a premium as the lot was regarded too small. We should do great injustice did we omit to mention a very superior article of sweet Spanish potatoes by Mrs. Louisa Hall. All of which is respectfully submitted.
THOROUGHBRED CATTLE. The committee consisting of G. Rives, D.C. Bellinger, Thomas Smith, Sr., Capt. James O. Long and Jno. W. Nobles, after carefully examining the young Bulls, presented to them as a committee on thorough bred cattle, beg leave to make

the following report: the pedigree, form and the condition in which we found the young Bulls, all extended into our consideration-we therefore award the highest premium of $10, to Nelson, the property of Joseph S. Reese Esq. Daniel Webster, the property of Maj. Bolling Hall though thorough bred, of the highest pedigree and well formed, being in bad condition did not on that account receive as favorable a consideration as he otherwise would have done. To him we award the premium of seven dollars the next highest.

J.S. Reese's Aldemy Bull Nelson, first premium, $10.00
Maj. Bolling Hall's Durham Bull Daniel Webster 2d premium, $7.00
Frank Peirce the property of R.J. Glenn Esq. beautiful well formed and in good condition, lost the award on account of not having a pedigree exhibited.
The committee are pleased to be able to remark that the young Bulls entitle their owners to great credit, and their fellow citizens should and no doubt will feel themselves under many obligations to those gentlemen for their exertions to improve the breed of cattle in the State.
NATIVE OR GRADE CATTLE. We the committee on native or grade cattle beg leave to make the following report. We find not a great many cattle native or grade upon exhibition, but those which are, are of superior quality. The premiums to be awarded on this class of cattle are but two, one for the best bull, and one for the best heifer or cow. The committee therefore do not feel at liberty to award a premium on calves, neither are they willing to class them with cattle that are grown, not being able to discriminate properly between cattle whose ages are so various, as calves they have classed them under a year old and recommend a premium to Washington Pollard for his bull calf Argyle, he being the best of that class on exhibition. The committee deem worthy of notice the calves exhibited by Mr. G. Hadnot and Mr. Duncan McKeethen, 6 months old, also, the twin calves of Mr. G. Gardner 5 months old, remarkably well grown and large of their age. Our friends who had milch cows on exhibition and who do not obtain a premium we hope will find some consolation for their disappointment in the fact that the committee could not decide without great difficulty in the award of the premium. There were none of inferior quality and the four gentlemen who composed the committee each had his favorite cow to whose owner he wished a premium awarded. It was decided by the chairman in favor of the cow Eliza, belonging to Dr. C. Bellinger, to whom a premium will be awarded, $3.00
A premium will be awarded to Geo. W. Hails for his bull Taurrus, $5.00
S.S. McWhorter chairman, A. McKeithre, John Witlenan, James Goodson, R. Smoot. (Concluded next week.)

Mortgage Sale. By virtue of a deed of mortgage executed to the undersigned by William Mills, and duly recorded in the office of Probate Judge of Autauga County in Book D. F. page 483. I will proceed to sell at public sale of cash at the late residence of said Mills on Saturday the 10th day of December next, the following property. To wit, Charles, a man about 33 years old, Tom a man about 28 years old, Curry a man about 20 years old, Mortu a man about 60 years old, Julia a woman about 50 years old, and John a boy about 10 years old, also two wagons, six mules, one carry log, one barouch and harness, one buggy, and harness, twenty-five head of cattle, and one mettal clock. Those wishing to buy good negroes, and particularly those in the lumber trade would do well to attend the above sale, as amongst them is one of the best sawyers in the State, also a good engineer, and an experienced wagoner. Sale positive. Titles good. A.C. Baker, Mortgagee.

The State of Alabama, Autauga County.
Taken up by A.J. Cooper and posted before Kenon Wells, a Justice of the Peace for said County, a brown Horse mule, thirteen and half hands high, twenty years old, white spots on both shoulders, blemish in the left eye. Appraised at forty dollars by R. Popwell and J.J.

Dawson, the 12th day of November, 1853. Henly Brown, Judge of Probate.

Vol. 1, Thursday, November 24, 1853, No. 43

Reports of Committees. Of the 2d Agricultural Fair held on the 2d, 3d and 4th days of November, 1853. [Concluded.]

JACKS, JANETTS AND MULES. The committee whom was upon the consideration of Jacks, Janetts and Mules, beg leave to report through their chairman that in discharging said duties they have awarded, to Capt. Joseph S. Reece a premium for his Jack York, $8.00
To E. Presley a premium for his Janett, $5.00
To W.A. Morgan a premium for a 2 year old mule, $3.00
To J. Goodson a premium for the best mule colt, $3.00
They take pleasure in stating that Dr. S.P. Smith exhibited a 2 year old mule, which the committee announced remarkably good and Mr. J. Goodson had on exhibition to other mule colts, besides the successful one which demand favorable notice, also the mule colt of Mr. E. Fay merits the applause of the committee, hoping that this branch of the exhibition of livestock will be enlarged by receiving that attention to which it is justly entitled to as intimately connected with the domestic and agricultural prosperity of the country, they earnestly trust that our next annual Fair will show a greater spirit of emulation and competition on a subject of such vast importance. All of which is respectfully submitted: M. Smith chairman.

HORSES. The committee upon horses has endeavored faithfully to discharge the duty assigned it. The number of horses upon exhibition was large and we are happy to say that a very great proportion deserve a favorable notice-in fact the committee had much difficulty in several instances in deciding upon the one entitled to a premium, so equally matched in excellence and merit, were the competing animals. We congratulate the society and the country at large upon the manifest improvement that is taking place in the breeding of horses and the increased attention bestowed upon objects so intimately connected with our interest.
To Frederick W. Jordan Premium for the best stallion, Dallas, $10.00 The only one on exhibition of his class but of decided merit and excellence.

Mr. P.D. Bibb exhibited a most admirable specimen of the pony stallion La Viga, and we regret that no premium was offered for horses of his class as we deem him eminently worthy of one.
To Robert H. Graham premium for the best pair of matched harness horses, $5.00
To Mr. F. Pope premium for the best single harness horse, $3.00
It is proper to remark that there were several horses of this class of decided merit. Messrs. M. Smith, J. McNiel Smith, T. Marks, Myers and others presented each an animal wealthy fitted to endure the shafts and harness, and acquitted themselves admirably in the drives about the grounds for. To Bolling Hall, premium for the best saddle horse, $3.00. The committee was unanimous in this award, yet the contest for this premium was a spirited one, there were several geldings of great beauty, firm action, and under the perfect control of their spirited riders. To Joseph B. Rogers first premium, for best brood mare, $3.00. The unsuccessful competitors for these premiums deserve our favorable notice. Mr. P.D. Bibb presented a beautiful brown mare, as did Mr. Tyus, both entitled to favor. To Malcolm Smith, premium for the best colt, $3.00. The committee respectfully suggest that whilst awarding the premium to Mr. Smith's bay colt as the best upon exhibition, irrespective of age, that Mr. David Myers Jr. brown colt was the best 2 of year old colt and R.J. Glenn's colt Flida was the best one year old colt, and in each case premiums would be awarded, had we the power to do so. The committee would further remark, that Capt. J.S. Reese's filly Sallie Taylor, was decided to be the best 2 year old Pony colt, and J.B. Carpenter's sorrel the best one year old pony colt. The number of this class, ponies, colts, and grown horses was considerable, but the committee would go beyond the sphere of its duty further to discriminate. The "rising generation" represented by several to the youths mounted upon ponies gave

evidence of ability "to rise in the world "and take care of itself. All of which are respectfully submitted: B. Fitzpatrick, chairman, B.C. Owen, J.B. Rogers, J.B. Carpenter, W.A. Morgan, J.G. Graham, W. Callaway

HOGS. The committee on hogs beg leave to report that they have examined those brought them for inspection. The committee regret that there was so few hogs for inspection. We have awarded the first premium to Washington Pollard for his Leicestershire boar Rip, $3.00. And the second premium is awarded to W.A. Morgan for a pair of Grazier and Woburn pigs, $2.00. P. Norris, A.C. Baker, John Wood, R.L. Logan, G.W. Benson, committee.

POULTRY. Report of the committee on poultry: consisting of Dr. T.D. Hall, chairman, Dr. J.H. Vincient, Dr. Goodwin, Dr. C.A. Edwards, Dr. R.H. Graham and Wm. C. Howell. The first premium is awarded to C.D. Pollard Jr. for the best pair of Shanghai fowls, $2.00. Mr. Pollard deserves great credit for the attention bestowed upon his fowls. The 2d premium is awarded to J.H. Vincent for the best pair of Bramah Pootras, $1.00. He exhibited also half dozen very large eggs from a cochin China hen-the hen that late to these eggs has laid so many as three eggs a day, and frequently two a day. Gen. C.M. Jackson exhibited the greatest variety of fowls, some of them very fine, he exhibited Shanghais of different colors, several varieties of Bantams, Bramahs, Pootras, &c. If the funds of the Society can permit the committee would very gladly award a premium to him. Mrs. P. Bibb's Fowls consisting of one pair of red and one pair of black Shanghais are very fine; she deserves a premium if the Finances of the Society will permit. Capt. J.O. Long's Thomson white game cock is very pretty, and no doubt would prove his blood right royal if an opportunity was afforded. E.A. Long exhibited 13 Shanghais of different sizes and ages. Col. Wm. B. Hall exhibited some fine Shanghais, his white pullet is especially fine. Capt. T.D. Ornsby and M.E. Pratt exhibited a pair of Oland fowls; they are quite a curiosity in this part of the country. Dr. S.P. Smith exhibited a pair of Bolton Greys, they were the best of the kind offered.

SHEEP AND GOATS. The committee on Sheep and goats, report that there were only 2 pair of sheep on exhibition; these were of the South-down kind; and brought by Maj. Bolling Hall from the neighborhood of Philadelphia; they are 18 months old and well grown. We award the premium to Maj. Hall, $2.00. and commend the spirit he has manifested in introducing a new and highly esteemed breed of sheep into our country. L.G. Robinson, H.D. Holmes, J. Merritt, committee.

HOUSEHOLD DEPARTMENT. The committee upon the Household department in the discharge of the duty assigned, take great pleasure in expressing their gratification at the general character and excellence of the various articles presented for inspection, we have awarded premiums because it was necessary to determine upon the relative merits of the articles, but the task was one frequently of difficulty because of the claims of the various competing items, we say emphatically to the ladies who have brought forward the varied excellent and useful collection exhibited in the Household department "well done," we hope others may do likewise. To Mrs. Louiza Hall premium best Ham, (plain cured), $1.00

To Mrs. Mary B. Hall premium best jar lard, $1.00

To Mrs. Judge Neal premium best hard soap,

To Mrs. Mary B. Hall premium best loaf wheat bread, $1.00

To Mrs. Mary B. Hall premium best pound cake, $1.00

To Mrs. Daniel Pratt premium best sponge cake, $1.00

To Mrs. Anne Elmore premium best jar pickles, $1.00

To Mrs. Shadrach Mims premium best bottle Tomatoe catsup, $1.00

To Mrs. Daniel Pratt premium best jelly (Scuppernongh), $1.00

To Mrs. Daniel Pratt premium best preserves (pear), $1.00

The committee would respectfully recommend that premiums be awarded

To Mrs. J.W. Nason for wax candles

To Mrs. Judge Neal for Tallow candles
To Mrs. Nancy Long for best pastry
To Mrs. Mary B. Hall for sweet pickles.
Other specimens of pickles were good and deserve credit.
To Mrs. Mary B. Hall for 2 samples of homemade Vinegar.
The Jellies exhibited by Mrs. Ben Fitzpatrick were fine and deserve notice.
To Miss Martha F. Rieves for best brandy peaches.
To Mrs. Anne Elmore for fruit in its own juice.
To Mrs. McWhorter for sugar cane syrup.
To Miss Martha Francis Rieves best domestic cologne.
To Mrs. Mary B. Hall for lemmon Syrup and candy.
Mrs. Eliza Rives, Mrs. Susan Lewis, Mrs. Lida P. Saxon.
DOMESTIC MANUFACTURES. The committee on domestic manufactures report as follows: having examined all the registered or presented and while we think all are very deserving, have awarded premiums as follows:
To Mrs. S.W. Nelson for best piece of wollen cloth, $2.00
To Mrs. Amos Smith for best piece carpet, $3.00
To Mrs. Dr. Mason for 2d best piece carpet, $2.00
To Mrs. Mary B. Hall best fly brush, $1.00
To Mrs. C. Myres best bed quilt, $2.00
To Mrs. Dr. Mason 2d best quilt, $1.00
To Mrs. Elizabeth Reener best coverlet (wool), $1.00
To Mrs. Rebecca Norris 2d best coverlet, $1.00
To Mrs. A. McKiethen best counterpane, $1.00
To Mrs. Mary B. Hall for best 1/2 dozen pairs of socks, $1.00
We recommend to the executive committee the following articles as highly deserving, and should by all means receive handsome premiums.
To Mrs. Mary Clopton for silk shawl,
To Mrs. Mary Clopton 1 pair of silk 1/4 hose
To Mrs. Mary Clopton specimen of sewing silk
To Mrs. C. Moncrief for Hearth rugg
To Mrs. F. Easterlin pair silk hose
To Miss S.E.W. Fay linnen hose
To Autaugaville Factory bale of Osnaburgs
To Messrs. Jordan and More bale of gagging
To Messrs. Jordan & More Coil of Rope
To Mrs. C.A. Gore Turft counterpane.
All of which is respectfully submitted.
John Nickles, Chairman, Mrs. Nancy Salton, Mrs. Nancy Long, Mrs. Sarah Bibb, Mrs. Mary B. Hall, Mrs. E. Reese.
DAIRY. The committee consisting of C.S. Pollard chairman, J.M. Smith, Mrs. J.W. Steel, Mrs. H. Goodwyn, Mrs. M. Smith, and Mrs. S. Mims appointed to examine the dairy department, beg leave to report that the samples of butter were all good, and deserving much credit, and form its peculiar flavor and sweetness, we award to Mrs. Daniel Holt for the best fresh butter, $1.00
To Mrs. Louiza Hall best butter over 6 months old, $1.00
To Mrs. George Myrick for best cheese, $1.00
To Mr. Wm. Walker for the largest yield of honey from one swarm of bees, and his superior management of the same, $3.00
NEEDLE AND FANCY WORK. The committee on needle and fancy work; D.C. Neal chairman, Mrs. H. Fitzpatrick, Mrs. Daniel Pratt, Miss Sallie Taylor.

The committee on needle and fancy work before reporting their awards, beg leave to say that they exceedingly regret the limited number of premiums assigned for their disposal, the number being only six, for in this particular department they have not hesitancy in saying that double the number could have been most meritoriously awarded. In discharging of the duties we make the following distribution of premiums,

To Mrs. S.P. Smith for the finest specimen of needle work, $1.00
To Mrs. John Carpenter 2d best needle work, $1.00
To Mrs. A. Elmore for finest specimen of fancy work, $1.00
To Mrs. S.H. Smith 2d finest specimen of fancy work, $1.00
To Mrs. E.J. Donnell best fire screen, $1.00
To Mrs. Laura Saxon best specimen of crochet work, $1.00

The committee further report and recommend premiums to Miss A.E. Rives for 2 purses, To Mrs. Judge Neal 2 seed bags, To Miss E. Faye 2 seed bags. In further discharge of the duties which the regard as legitimately within their scope they cannot conclude this report without making honorable and a distinguished mention of the articles following, a pair of ottomans by Miss S. Rice, and other articles by Miss Mary E. Ornsby, fancy work by Miss Kirkland, a very handsome and embroidered mantilla by Mrs. Howell, also a pair of ottomans by Mrs. Howell, a pair of lamp mats by Mrs. Brock, a pair of mats by Mrs. Ben Fitzpatrick, wax work by Mrs. Claborne Myers, a lot of beautiful needle work by Mrs. W.S. Hadnot, a number of mats by Miss Mary McKeethen, a fire screen by Miss Mary Townsend, a table cover by Mrs. Adaline Loyd, a port folio by Miss Sarah Reese, a pair of slippers and other articles by Mrs. S. Pearce, a shirt made by Miss Amanda Hall being 10 years of age, a very handsome ottoman by Mrs. A. Snodgragss, a pair of silk stockings of home made silk by Mrs. Easterlin. All of which is respectfully submitted to the President of the Agricultural Association of Autauga County.

FRUITS. The committee on fruits in the absence of their chairman have instructed me to report that they and attentively considered and experimentally tested the various specimens presented for their inspection, and our gratified to witness the increasing interest taken in this department of horticulture, and while they are highly pleased with the 4 varieties of apples of Gen. C.M. Jackson, the one of Col. Griffin, the 4 of Mr. W.B. Scoggins, they feel bound to award the prize to the 9 varieties of Dr. S.P. Smith as the greatest number of varieties, and some of them, with the exception of one presented by Mr. Scoggins called the mammoth apple, the largest and equally as well flavored, $1.00. But to specimens of peaches were offered, one by Dr. Joseph H. Vincent, the other by Dr. Baldwin, those by Dr. Baldwin, called November peaches were the finest specimen of late peaches we have ever seen, but the number will not justify a premium according to the conditions previously imposed by the Society of not less than a dozen. Dr. Vincent therefore takes the prize for his of October peaches, $1.00. The committee regret that neither pears oranges or dried fruits were presented most of which they are confident, might have been exhibited of the productions of our own county if they had been thought of by those who have them. The committee take the liberty specially to notice though not particularly requested to do so, a fine specimen of pears raised by R.J. Glenn, and a peculiar and to them and unusual production under the name of vegetable pear presented by Mrs. Nancy Long, also a beautiful bouquet of flowers by Misses Amanda Hall, Eliza H. Withers and Eleutheria Fay. All of which is respectfully submitted, E. Fay chairman.

MECHANICAL DEPARTMENT. The committee two which was referred the inspection of the mechanical department beg leave to report that in discharging said duty they award the following premiums.

To Daniel Pratt & Co. for the best cotton gin, $5.00
To Francis Pope for the best Iron Ploughstock attached, $3.00

To E.S. Morgan for the best lot of panel doors, blinds and sashes, $3.00

They also recommend the following articles, a straw cutter from the Messrs. Fletchers, from W.A. Franks the best grist horse mill, from W.B. Hall the best chicken koop, from J.D. Whetstone the best cotton basket, from Messrs. Wainwright the best cooking stove. The committee regret to state that very few of the above articles were on exhibition and would be very happy to see this branch of industry receive that encouragement and patronage at our next annual Fair, which its importance deserves. All of which is respectfully submitted, L. Spigner acting chairman.

VEGETABLES. The committee on vegetables with pleasure report that the amount and variety of vegetables on exhibition would do credit to the months of June and July, particularly the varieties exhibited by Mrs. Louiza Hall, Mrs. Glenn and Mrs. M. Pope, Mrs. Louiza Hall's being the largest, to her we award a premium, $3.00. Mrs. Mary B. Hall exhibited 33 varieties of garden seed, Mrs. Lanier 50 varieties to whom the committee award a premium, $2.00.

To Mrs. Lanier 1st premium, $2.00

To Mrs. Mary B. Hall 2d premium, $1.00

On garden seed.

Capt. Long exhibited the largest turnip, to whom the committee award a premium, $1.00. The largest radish was that of Mrs. Glenn, Irish potatoes those of Dr. Bellenger to whom the committee award the premium, $2.00. Sweet potatoes, the two largest on exhibition were those of B.S. Griffin of the red species, but the best bushel was exhibited Mr. Wm. Walker to whom the committee award the premium. (Note by the secretary. The appropriate committee, that on the field crops awarded the premium on sweet potatoes, though this committee acted according to their register and noticing this article.) There was on exhibition a vegetable pear by Mrs. Nancy Long being a new vegetable to the committee, they could not tell whether a good specimen or not. Beets, large specimens were on exhibition by Mrs. Hale and Mrs. D. Hall Esq., all good. The largest collard on exhibition was that of Mrs. D Holt. Fine specimens of sugar cane were exhibited by Mr. G.W. Hadnot. Wm. Walker and J. McNiel Smith in which there was but little difference that the committee thought that of Mr. G.W. Hadnot the heaviest; it was all of the ribbon species. Respectfully, L. Long chairman, A.Y. Smith, W.P. Pollard, Mrs. M. Pope, Mrs. T. Young, Mrs. C. Myers, Mrs. J.M. Gordon.

MISCELLANEOUS. The committee on miscellaneous articles award to Alfred Hubbard a premium for a most excellent article of shingles, $2.00. We also award to R.J. Glenn a premium for a very good lot of pine lumber, $3.00. Evan Presly, R. Spigner, Wm. Zeigler.

FINE ARTS. The committee on fine arts entered upon its duties with much diffidence from a conscious wane of qualification to act as judges in this department. We would say considering that this is but the 2d Fair held by your body, there was quite a collection of specimens in this department, and many of them executed with most exquisite taste. We were very much pleased with the paintings on Ivory by Mrs. Laura Holt of Montgomery, in the estimation of the committee they were considered specimens of extraordinary merit and would recommend a prize to be awarded. We were next attracted by 2 very finely executed drawings by Miss S. Elmore of Montgomery. The committee is unanimous in saying they can not sufficiently express their admiration for these specimens of art, and would recommend them as deserving your highest praise, the drawings of master Eugene A. Smith of Prattville a lad of eleven years of age, next occupied our attention; there was quite a collection of specimens, we discovered in them a display of great skill for one so young and a promise of great excellence here after, with much cheerfulnes we recommend a prize to be awarded to him. We were very much gratified to see the number of oil paintings which adorned your walls, as they were only intended for exhibition, we forbear further notice. A plaster cast by Dr. Reese of Montgomery, we would recommend as worthy of honorable notice. Avery superior lot of Daguerreotypes, specimens was exhibited by Mr. McIntyre of Montgomery, but come after the committee has concluded its decisions. The committee congratulates the Society and the interest taken and display made in this department of your exhibition. Respectfully submitted, L. Owen, M.J. Bibb, C. Bellenger and E.F. Montgue.

LEATHER. Mr. Pope presented a beautiful specimen of wood bottomed shoes of singular construction, but as there is but one pair of them the committee could not consider them as entered for premium. D.A. Benjamin & Co., presented a beautiful sett of harness, which we recommend to the consideration of the executive committee as worthy of a premium also a fine summersett saddle, bridle, and martingales. The committee regret exceedingly that his leather was on exhibition. B.M. Baker exhibited two setts of beautiful buggy harness. W.S. Comstock, J. Gool, P.D. Bibb, J. Zeigler, J.D. Graves, B. Easterlin.

SPECIAL COMMITTEE. The executive committee acting as the special committee, ex-officio, award a premium to Messrs. Jordan and More for a most excellent article of bagging and rope, far exceeding the Kentucky, India or any other manufacture of these article it has ever seen. To Malcom Smith a premium is given for a bolt of superior osnaburgs of this Autauga factory, $4.00, to O.W. Mathany for a good of article of blacking of his own manufacturer, $2.00. To Tallasee Manufacturing Company for specimens of lincey, Kerseys, twilled and plain osnaburgs, and sewing thread. It takes great pleasure in stating that these articles for texture durability and appearance deserved the highest commendation, $5.00. To D.A. Benjamin & Co. for buggy harness, saddle, bridle and martingales as recommended by the committee on leather. These articles were the elaborate and more beautiful workmanship. To Mrs. Mary Clopton for a beautiful silk shawl, silk stockings and sewing silk, all manufactured from home made a silk, Mrs. Clopton is entitled to much praise for the attention and skill bestowed upon these really handsome articles, $3.00. The committee very cheerfully adopt the recommendation of the comedian on Fine Arts and award a premium to master Eugene A. Smith for his pencil drawings, $3.00. As Hadnot did not have an entry made of a certificate of the yield of his acre of upland corn the committee on field crops could not give him a premium, but as it has been represented to the executive committee that he had a certificate but omitted to register it. The executive committee consider the case as requiring his notice and has accordingly awarded to him the premium for which he competed, $5.00. The yield was 74 bushels 2 pecks and 2 quarts, the committee further report that there were several varieties of wine on exhibition. The specimen of Georgia wine presented by Dr. Cloud was admirable, and would be entitled to a premium had it been manufactured within the state; it deserves great commendation. A premium is awarded to Dr. W.O. Baldwin for his excellent wine, $2.00. Dr. Wm. M. Bolling, R.J. Glenn, Mary B. Hall, and Mrs. Dr. S.P. Smith, also presented specimens of wine. The committee awarded a premium to Mrs. Judge Neal for citron preserves, the carving of which was exquisitely beautiful, $3.00. To President of the Agricultural Association.

Many thanks to Maj. Bolling Hall for a copy of the Governor's Message.

The Corn Law. The bill introduced in the Senate on the first day of the session, by Gen. Kelly, of Jefferson, to exempt 100 bushels of corn from execution, passed the House, and is now the law of the land. This fact will be hailed with universal joy throughout the State.

The large dry goods establishment of A.F. Stewart, Broadway, New York, it is stated, pays annually more than a million of dollars for a duty into the Treasury of the U.S.

The Legislature. The present session of the Legislature, no doubt, will be one of much interest, and, if we could spare the room, would like extremely well to publish the entire proceedings of both Houses; but as it is not in our power to do so, we can only furnish our readers, from week to week, with a synopsis of its doings-such as are of a general character, and such as relate to our own county. We extract the following from the proceedings of the Senate on the 19th inst: Mr. H.C. Jones moved to take from the table the Resolution providing for the election of a Judge of the Supreme Court on Tuesday 22d inst. to fill the vacancy that will occur by the expiration of the term of office of the Hon. W.P. Chilton, adopted. Mr. Bethea moved to strike out 22d and insert 26th inst. motion was lost, the Resolution was adopted. Mr. Kelly moved to take from the table the message from the Senate, which was adopted. The bills which originated in the Senate amending the exemption law by inserting 100 bushels of corn, was reported back from the House, with an amendment striking out "is" and in searching "are" the Senate, on motion concurred in said amendment. The bill to repeal an act approved Feb. 18-50, so far as it authorizes the loaning of a portion of the 3 per cent fund to Plank Road companies was read a 2nd time and referred to the committee on Internal Improvements and Inland Navigation. The bill to amend the Estray Law, was read a second time and referred to the Judiciary Committee. The President announced the following committees to lay off Congressional Districts-Messrs. Bethea of the 1st; Watts 2d; Powell 3d; Woodward 4th; Patton 5th; McLemore 7th. the bill to repeal some much of section 3439 of the New Code , as prohibits persons from serving on Juries who cannot read and write, was read a third time, bill passed, yeas, 27, nays, 3. The bill from the House to amend the incorporating the Mechanic's Savings Company of Mobile, by changing the name and giving Co. authority to lease or rent property, was taken up read and rule suspended and passed forthwith. The bill to incorporate the Tennessee and Alabama Central Railroad Company was read, and on motion of Mr. Malone referred to the committee on Internal Improvements and Inland Navigation. The following are taken from proceedings of the House on the 19th: by Mr. Curry: A bill to repeal an act to dispose of the unappropriated portion of the two percent fund. Mr. Curry moved that the constitutional rule be suspended that the bill may be read a second time, with a view to its reference, which was adopted, an the bill was read the second time and referred to the committee on Internal Improvements. A message was received from the Senate informing the House that it had passed a resolution to elect United States Senators on Friday next. By Mr. Benners: A bill to provide for the payment over to the overseers of roads all monies on account of fines for default in working on roads. By Mr. Vest: A bill to amend the exemption law-so as to exempt one additional horse or mule or yoke of oxen. The bill to reduce the fees of Probate Judges, in case of runaway slaves to 50 cents, was read it and referred to the committee on retrenchment. The bill to amend the law in relation to estrays, was read a second time, and referred to the Judiciary committee. The bill to amend the road law in Pickens was read a second time. Mr. Hall moved to include the county of Autauga within the provisions of the bill. The bill was then referred to the committee on roads, bridges and ferries. Mr. Belser introduced a resolution referring so much of the Governor's message as refers to the boundary line of Georgia and Alabama referred to the committee on the Judiciary. Mr. Reynolds: A resolution referring to the committee on the Judiciary the statute of limitating and instructing them to report a declaratory law. The bill to increase the salaries of the Circuit Court Judges and Chancellors, to $2,000 instead of $15,00, was read a second time, and referred to the committee on Retrenchment. A message from the Senate informing the House that it had passed a resolution to go into the election of a Judge of the Supreme Court on Tuesday next, the 22d inst., was taken up. The bill to restrict the session of the Legislature to 60 days, was read and referred to the committee on retrenchment. The bill to prevent the levy a garnishment in certain cases, was read a second time and referred to the Judiciary committee. The bill to amend the law exempting certain property from levy and sale, was read and referred. The bill to authorize Probate Judges to direct the sale of slaves of guardian wards in certain cases, was read a second time and referred to the Judiciary committee. By Mr. Henry: a petition of A.B. Clitherall and fifty others, of Pickens county, for a prohibiting anti-licens law. The bill to authorize the Bank of Mobile, the Southern Bank of Alabama and the Northern Bank of Alabama to issue bills of a less denomination than $5, was read the second time and referred to the committee on Banks. The bill to regulate the sale of real and personal property by administrators and executors, was read and referred. Mr. Yelverton introduced a resolution to appoint a committee of one from each Judicial Circuit to arrange and equalize the duties of the Circuit Judges in the State, which was adopted. From present appearances it is evident the members intend, or will try, to make a hotch potch affair of the new code, before they get through with it. It seems to be the height of their ambition to pitch into it. Of course there are some defects in the Code but otherwise it contains many wholesome laws, they should handle it carefully, lest they make the matter worse. The following are a few of the engrossed bills passed in the House on the 21st: the bill to repeal section 2491 of the code was read a third time and passed. The bill to repeal so much of section 3436 as prohibits persons who cannot read and write from serving on juries. The bill to exempt certain property from sale by Administrators and Executors of deceased persons. The bill to authorize Executors, Administrators and Guardians to compromise or sell all bad and doubtful debts belonging to the estates under their control. The bill to make copies of deeds evidence in certain cases. The bill to change the time of holding the fall term of the Circuit Court of Barbour County third Monday after the fourth Monday in September.

Editorial Brevities. The Cincinnati *Atlas* states that on Thursday night in that city, while Thomas Smith, James Freely and James Dickson were standing at the corner of a street, John Hannegan rushed out of his house, and with an ax in his hand pitched into them, striking at their heads, and cutting them all down. Freely had two cuts in his head and died in an hour or so. Smith had a deep cut in his head, considered dangerous, and Dickson was slightly wounded. Hannegan, who escaped, mistook one of them for a man named Cann, whom he had threatened.

The Louisville *Courier* says that a man by the name of Wingo was executed by the populace of Missouri, on the 15th ult., for the murder of a very estimable citizen named Allen. Wingo was lodged in jail, where he remained until the 15th when he was brought out for trial. The court, in consequences of the universal prejudice against the culprit, granted a change of venue; that the populace anticipating the event and predetermined that he should not escaped, assembled in mass in front of the courthouse, and as soon as the prisoner, in custody of the sheriff, made his egress a rope was thrown about his neck, and in spite of the remonstrance and efforts of the officers, he was hastily dragged off with such violence as nearly deprived him of life ere reaching the place of execution, when the rope was thrown over the branch of a tree, and the prisoner swung up by the neck.

Information Wanted. If James K. Stephens, a Printer, who left Wetumpka, Ala., about the 20th of July last, and the last heard of was in Mississippi, will address the editor of the Sentinel, Selma, Ala., he will learn something to his advantage.

Tired of Liberty. We mentioned yesterday, says the Savannah *Republican* that Shelley, a slave, property of Mr. Edward Padelford, had thought proper while in Philadelphia to take an excursion on the underground railroad. We are now informed that he soon became wearied of that species of travel, and returning to his master, pleaded long and earnestly to be taken back to home and happiness at the South. To this his master at length consented, and

Shelley accordingly returned home last night in the *Keystone State*.

The State of Alabama, Autauga county, Court of Probate, November 16, 1853.
This day came Aaron G. Stewart, administrator of the estate of Samuel Fleming, deceased, and filed his petition in writing praying for an order to sell the capital S. W. 1/4 of the N.W. 1/4 and the S. E 1/4 of the N. W. 1/4 of Section three, T. 17, R. 15, situated in said County, for the purpose of making a division among the heirs at law for said deceased. It is a ordered that the 27th day of December next be set for a hearing of said petition, and that notice of this application be given to Robert Fleming, Samuel Fleming, and the heirs of Elizabeth Jackson, who reside in the State of Georgia, and Mary Stewart, wife of George A. Stewart, who resides in the State of Texas, and Mary F. Reddick, who resides in the State of Louisiana, by publication for three successive weeks in the Autauga Citizen, notifying them to be and appear at a court to be held on the 27th day of December next, to show cause why said land should not be sold. Henly Brown, Judge of Probate.

The State of Alabama, Autauga county, Special Court of Probate, November 4, 1853.
This day came Arenia Whetstone, Administratrix of the estate of Wm. W. Whetstone, deceased, and filed her accounts and vouchers for the annual settlement of the estate of said deceased, which was examined, and ordered to be filed for the inspection of all concerned. It is therefore ordered, that notice be given for forty days, by publication for three successive weeks in the Autauga Citizen, a newspaper published in said county, notifying all persons interested to be and appear at a court to be held on the 18th day of December next, to show cause why said account should not be stated and allowed, and said settlement be made. Henly Brown, Judge of Probate.

The State of Alabama, Autauga county, Special Court of Probate, November 10, 1853.
This day came Jacob A. Murph, guardian, Amos Rast, Emma J. Rast, and Martha G. Rast, minors, and filed his accounts and vouchers for the annual and final settlement of his guardian ship of said ward's estate, which was examined, and ordered to be filed for the inspection of all concerned. It is therefore ordered, that notice be given for forty days, by publication for three successive weeks in the Autauga Citizen, a newspaper published in said county, notifying all persons interested to be and appear at a court to be held on the eighteenth day of December next, to show cause why said account should not be stated and allowed, and said settlement be made. Henly Brown, Judge of Probate.

Administrator's Sale. I will sell and the Town of Prattville on Saturday the 17th day of November next, the following property to wit. Two Ward Robes, one sulkey and harness, one buggy and Harness, and a lot of Jars, Jugs, and Medicines. sold as the property of the estate of James Townsend dec'd by order of the Probate Court of Autauga County. Said sale on a credit of six months. James A. Lawler, Shff., Ex-officio Admin'r.

The State of Alabama, Autauga County.
The Judge of Probate of said county has granted to me letters of administration on the estate of James Townsend, dates the 8th day of November, 1853, all persons holding claims against the estate are requested to present them as required by the statue, or they will be barred. James A. Lawler, Shff. and Admr. Ex-officio.

The State of Alabama, Autauga County, Special Court of Probate, October 17, 1853.
The estate of Alfred Parker, deceased, having this day been declared insolvent, it is therefore ordered by the court that the 15th day of December next be appointed and set apart for

the settlement of the accounts of James A. Lawler, administrator of said the state, at the Probate Court room in Kingston in said county. Henly Brown, Judge of Probate

Vol. 1, Thursday, December 1, 1853, No. 44

The inauguration of the new Governor, Mr. Winston, is to take place on the 20th of December. There will be, as usual, a grand ball.

Pork! Pork! We are authorized to state that Wm. Lynch, Esq., from Tennessee, will be in Prattville between the 15th and 20th of the present month, with a drove of some five hundred of the finest hogs ever brought to this market. He has expressed his determination to sell at the lowest market prices, and such being the fact, we would advise all those who expect to endure their own meat, to defer buying until Mr. Lynch arrives-if they don't, they may, perhaps, miss good bargains, as he is determined to sell as cheap as the cheapest.

The Agony is Over. The election of U.S. Senators came off promptly on Monday at 12 o'clock. Hon. Benj. Fitzpatrick was elected to fill the unexpired term of the late Hon. Wm. R. King, (two years)-receiving 100 votes. For the long term, (to fill the vacancy occasioned by the expiration of the term of Mr. Clemens,) the Hon. C. Clay, Jr., was elected, receiving 85 votes. We copy the full proceedings of the election from the *Advertiser*, which is as follows: Mr. Scott, of the House, at the hour of 12, M. moved that the Senate be now invited into the house to proceed to the election of United States Senators. Mr. Pickett asked of the Chair if it was in order to give reasons why the Senate should not be invited into the Hall of the House. Mr. Speaker decided that it was not in order. Mr. L.P. Walker suggested that the motion of Mr. Scott was not necessary, it was competent for the Speaker to order the Clerk to invite the Senate whenever the hour arrives. Mr. Speaker so decided, and ordered the Clerk to invite the Senate into the Hall of the House.

ELECTION OF U.S. SENATORS. The Senate, then by invitation, appeared within the Hall of the House; and the two Houses, in convention, proceeded to the election of- 1st. A Senator to fill the vacancy occasioned by the resignation of the Hon. Wm. R. King. Mr. Meek placed in nomination the Hon. Benj. Fitzpatrick. Mr. Watts nominated the Hon. R.W. Walker, of Lauderdale. Mr. Percy Walker requested Mr. Watts to withdraw the nomination. Mr. Watts withdrew the nomination for the present. Mr. Creagh nominated the Hon. Wm. D. Dunn, of Mobile. Those of the Senate who voted for Mr. Fitzpatrick, were: Messrs. President, Acklen, Baker, Bethea, Blake, Bradford, Brindley, Clanton, Cocke, Crenshaw, Dickinson, Frazier, Gay, Hendricks, Hobdy, Hewlett, E.P. Jones, H.C. Jones, Kelly, Kimball, Lamar, Malone, Patton, Peterson, Powell, Scarcy, and Woodward. Those of the House, were: Messrs. Speaker, Abercrombie, Agee, Alldredge, Allen, Bell, Belser, Bishop, Brown, Burnet, Camp, Calhoun, Carrol, Clifton, Cochran, Comer, Cowan, Cook, Curry, J.W. Davis, William P. Davis, Ervine, of Wilcox, Farrior, Fletcher, Foreman, Foscue, Fox, Garth, Gibson, Gibreath, Gillam, Gordy, Greene, Hall, Hanserd, Haye, Hill, R.H.J. Holley, A. Holly, Horn, Hubbard, Humphreys, Irvine, of Walker, Johnson, Judge, Lawrence, of Fayette, Lawrence, of Cherokee, Lawrence, of Shelby, Lindsey, McBryde, McCall, of Barbour, McCall, of Choctaw, Meek, Murphey, Musgrove, Nelms, Newell, Newman, Owen, Payne, Phillips, Portis, Reynolds, Rhodes, Robinson, Sanford, Scott, Skelton, St. John, Sterrett, Talbert, Thornton, Todd, Vest, Walker, of Lauderdale, Walker, of Mobile, Watkins, Weaver, Whitsett, Wills, Yeldell and Yelverton-100. Those of the Senate who voted for Mr. Dunn, were: Messrs. Ashly, Jemison, Lee, McLemore, Watts and Webb. Those of the House, were: Messrs. Benners, Cole, Creagh, Hatcher, Inge, Jay, Webb, and Wilkins-14. Messrs. Henry and Ward voted for Mr. Clemens, and Messrs. Pickett and Shelley for Mr. Lyon. Mr. Fitzpatrick was elected for the short term. 2d. A Senator to fill the full term of six years from the 4th of March last. Mr. Skelton nominated the Hon. C.C. Clay, Jr. Mr. Watts nominated the Hon. R.W. Walker, of Lauderdale. Mr. Percy Walker renewed his request to Mr. Watts to withdraw the name of Mr. R.W.

Walker. He asked it as a personal favor. Mr. Watts declined. Those of the Senate who voted for Mr. Clay, were: Messrs. President, Acklen, Bethea, Blake, Bradford, Brindle, Dickinson, Frazier, Gay, Hendricks, Hobly, Hewlett, E.P. Jones, H.C. Jones, Kelly, Lamar, Malone, Patton, Powell, Webb, and Woodward. Those of the House, were: Mr. Speaker, Agee, Alldridge, Allen, Bell, Benners, Bishop, Brown, Burnett, Camp, Carroll, Clinton, Cochran, Comer, Cowan, Cook, Curry, J.W. Davis, W.P. Davis, Ervine, of Wilcox, Farrior, Fletcher, Foreman, Foscue, Fox, Garth, Gilbreath, Gordy, Greene, Hall, Hanserd, Hays, Hubbard, Humphries, Irvine of Walker, Lawrence, of Fayette, Lindsey, Martin, McBride, McCall, of Barbour, Meek, Murphey, Musgrove, Newell, Newman, Owen, Portis, Reynolds, Rhodes, Sanford, Scott, Skelton, St. John, Sterritt, Talbert, Thornton, Vest, Walker, of Lauderdale, Walker of Mobile, Watkins, Weaver, Whitsitt, Wilkins, Wills, Yelverton.-85. Those of the Senate who voted for Mr. Walker, were: Messrs. Ashly, Baker, Clinton, Cocke, Crenshaw, Jemison, Lee, McLemore, Peterson, Searcy and Watts. Those of the House, were: Messrs. Abercrombie, Belser, Calhoun, Cole, Gibson, Hatcher, Hill, R.H.J. Holly, Inge, Jay, Johnson, Judge, Lawrence, of Cherokee, Lawrence, of Shelby, McCall, of Choctaw, Nelms, Odom, Payne, Phillips, Pickett, Robinson, Shelley, Todd, Ward, Webb, and Yeldell-36.
Mr. Kimball, of the Senate, and Messrs. Gillam, Gooden, Henry, A. Holly, Horn, and Laughinghouse, of the House, voted for Mr. Clemens. Mr. Clay was declared elected for the long term. The Senate then withdrew.

Editorial Brevities.
The negro Morris, belonging to Thomas H. Snow, convicted at the late term of the Circuit Court of Lowndes county, on a charge of "assault with intent to kill," and sentenced to be hung, has been pardoned by Gov. Collier.

Great Liberality. The N. Y. Commercial states that the collection in the Rev. Dr. Alexander's church, on the Fifth Avenue, on Sunday week, for the Bible cause, after an appropriate discourse by the pastor, amounted to three thousand and eighty-three dollars. This, it believes, is the largest sum ever collected on a singular occasion.

Telegraph Operators. Mr. Justice Meredith, in the Superior Court at Quebec, recently decided that the operator of a telegraph company cannot be compelled to divulge within a Court of Justice, the contents of telegraph dispatches sent or received by him.

The last New York letter of the New Orleans Bulletin says: "another forgery to the tune of $50,000, is revealed today upon the failure of Graham & Co., druggist of Maiden Lane. The name of Joseph B. Varnum, was used."

On the 16th inst. the Hon. Charles J. McDonald, (late Governor) was nominated for United States Senator, by a democratic caucus of the Georgia Legislature, on the seventh ballot. A few of the friends of ex-Governor Cobb left the caucus in a rage. Cobb only got ten votes.

The Philadelphia Bulletin states that Francis de Silva, now in prison at Havana, on a charge of being connected with the Cuban Junta in New York last summer, is a naturalized citizen of the united states, and calls upon Secretary Marcy to interfere.

It is stated that the Rev. Henry Chase, of New York, lately deceased, united in the holy bands of matrimony upwards of 9000 couple.

Mississippi. A New Orleans paper says that the returns from thirty five counties shows

McRae's majority to be 1, 668 over the Whig candidate. The Union loss since 1851 is 3,618 and the Whig gain since the Presidential election 4.465. The next Senate will probably stand 11 Whig 1 Union democrat and 20 States Right democrats. The House as far as heard from stands 37 Whig and Union, 44 democrats.

The Vicksburg Sentinel says that the democratic majority on joint ballot in the legislature will be between 35 and 50. The Sentinel says also that Rev. D.B. Nabers (independent democratic Union candidate) is defeated for Congress by five or six hundred votes. It rejoices over the fact, because the gentleman is Foote's lieutenant, and next to defeating Foote, the best thing is defeat.

The Legislature. The following are taken from the proceedings of the Senate on Saturday last. At present Legislature, it seems, has gone to work earnestly, and, no doubt, will perform much useful labor before its adjournment: Mr. Blake, from the Judiciary Committee, to whom referred the bill to amend the Estray Law, reported a substitute-same in substance, differing in phraseology. Substitute adopted and ordered to a third reading. Same, from the same, reported back the bill to amend section 1065, of the Code, as inexpedient. Concurred in. Same, from the same, reported back to the bill making copies of the deeds evidences in certain cases, without amendment, and recommended its adoption. Concurred in and ordered to a third reading. Same, from same, to whom was referred the bill to amend the law in relation to issuance Marriage Licenses, reported it inexpedient to legislate. Mr. Brindley opposed the adoption of the report of the committee. Report concurred in. From the same, reported that it was inexpedient to legislate upon the bill to authorize executors, administrators and guardians to sell or compromise bad and doubtful debts belonging to the estate of which they are representatives, as the law made ample provisions. Concurred in. Mr. Crenshaw, from the Judiciary Committee, reported a substitute for the bill to increase the pay of Jurors in Lowndes county, (substitute allows $2.25 per day,) which was adopted, and bill ordered to a third reading. A bill to give the election of County Treasurer in Chambers county to the people.

Mr. Crenshaw. A bill in relation to the burnt records of the county of Butler. Also, a bill to repeal in part an act making the Treasurer of Madison county elective by the people. Also, a bill to reduce the number of Supreme Court Judges. Also, a bill to repeal certain sections of the Code in reference to election precincts.

Mr. Blake. A bill to amend the charter of the Alabama and Tennessee River Railroad Company.

Mr. Hewlett. A bill for the relief of John A.L. DeBornie, of Walker county.

Mr. Blake. A bill to exempt certain persons from working on the roads.

Mr. Baker. Joint resolution, relating to the claim of Dr. John J. Boswell against the State. Referred to a Select Committee, consisting of Messrs. Baker, Powell, Peterson, Watts and Kimball.

Mr. Bethea. A bill to increase the salaries of Judges of the Supreme Court to $3,000, Chancellors to $2,500, and Judges of the Circuit Courts to $2,500.

Mr. Peterson. And resolution that a committee of one from each Judicial Circuit be appointed to inquire about the expediency of abolishing the militia system, and levying a poll tax, to be applied to the establishment of a Polytechnic School. - Adopted.

Mr. Hendricks. A bill to authorize the court of county commissioners to change bounds of election precincts. Read and ordered to a second.

Mr. Searcy. A resolution to go into the election of a Supreme Court Judge, to fill the vacancy of Judge Dargon. On motion, of Mr. Acklen, laid on the table. Also, a bill to provide for electing County Treasurer in the counties of in Henry and Dale. Read and ordered to a second.

A bill to compensate Jailers in certain cases. Passed. The bill to amend sections 1744 1746, of the Code. Passed. The bill to authorize the Governor to the issue at patent to George Myers. Passed. The following are taken from the proceedings of the House on the same day: Mr. Speaker announced the following Select Committee on the subject of Temperance: Messrs. Henry, Creagh, Conners, Sanford, Owen, Yelverton, Lindsay, Bishop and Burnett. Mr. Speaker laid before the House a communication from his Excellency the Governor, transmitting Resolutions of the Agricultural Convention of the Southern States; also Resolutions of the General Assemblies of Connecticut and Louisiana, and accompanying documents. Referred to the committee on Agriculture. Mr. Percy Walker day notice that he would move to reconsider the vote by which the Report of F.S. Lyon, Commissioner, &c., was preferred to the committee on the State Bank and Branches. Mr. Benners asked to be excused from serving on said committee; he was a member of several other committees, and had as much as he could attend to. Mr. Burnett make the same request. Neither of the gentleman was excused. Mr. L.P. Walker move to that Mr. Burnett be excused from serving on the Temperance Committee. The motion prevailed. Mr. Judge moved to excuse Mr. Benners. The motion failed. Mr. Cole presented the petition of R.A. Woolsey and others, G.W. Carroll and others, of Perry, for an anti-liquor law referred to Committee on Temperance.

Mr. Talbert. A petition of resident citizens of a certain township in Perry county. Referred to the Committee on the 16th Section Fund. Also, the petition of Ladies of Perry county for an anti-liquor law. Referred to Committee on Temperance.

Mr. Johnson introduced joint resolutions in relation to the public lands. Laid on the table for the present, on motion of Mr. Hubbard.

Mr. Henry. A bill to ammend an act to incorporate the Alabama and Noxubee Co. Miss. Railroad Company.

Mr. Henry. Petition of Mr. F. Cook and 24 others, of J.T. Gardner and 27 others, of Pickens county, for an anti-liquor law. Referred to the Committee of Temperance.

The resolution from the House, amended by the Senate proposing to elect U.S. Senators on Monday next, at 12 o'clock, M., was taken up, and a House concurred therein.

Mr. Sterritt petitions from citizens of Shelby county for an anti-liquor law, (Edmund King and 215 others.) Referred to Committee on Temperance.

Mr. Whitsitt. A bill to enlarge the jurisdiction of the Probate Court.

Mr. Curry. A bill to aid the Alabama and Tennessee River Railroad Company. [the bill authorizes a loan of $500,000 to the Alabama and Tennessee River Railroad Company at six percent, per annum, principal payable in 1860, interest semi annually, and secured by a lien on the iron purchased by the company, with the money-and by contributions, ratably, from the stockholders, in the event of deficiency.]

Mr. Curry moved to suspend the rule in order to refer the bill.

Mr. Henry had made a like motion in reference to the bill he had introduced in the morning; the rule should work equally.

Mr. Hubbard desired the bill printed.

Mr. L.P. Walker opposed to the printing until the bill was returned from the committee.

Mr. Scott opposed the suspension of the rule, as a matter of principle, unless it be in a case of emergency, as indicated by the Constitution.

Mr. Meek agreed with Mr. Scott in his view of the constitutional rule, but insisted that this is just such a case as comes within the pervieu of the rule.

Mr. L.P. Walker moved to lay the bill on the table and print 133 copies. The motion prevailed.

Mr. L.P. Walker moved to take the bill from the table and give it a second reading with a view to its reference. The motions severally prevailed, and the bill was referred to the Committee on Internal Improvement.

Mr. Curry introduced a bill to amend section 634 of the Code. Also, the account of Andrew Lawson. Referred to the Committee on Accounts.

Mr. Martin presented petitions of voters and ladies of Tuscaloosa county, for an anti-liquor law. Referred to Committee on Temperance.

Mr. Brown. A bill to amend the law of trading with slaves, (under section 3227 of the Code.)

Mr. Pickett gave notice that he would on Monday next move to reconsider the vote by which the House, proposing to elect United States Senators, on Monday next at 12 m.

And then the House adjourned until Monday morning at 10 o'clock.

Public Meeting. At a meeting of planters and others, at Mulberry P. O. Autauga county, on Monday, the 28th of November, 1853, the following preamble and resolutions were adopted: Whereas, The steam boat owners on the Alabama river, in connection with others, have, by combination, advanced their tariff of freights fifty per cent upon the rates heretofore paid, an inasmuch as the causes which they assign for the advance in our judgement are not sufficient to justify them. Be it resolved; That we promisee our patronage to any good boat or boats that will take our cotton at $1 per bale, and up freight at 50cts per barrel, and pledge ourselves to sustain, regardless of any reduction that may be made by the boats engaged in the combination, even if they propose to take it for nothing. Resolved, that the foregoing resolution be signed by the chairman, secretary and all others present, and sent to our country papers, and the Mobile Evening News for publication. John Steele, Chairman
Leonidas Howard, Secretary.

C.G. Lanier, Nelson Clark, A.C. Houston, H.D. Homes, Jno. Bates, Wm. T. Hale, A.C. Taylor, Thos. Underwood, Wm. Jones, Charles Golsan, Wm. Limbrek, J. Wood, Richard Morton, C.C. Dickerson, O.D. Steele, Wm. Wiley, J.H. Dickson, J.C. Morgan, J.J. Chappell, J.M. Langford, C.M. Howard, J.A. Scarbro, P.H. Whetstone, E. Sherer, R. Jones, G. Wallace, J.W. Wilson, R. Ross.

Joshua Bates, of the firm of Baring Brothers, has been appointed umpire, to the Mixed Commission upon Claims, now in Session at London, in the place of Ex-President Van Buren declined.

Vol. 1, Thursday, December 8, 1853, No. 45

Election of Solicitors. On the 30th ult. the Legislature elected Solicitors for the 2d, 7th and 9th Circuits. For the 2d, James A. Stallworth, of Conecuh, was re-elected; for the 7th, Alfred E. Van Hoose, of Tuscaloosa, was elected; and for the 6th, John J. Woodward, of Talladega-all Democrats.

Death of the Hon. Dougherty. The Columbus Enquirer announces the death of this distinguished citizen of Georgia, who died very suddenly at his residence in Athens on Saturday morning last. "Judge Dougherty has long filled an important place in the regards of the people of this his native State. Having been frequently Representative and Senator in our State Legislature, for several terms Judge of the Superior Court for the Western Circuit, and the nominee of his party for Governor and United States Senator. With distinguished ability and incorruptible integrity he discharged all the duties of the many and important public stations to which he was called by his fellow citizens. Loved by all who had the good fortune to know him, his death brings deep grief to the hearts of his numerous friends throughout the State, and his loss will be much felt, especially in that section of the State in which he lived." The deceased was a brother of Judge Robert Dougherty of this State.

Editorial Brevities.
Gen. Robles, Mexican Minister of War under Arista, and banished by Santa Anna, is at Rome, about fifteen miles from Ringgold Barracks, Texas, and designs to take up his residence in New Orleans. He narrowly escaped arrest and trial as a conspirator.

The ship *Defiance*, whose Captain McCerrin, was so cruelly maltreated at the Chincha Islands has sailed from Calloa for New York. Capt. McCerran is slowly recovering from his wounds. The Peruvian Government has paid damages for the detention of the *Defiance*, that the rest of the matter remains unsettled.

President Pierce has been ill for several days from a billious attack, but at last accounts he was convalescent.

P.S. Shelton, a merchant of Boston, largely engaged in the East India trade, has failed to a heavy amount.

The forgery case at Troy is heavier an at first supposed. The party is the present Mayor and Postmaster.

Death of Another Consul. A New York letter says that much sympathy is felt in the death of Henry de Wolfe, lately appointed Consul to Dundee, Scotland. He left for Europe in the Baltic only a month ago, but illness obliged him to return immediately. He was a native of Rhode Island, and in 1823 married a daughter of Professor Rogers, of the Pennsylvania University, who with seven children, survive him. His death is the seventh that has occurred among the Consul appointments made by President Pierce, during the eight months he has been in office.

From Texas. Advices from Galveston to the 25th that yellow fever was still prevailing and Brownsville and Matamoras, though on the decrease. There had been fifteen deaths and the garrison at Brownsville, including Lieut. Whiting, Lieut. Duncan and Colonel Webster. The fever had again appeared in Houston, and with increasing malignity.

Letters from Santa Fe. Late advices from Santa Fe states that General Garland has left the Mesilla Valley, and that no authority will be exercised over it.

Lieut. Aubrey had started on his expedition to explore a new route to California.

Legislative Proceedings. In the Senate, on Friday, December 2d, several reports were made from standing committees. Mr. Patton, from the Committee on Internal Improvements and Inland Navigation, to whom was referred the bill to incorporate the Tennessee and Alabama Central Railroad Company, reported the bill, some amendments, and recommended its passage. Amendment requires stock to the amount of one hundred thousand dollars before they commence work, and that at least twenty miles shall be let out to contract for grading and crossties within twelve months. Amendment adopted, after strong opposition by Mr. Malone, who wished the charter passed as introduced. On the second amendment, a considerable discussion ensued, in which Messrs. Malone, Webb, Patton and Bethea engaged. Mr. Patton stated that his object was to bring about speedy action about the company. On motion of Mr. Malone, twelve months was stricken out, and two years inserted. Mr. Malone moved to lay the amendment of committee, as amended, on the table, and called for the yeas and nays. Yeas 7; nays 21. Amendment was then adopted. Mr. Blake, from Judiciary to whom was referred the bill to amend section 5251-(said bill change the penalty for exhibiting faro tables; and, also, from imprisonment in the penitentiary to a fine of five hundred dollars)- report it inexpedient to pass said bill. Mr. Baker desired to say that he had introduced this bill, not to give license to gaming; he was anxious to see gaming up every kind suppressed; but the law now in existence is so bloody that it will never be enforced. He never knew one man convicted under this law, and he was led into it in a moment of intoxication, and was not morally guilty. Mr. Webb advocated the adoption of the report. Mr. H.C. Jones opposed to it. Mr. Baker moved to lay the report on the table. Lost. Yeas 12; nays 14. Mr. Blake, from the Judiciary Committee, reported that it was inexpedient to pass the bill to amend section 2257, of the Code. Report concurred in. Mr. Hewlett, from the committee on Federal Relations, reported favorably on memorial to Congress to make an additional appropriation to improve the navigation of Mobile bay. Report concurred in and memorial adopted. Mr. Blake, from the Judiciary Committee, reported back the petition from the citizens of township 20, in Perry, and recommended its reference to the Committee on Sixteenth Section. Concurred in. Mr. Jemison, from the Joint Committee, to whom was referred the report of Mr. F.S. Lyon, reported, which was laid on the table, and 1800 copies ordered to be printed. They also, reported resolutions highly complementary of Mr. Lyon-which where unanimously adopted.

Mr. Jemison. A bill to charter the Bank of Tuscaloosa, which was, rule suspended, referred to the Committee on Banks and Banking.

Mr. Patton. A bill to amend the charter of the Northern Bank of Alabama, which was read, and ordered to a second reading.

On motion of Mr. H.C. Jones, the bill in reference to Sheriff's sales in Franklin county, was taken from the table and passed.

Mr. Blake. A bill to regulate the taking of testimony before Chancery Courts.

Mr. Acklen. A joint memorial, asking the Mississippi Legislature to grant the right of way to the Memphis and Charleston Railroad Co.

Mr. Webb. A resolution (by the request of Mr. H.C. Jones,) to adjourn *sine die*, on the 26th inst., which, on motion of Mr. Bethea, was laid on the table.

Mr. Brindley offered the following resolution: *Resolved*, That a Committee on Inland Navigation and Internal Improvement, inquire into the expediency of building a *main Central*

Railroad through the center of the State, or as nearly so as practicable, across the mountainous part of the State, the distance of, say sixty miles, to include the worst part or the part which is hardest to build, for the purpose of connecting the North and South sections of the State; and of applying either by investing as stock, or by loaning to a company, in sums of five or ten thousand dollars, to be secured by mortgages on real estate: all such funds as are held by the State, not otherwise appropriated, now on hand, or here after to be received in trust, and especially such as now do, or are hereafter likely, to burden the people with the annual taxation: and report by or otherwise. The Senate then adjourned. The proceedings of the House the same day we have omitted, as little of interest transpired in that department.

The Pacific Railroad Company, recently organized, with "such a flourish," in New York is looked upon as somewhat of a humbug. The Press, in various sections of the country, is down on it very heavily. The Washington correspondent of the *Charleston Courier* gives it a "first rate notice," thus: "The Pacific Railroad, (which some one maliciously designated the Moonshine Company,) with a capital of one hundred millions of dollars, has perfected its organization. The manner in which the stock was subscribed tended rather to shake public confidence in the enterprise. Mr. Walker, the distinguished Ex-Secretary of the United States Treasury, whom no one regards as an eminently wealthy man, by a single dash of his pen, put down his name for ten millions. A young newspaper man of our acquaintance, whom we met a short time ago, remarked that he felt like a rich man! He was asked why so, and he playfully said that he had just subscribed at the Metropolitan Hotel, one hundred thousand dollars to the great Pacific Railroad. The sum total of his worldly possessions, will not exceed five hundred dollars. However, the organization has been perfected, and" solid "names are connected with its management. Among the principals are those of L.S. Chatfield, Attorney General of the State, A.C. Flagg, our worthy City Comptroller, Robert J. Walker, Isaac E. Holmes, T. Butler of this city, W.W. Leland, of the Metropolitan Hotel, and various Members of Congress, Governors of States, and some large capitalists. How some of the minor capitalists, who are investing millions in it, can be unable these tight times to pay up their regular installments, is a matter of their own business, not ours. Engineers and surveyors has been engaged, and it is said will soon start to the Southwest, with a view of fixing the line of the road. Their descendants to the fourth generation they probably travel over the great Pacific road, and probably not." "The New York *Herald* is its puffer, and the New York *Tribune* calls it the 'Moonshine Company.' "

Beware of the Villain! There came to this village last summer a Daguerrean Artist, calling himself *B.S. Morrill*, who remained here several months, and during the time addressed a young lady of the village who consented to marry him. The day for their marriage was fixed upon, and the ceremony was about being performed, when a letter came to hand informing her parents that he had two wives living, one in Massachusetts and the other and Canada. Not at all abashed by this sudden interference with his hopes, the villainy unequalled to, he offered to pay the expenses of the young lady's father to New York, and elsewhere, that he might fully satisfy himself that the information was false, and the letter the offspring of some malicious foe. His loud protestations of innocence and boldness, he imagined, would settle the question at once, and his hellish purpose of blasting the happiness of another innocent one be accomplished. But the father not being so easily satisfied, availed himself of the money, and a few letters which Morrill gave him to his friends to *establish his innocence!* and started for the North. As soon as Morrill, who had removed to Selma, was assured of his leaving, he packed up and left for parts unknown. The father of the young lady on arriving in New York, called upon one of Morrill's references, who gave him, in substance, the following information in writing: - that B.S. Morrill is an assumed name-his true name is *S.M. Bradley*-that he married in Massachusetts a lady by whom he had four children-that he cruelly deserted her and when to Canada, where he married a Miss Gibbs by whom he had three children, and that both of the wives are now living. He was also found to be largely in debt and New York, having obtained goods by false pretenses under different assumed names. He came south last May with some gentlemen of Montgomery, who, deceived by his pleasant address and accomplished manners, were disposed to show him some attention. He so far gained the confidence of one of these gentlemen as to obtain the loan of a valuable horse which he sold and appropriated the proceeds to his own use. He also left a large Hotel bill unpaid in Montgomery. *S.M. Bradley*, alias B.S. Morrill, is in appearance about 35 years old, about 5 feet 10 inches high, will weigh about 170 pounds and has dark hair and blue eyes. On the whole, is a fine looking man, can readily assume the manners of the gentleman, and render himself agreeable to all-in fact, is not wanting in any essential for an *accomplished villain.* Before leaving Selma he expressed a determination to go to Florida. His arrival has recently been noticed in New Orleans, but where ever he may be he is a *dangerous man, and a villain of the deepest dye!* These statements are made from undisputed authority, and knowing them to be correct, I am in hopes that the Press all over the Union, will pass him around, and warn communities against him. Geo. W. Coe

Administrator's Sale. By virtue of authority vested in me by an order from the Honorable Henly Brown, Judge of Probate in for the County of Autauga, I will sell to the highest bidder at the late residence of Mrs. Anderson, near Prattville, on the 9th day of January next, 1854, all of the perishable property belonging to the estate of Margaret A. Mitchell, deceased consisting of six negroes, too valuable women and four children from four to ten years old, well formed an very likely, household and kitchen furniture, plantation utensils, a two horse wagon and harness, two mules, nine head of cattle, corn, fodder, peas, potatoes &c., &c., Terms-Two of the negroes will be sold for cash, and the residue of the property will be sold on a credit until the first day of January 1855, provided the amount purchased exceeds ten dollars-for all purchases less than that amount the cash will be required. Those purchasing on time will be required to give notes with at least two approved securities. Wm. H. Northington, Adm'r.

Administrator's Notice. Letters of administration upon the estate of Margaret A. Williams, deceased, were granted to the undersigned on the 30th day of November, 1853, by the Honorable Henly Brown, Judge of Probate in and for the County of Autauga. All persons having claims against said deceased are here by notified to present them to him duty authenticated within that time prescribed by law, or they will be barred. Wm. H. Northington, Adm'r.

Administrator's Sale. By virtue of an order granted by the Probate Court of Autauga County, I will sell at my house near Pine Flat, on the 7th day of January next, all the perishable property be longing to the estate of Tabitha Massingale, deceased: to wit, one negro by the name of Lewis, 20 years of age, boy Jordan, 10 years of age, boy Riley, 7 years of age, and a woman, Ann, 24 years of age, and her child, Patsey, 8 months old, and one bed and furniture, on a credit until the first day of January 1855. John Massingale, Adm'r.

Administrator's Sale. I will offer for sale to the highest bidder, on Monday, the 7th of January next, 1854, on a credit of six months, at the late residence of Abner Hill, deceased, near Prattville, in the County of Autauga, all the perishable property belonging to the estate of said deceased, consisting, in part, of household and kitchen furniture, hogs, horses, mules, cows, plantation utensils, corn, fodder, oats, potatoes, &c. &c. the purchaser will be required to give small notes, with at least two approved securities. Wm. Montgomery, Adm'r.

Notice. Letters of administration was granted to the under signed by the Judge of Probate of Autauga County upon the estate of Tabitha Massingale, on the 28th day of November, 1853, all persons having claims against the estate of said Tabitha Massingale are required to present the same within the time allowed by law, or the same will be barred. John Massingale, Adm'r.

The State of Alabama, Autauga County, Special Court of Probate, November 30, 1853.
This day came William Montgomery, administrator of the estate of Abner Hill, deceased, and filed his application in writing praying for an order to sell the six following Negro slaves, to wit, Daniel, Mary, Violet, Lucy, Ellen and Rexana, for the purpose of paying the debts of said deceased. It is therefore ordered that the 23d day of December next be set apart for the hearing of said petition-all persons interested are hereby notified to be and appear at a special Term of the Probate Court to be held on the 23d day of December next, to show cause, if any, why said negroes slaves should not be sold. Henly Brown, Judge of Probate

The State of Alabama, Autauga County, Court of Probate, December 5, 1853.
This day came Wm. H. Northington, administrator of the estate of Eugenia E. Knox, deceased, and filed his application in writing praying for an order to sell the west half of the northwest corner of Section 20, Township 17, Range 16, also 26 1/2 acres running east and west, and in the center of the east half of the southwest corner of Section 20, same Township and Range as above, lying and being situated in the County aforesaid, for the purpose of making a division amongst the heirs at law of said deceased. It is ordered that the 3d Monday in January next, 1854, be set to for the hearing of said application, and that notice of this the application be given to Henry C. Laughter, and Madora C. Laughter, wife of said Henry C. Laughter, who reside in the State of Texas, by publication for three successive weeks in the Autauga Citizen, notifying them to be and appear at a court to be held on the third Monday in January next, 1854, to show cause, if any, why said land should not be sold. Henly Brown, Judge of Probate

The State of Alabama, Autauga County, Special Court of Probate, December 5, 1853.
This day came William H. Northington, administrator of the estate of Green Hampton, deceased and filed his accounts and vouchers for the final settlement of the estate of said deceased, which was examined, and ordered to be filed for the inspection of all concerned. It is therefore ordered, that notice be given for forty days, by publication for three successive weeks in the Autauga Citizen, a newspaper published in said county, notifying all persons interested to be and appear at a court to be held on the 17th day of January next to show cause why said account should not be stated and allowed, and said settlement be made. Henly Brown, Judge of Probate

The State of Alabama, Autauga County, Special Court of Probate, December 2, 1853.
This day came Joel Zeigler, executor of last will and testament of William Zeigler, deceased and filed his accounts and vouchers for the annual and final settlement of his said executorship which were examined, and ordered to be filed for the inspection of all concerned. It is therefore ordered, that notice be given for forty days, by publication for three successive weeks in the Autauga Citizen, a newspaper published in said county, notifying all persons interested to be an to appear at a court to be held on the 16th date of January next, to show cause why said account should not be stated and allowed, and said settlement be made. Henly Brown, Judge of Probate

Vol. 1, Thursday, December 15, 1853, Nov. 46

Legislative Proceedings. Local of interest transpired in the two Houses of the Legislature on Friday and Saturday, with the exception of the election of Secretary of State. At 12, M., the Senate appeared within the House, when the two Houses preceded to an election for Secretary. The names of Messrs. Benham, Higgins and Caldwell were placed in nomination. After the 6th balloting the name of Mr. Higgins was withdrawn, neither of the candidates having received a majority of the votes cast. Twelve votes were cast for P.H. Brittan on the 4th ballot, after which his name was withdrawn. A motion was made to adjourn. Lost. Mr. Greene renewed the nomination of Mr. Higgins. Mr. Lindsay moved to an adjournment, and the motion prevailed. The Senate withdrew and the House adjourned. On Saturday morning the Senate appeared within the Hall of the House, and the two Houses in convention resumed the ballotings for Secretary. After the tenth balloting the names of Messrs. Clitheral and Harrison were placed in nomination. After the sixteenth balloting the names of Messrs. Higgins, Clitheral and Harris were withdrawn, when Mr. Benham was declared duly and constitutionally elected Secretary. The Senate then withdrew. In the House, Mr. Hall (by leave) introduced a bill for the relief of John T. Weaver, which was read twice and referred to the Committee on Propositions and Grievances. The House then adjourned until Monday morning, 10 o'clock.

Married. In Prattville, on the 8th of December, 1853, by Charles S.G. Doster, Esq., Thomas M. McClelen, of Talladega County, Ala., to Martha J. Houston, of Prattville.

Administrator's Notice. Letters of administration upon the estate of Margaret A. Anderson, deceased, were granted to the undersigned on the 5th day of December, 1853, by the Honorable Henly Brown, Judge of Probate in and for the County of Autauga. All persons holding claims against said deceased are here by notified to present them duly authenticated within the time prescribed by law, or they will be barred. Joseph M. Williams, Adm'r.

Administrator's Sale. By virtue of an order of sell granted me by the Honorable Henly Brown on, Judge of Probate Court Autauga County, on the 26th day of November, I will proceed to sell in front of the courthouse at Kingston, on Monday, the 25th day of January next, all of the real estate of A.T. Harris, deceased, to wit: lots no. 1,2,3,4,5,6,7 & 8, of original lot no. 187, situated in West Wetumpka, and the balance of said lot no. 187, except about one lot in the South East corner of said lot, for one half cash, the balance on a credit of 12 months, the purchaser to give notes with two approved securities. John F. Horton, Adm'r.

Negro Dogs! The undersigned would take this method to inform the public generally, that he has one of the best pack of Negro Dogs to be found in the State. Those who have negroes to run away would do well to test the skill of his dogs. His charges are three dollars per day, or fifteen dollars for catching. He can always be found at his residence, seven miles from Prattville. F.F. DeBardelaben.

Vol. 1, Thursday, December 22, 1853, No. 47

The two Houses of the Legislature met on Saturday, and proceeded to the election of Treasurer, and Comptroller of Public Accounts. Hon. Wm. Graham, of this county, was re-elected Treasurer, without opposition, and Joel Riggs re-elected Comptroller, without opposition.

Editorial Brevities.
It is understood now that Secretary Davis will ask Congress for some additional military force-perhaps three regiments to, of 800 men each. The necessity for this enlargement of the peace establishment has become so great, in consequence of our greatly increased frontier, that it is impossible longer to resist it.

Mr. A.T. Stuart, the purchaser of the Metropolitan Hotel, on Saturday last paid down $400,000 of the purchase money. The remaining $400,000 is to be paid at the expiration of a year from the term of the purchase.

Gov. Foote, of Mississippi, it is said, is about to take up his residence in New Orleans. We see from the papers of that city that he is now on a visit there.

A difficulty occurred on Tuesday between Senator Gwin and Secretary Guthrie, in Washington, on account of alleged incivility on the part of the latter and a duel was at first anticipated, as Mr. Gwin demanded an apology but ultimately, it is said, the matter was amicably adjusted.

Congressional. Baltimore, December 15. - in the U.S. Senate on Wednesday no business of any importance was transacted. In the House of Representatives the resolutions to purchase Mount Vernon were warmly discussed, but no decision was arrived at. The Senate resolution to change the mode of appointment of Assistant Secretary of the Treasury, elicited considerable discussion, Mr. Pressly Ewing of Kentucky, regarding it as an indirect assault on Mr. Guthrie, which Mr. Thos. H. Bayly, of Va., and Mr. Geo. S. Houston, of Alabama, denied.

Gen. Cass, it is said, approves of the postponement of the five anti-demonstration resolutions offered in caucus by Mr. Stanton, but reserves his opinion as to pressing them hereafter.

Murder in Shelby County. We have seen a private letter for Montevallo, stating that a man named Chapman Horton shot another named Danl. Sumner through the heart with a gun, killing him instantly. This transaction took place a few days ago. If the particulars given in the letter are true, it was than most cold blooded murder. Horton made his escape. The letter says: Horton is about 45 years old, about 5 feet 8 inches high, walks erect, light complected, and has a habit of batting his eyes, (that is, winking.) He is a man of fine education, but of very bad countenance. It is thought he may go through Montgomery. He weighs 150 pounds.

F.G. Ruffin, editor of the Southern *Planter*, has been elected Secretary to the Virginia Agricultural Society, at a salary of $1,500 per annum.

Married. On the 14th inst., by the Rev. Mr. Norton, of Montgomery, David R. Myers to Miss Mary C. DeJarnette, both of this county.

Administrator's Notice. Letters of administration having been granted by the Honorable Judge of Probate of Autauga County, to the undersigned, on the 17th December, 1853, on the estate of John M. Boothe, deceased, all persons indebted to said estate will make immediate payment to me, and those having claims against the same will present within that time prescribed by law or they will be barred. Charles Boothe, Adm'r.

Negroes for Hire. A negroes belonging to Charles W. Durden, a minor heir of Jacob W. Durden, deceased, will be hired out in Prattville on Monday, at 26th day of December, 1853. Wm. H. Northington, Guardian.

The State of Alabama, Autauga County, Special Court of Probate, December 12, 1853. This day came Amos C. Baker, formerly Guardian of Catharine E. Zeigler, now deceased, and filed his accounts and vouchers for the final settlement of his guardianship of the estate of said deceased, which was examined, and ordered to be filed for the inspection of all concerned. It is therefore ordered, that notice be given for forty days, by publication for three successive weeks in the Autauga Citizen, a newspaper published in said county, notifying all persons interested to be and appear at a court to be held on the 24th day of January next, to show cause why said account should not be stated and allowed, and said settlement be made. Henly Brown, Judge of Probate.

The State of Alabama, Autauga County, Special Court of Probate, December 19, 1853. This day came John D. Fralick, surviving executor of the last will and testament of Henry Fralick, deceased, and filed his accounts and vouchers for the final settlement of the estate of said deceased, which was examined, and ordered to be filed for the inspection of all concerned. It is therefore ordered, that notice be given for forty days, by publication for three successive weeks in the Autauga Citizen, a newspaper published in said county, notifying all persons interested to be and appear at a court to be held on the 7th day of February next, to show cause why said account should not be stated and allowed, and said settlement be made. Henly Brown, Judge of Probate.

The State of Alabama, Autauga County, Special Court of Probate, December 19, 1953. This day came Clinton Thompson, administrator of the estate of Burket Thompson, deceased, and filed his accounts and vouchers for the final settlement of the estate of said deceased, which was examined, and ordered to be filed for the inspection of all concerned. It is therefore ordered, that notice be given for forty days, by publication for three successive weeks in the Autauga Citizen, a newspaper published in said county, notifying all persons interested to be and appear at a court to be held the on 25th day of January next, to show cause why said account should not be stated and allow, and said settlement be made. Henly Brown, Judge of Probate.

Vol. 1, Thursday, December 29, 1853, No. 48

Much obliged to our kind *confreres*, Messrs. N. J. & L.T. Blome, for an imitation to attend their Egg-Nogg Party on last Tuesday evening, and regret very much we could not be on hand. We hope, gentleman, that you had a merry time of it.

Editorial Brevities.
We notice that the Washington *Union* announces that the Hon. Benj. Fitzpatrick had taken his seat in the Senate. All the members of Congress from this State are now at their posts.

Gov. P.H. Bell has resigned the office of Governor of Texas, in consequence, we suppose, of being elected to Congress, and the duties of that station have therefore devolved upon the present Lieutenant Governor, J.W. Henderson, by whom they will be discharged until the 21st December, when a new Governor will be elected.

Mrs. Nichols, of Vermont, and Mrs. Fowler, of New York, are canvassing the State of Wisconsin in favor of the Maine law.

Married. On the 20th inst., by Rev. Jas. Foster, Frank Pope to Miss Mary A. McKeithen. On the 21st inst., by Rev. Jas. Foster, Joseph A. Smith to Miss Isadore C. Pope.

Guardian Sale. By virtue of authority vested in me by a decree of the Probate court of Autauga County, rendered on the 26th day of December, 1853, I will sell to the highest bidder, in Prattville, on the 28th day of January next, 1854, the interest of the minor heirs of Margaret A. Mitchel, deceased, (being 5-6) in the following property, to wit: household and kitchen furniture, cows, hogs, plantation utensils, and three negroes, viz.: Eliza, a woman, Ameia and Amanda, two very likely girls, and two mules. Terms, the negroes will be sold for cash, and the balance on a credit until the 1st day of January, 1855. Joseph M. Williams, Guardian.

Index

A

Aaris, Iverson L. 22
Abercrombie 192
Abercrombie 123, 130, 191
Abercrombie, James 5
Abrahams, Dorothea 24
Acklen 130, 191, 192
Acklen, Mr. 193, 198
Adams, Jas. 147
Adams, Miss 3
Adams, Mr. 87
Adams, President 24
Adams, S. 163
Adams, W.R. 113
Adkins, W.M. 147
Agassiz, Professor 165
Agee 191, 192
Aguilar, Senor 112
Alexander, Benjamin B. 174
Alexander, Dr. 192
Alexander, James L. 14
Alexander, Jas. I. 114
Alford, J.H. 163
Alldredge 191
Alldridge 192
Allen 163, 188, 191, 192
Allen, James 141
Allen, Jas. 3, 48
Allen, W.C. 126, 141
Allgoo, A. 147
Amanda 207
Ameis 207
Anderson, Agnes 66, 101
Anderson, D.C. 5
Anderson, George W. 65
Anderson, J. 147
Anderson, Margaret A. 203
Anderson, Mrs. 200
Anderson, O.L. 1
Anderson, Walker 74
Andrews, A. 40
Ann 200
Anna, Santa 8, 51, 63, 66, 84, 112, 197
Arista 197
Arista, Gen. 84
Arista, President 13
Armstrong, H.H. 92
Arnold, Major 169
Ashby, T.W. 41
Ashley, John 95
Ashly 130, 191, 192
Ashly, Wm. A. 80
Atchison, David R. 32
Atchison, Mr. 45
Atchison, T.A. 75
Atkinson, Miss Ann M. 21
Aubrey, Lieut. 198
Austin, J.C. 177
Austin, Stephen F. 19
Austria 11
Avalos, Gen. 13
Averhart, John 3
Avery, Maj. 1
Axon, A.F. 16
Axson, A.F. 15

B

Bache, A.D. 105
Badger, Mr. 31
Bagby, A.P. 56
Bagby, Mr. 157
Baggett, James M. 113
Bagly, P. 147
Baire, R. 147
Baker 191, 192, 193
Baker, A. 167
Baker, A.C. 57, 62, 179, 182
Baker, Amos C. 206
Baker, B.H. 129
Baker, B.M. 186
Baker, Benj. M. 23
Baker, J.H. 147
Baker, Mr. 193, 198
Baker, R.A. 147, 149
Baldwin, A.M. 167
Baldwin, Dr. 184
Baldwin, M.A. 4, 5
Baldwin, Oliver P. 1
Baldwin, W.O. 186
Bancroft, George 2
Bancroft, Mr. 141
Banwell 72
Barber, Green 114
Barber, Greene B. 81
Barber, James J. 57
Barber, Jas. J. 57
Barclay, T.C. 148
Barclay, Thos. C. 147, 150
Barclay, Tom 147
Barlow, John H. 109
Barnard, John L. 13
Barnes, Mr. 3
Barrell, G.G. 24
Basare, Col. 13
Bassel, Caroline 98
Bates, Flemming 48
Bates, James B. 99
Bates, Jno. 195
Bates, Joshua 195
Battle, W.A. 147
Baylor, C.G. 91
Bayly, Thos. H. 205
Baynton, Mrs. 48
Beal, Lieutenant 169
Beale, Mr. 83
Beatsell, Isaac 114
Beaumont, Victor 175
Beck, Chas. A. 150
Beck, F.E. 65
Beecher, Henry Ward 161
Beers, Oliver S. 67
Begelow 89
Belcer, J.E. 93
Bell 130, 191, 192
Bell, Henry 48
Bell, John 97, 173
Bell, P.H. 207
Belleinger, Dr. 185
Bellenger, C. 186
Bellinger, C. 74, 166, 179
Bellinger, D.C. 178
Belser 130, 191, 192
Belser, James E. 79
Belser, JamesE. 133
Belser, Jas. E. 134
Belser, Mr. 187
Benford, James 57
Benham 203
Benham, Mr. 203
Benjamin, D.A. 186
Benjamin, J.P. 35
Bennard, F.A.P. 147
Benners 130, 191, 192
Benners, Mr. 187, 194
Bennett, James Gorden 175
Benson, G.W. 182
Benson, Nimrod E. 13
Benton 137
Benton, Col. 23, 83, 169
Benton, Thomas Hart 23
Berkeley, Mr. 110
Bernard, F.A.B. 148
Bernard, F.A.P. 147
Berrian, J.M. 84
Berry 158
Bethea 187, 191, 192, 198
Bethea, Mr. 187, 193, 198
Bethea, T.B. 129
Betts, E.F. 163
Beyington, Mr. 137
Bibb, B.S. 74, 92
Bibb, Governor 157
Bibb, Judge 65
Bibb, M.J. 186
Bibb, Mrs. P. 182
Bibb, P. 167
Bibb, P.D. 181, 186
Bibb, Peyton 157
Bibb, Sarah 167, 183
Bigger, T.B. 41
Bigler, Gov. 153
Birdsong, Henry 129
Bishop 130, 191, 192, 194
Bishop, Abram 98
Blackman, J.F. 113
Blackman, Jas. F. 113
Blake 191, 192
Blake, Gov. 18
Blake, Mr. 193, 198
Blake, S.R. 129
Blevins, George P. 93
Blome, L.T. 83, 207
Blue, M.P. 73
Boisseaw, William E. 68
Bolling, Wm. M. 186
Boniface, Mrs. Delpha 21
Booker, N.P. 33
Boon, Britan 161
Booth, Charles 206
Booth, H. 81
Boothe, John M. 206
Borland, Mr. 135
Boston, John 42
Boswell, John J. 193
Bowen, John 41
Bowen, Levi K. 174
Bowlegs, Billy 14
Bowles, Joseph 3, 48
Boyed, James 33
Boyless, J.A. 3
Bradford 191, 192
Bradford, Jas. M. 62
Bradley, S.M. 200
Bragg, John 5
Brandon, Mary 166
Breckenridge, Mr. 137
Bremer, Frederika 116
Brevard, T.W. 96
Brewer, Mr. 109
Brigham, Waitsill 131
Bright, Senator 32
Brindle 192
Brindley 191
Brindley, G.L. 147
Brindley, Mr. 193, 198
Britt, Ira 48
Britt, Malinda 3
Brittan, P.H. 203
Brittan, Mr. 73
Brittum, James 48
Broadnax, Robert 95
Broadnax, Robt. 96
Brock, Mrs. 184
Brogan, John 135
Bronson, Ex-Collector 178
Bronson, Mr. 169
Brooke 19
Brooke, Mr. 19
Broomer, Cornelius 107
Brown 130, 191, 192
Brown, 48
Brown, Eliza 167
Brown, Frederick H. 102
Brown, Henley 5
Brown, Henly 4, 8, 9, 14, 15, 21, 25, 30, 40, 43, 49, 52, 57, 59, 68, 77, 81, 85, 88, 89, 93, 94, 95, 98, 99, 102, 108, 113, 132, 136, 139, 140, 143, 151, 152, 158, 159, 166, 170, 172, 180, 189, 190, 200, 201, 203, 206
Brown, Jesse R. 102
Brown, Joseph 112
Brown, Miss 109

209

Brown, Mr. 69, 131, 195
Brown, Mrs. Stephen 48
Brown, R. 163
Brown, S.G. 147
Brown, S.T. 73
Brown, Saml. 174
Bruhns, C. 172
Brundridge, James 177
Buchanan, 116
Buchanan, A.M. 51
Buchanan, Mr. 1, 87
Buckler, John 147
Bugg, William R. 43
Bullard, James S. 24, 56
Bulloch 69
Bulloch, Uriah J. 70
Bunch, Mrs. Marion 109
Bunsell, O.S. 147
Burgess, Tristam 172
Burke 69
Burke, Mary A. 3
Burn, John 76
Burnes, James H. 172
Burnes, Robert F. 172
Burnet 191
Burnett 130, 192, 194
Burnett, Mr. 194
Burr, W.S. 147
Burrows, Epaphras 89
Burt, William 96
Burt, Wm. 96
Bushnell, Father 126
Butler, Adelis 178
Butler, Benj. F. 80
Butler, C.M. 31
Butler, John 3
Butler, N. 163
Butler, T. 199
Buyck, E.S. 163
Buyr, Mrs. J. 163
Byars, W. 147
Byrd, W. 147

C

Cain, A. 147
Caldwell 203
Calhoun 130, 191, 192
Calhoun, J.C. 46
Calhoun, Mr. 45, 46, 79, 87
Callahan 72
Callaway, W. 167, 182
Calvert, C.B. 42
Calvert, J. 147
Calvin, Rachel 8
Camak, Dr. 22
Camak, M. 147
Camp 191, 192
Camp, F.T. 48
Camp, J. 147
Camp, T.J. 3, 163
Campbell, A.J. 109
Campbell, George H. 97
Campbell, J.A. 67

Campbell, James 51
Campbell, Jas. 28
Campbell, John H. 42
Campbell, Judge 32
Cann 188
Cantley, Octavius G. 150
Capers, S.O. 103, 119, 170, 173, 174
Carew, E.G. 92
Carnes 73
Carnes, Geo. 147
Carpenter, Gillum 48
Carpenter, J.B. 106, 181, 182
Carpenter, John 57
Carpenter, Mrs. John 184
Carrol 191
Carroll 192
Carroll, G.W. 194
Carroll, Mr. 55
Carter, Alexander 93
Carter, J. 41
Cartledge, Augustus 169
Cass, Gen. 205
Cass, Lewis 31, 32
Cavellos 19
Caver, Henry 4
Caver, L. 114
Caver, Mary A.E. 4
Caver, Samuel 4
Caver, Sarah F. 4
Caver, Waid H. 4
Caver, Wm. 56
Cevelos 13
Cevelos, 13
Chambers, J.L. 167
Chambers, James M. 21, 74
Chambers, Thomas J. 40
Chambliss, Mrs. D. 163
Chapman, Jos. 167
Chapman, N. 112
Chappell, J.J. 195
Chapron, Mr. 51
Chapson, Miss E. 163
Charles 179
CHARLOTTE 132
Charlotte 12
Chase 75
Chase, Henry 192
Chatfield, L.S. 199
Cheatham, William 165
Cheek, Brantly J. 77
Cheek, Elizabeth 77
Cheny, R.S. 41
Cherry, R.M. 166
Childress, J.L. 147
Childress, Jas. L. 148
Chilton, W.P. 187
Chilton, William F. 4
Chitwood, C. 163
Chubb, Mr. 134
Churchwell, W.M. 24
Clanton 191
Clanton, Mr. 93
Clanton, N.H. 129

Clare 173
Clark, G.W. 147
Clark, J. 163
Clark, Mr. 92
Clark, Nelson 195
Clark, W.E. 5
Clark, W.G. 93
Clarke, James R. 5
Clarke, John W. 105, 123
Clarke, W.E. 134
Clay, C., Jr. 191
Clay, C.C., Jr 191
Clay, Cassius M. 58
Clay, Elizabeth 165
Clay, Henry 58, 88
Clay, J.M. 92
Clay, Mr. 87, 192
Clayton, Sampson 13
Clegg, David 99
Clemens, Jere. 165
Clemens, Jeremiah 5
Clemens, Mr. 23, 191, 192
Clemens, Senator 88
Clenatham, Col. 169
Cleveland, James A. 95
Clifton 191
Clinton 192
Clinton, J.H. 93
Clitheral 203
Clitherall, A.B. 188
Clopton 123
Clopton, Mary 183, 186
Cloud, Dr. 11, 65, 186
Cloud, N.B. 74
Clough 89
Cobb, Col. 65
Cobb, ex-Governor 192
Cobb, Joseph B. 48
Cobb, Mr. 141
Cobb, W.R.W. 5
Cochran 130, 191, 192
Cockburn, George 153
Cocke 130, 191, 192
Cocke, Mr. 177
Cockrell, S.W. 147
Coe, Geo. W. 200
Coe, George 23
Cogburn, J.H. 135
Coggin, Daniel 5
Coker, Malinda 3
Colcock, Mr. 45
Cole 130, 191, 192
Cole, Lewis 147
Cole, Mr. 194
Coleman, Thomas 158
Collier, Gov. 57, 192
Collier, Governor 41, 146
Collier, H.W. 154
Collier, Henry W. 4
Collins, A.J. 178
Collinson, Capt. 2
Collyer, Mr. 177
Comegys, John 14
Comer 130, 191, 192
Comstock, Mr. 167

Comstock, W.S. 186
Conkling, Judge 66
Connell, Mrs. 131
Conners 194
Converse, A.P. 113
Conway, C.J. 91
Conyers, J.R. 135
Cook 130, 191, 192
Cook, Edward H. 5
Cook, F. 194
Cook, J.M. 163
Cook, James 158
Cook, James M. 62, 114, 158
Cook, John N. 62
Cook, Judge 62
Cook, N. 75
Cooker, J.B. 147
Cooper, A.J. 179
Cooper, Peter 167
Copread, Jane 48
Corum, Thornton 157
Corwin, ex-Secretary 58
Costa 130
Cotton, Catherine 14
Cottrell, Col. 65
Cottrell, J.L. 65
Cowan 191, 192
Cowden, J.P. 147
Cowden, R.D. 147
Cowles, E.A. 30
Cowles, Geo. 27, 30
Cox, Isaac W. 114
Cox, Jesse J. 29
Cox, Wm. H. 3
Coxe, G.S. 92
Coxe, Robt. E. 79
Coy, Mr. 73
Cozart, Sheriff 81
Cragon, Col. 142
Craig, B. 147
Craig, R. 147
Crandall, Isaac 102
Crapau, John 52
Crawford, Captain 33
Crazel, Mr. 157
Creagh 191, 194
Creagh, Mr. 191
Crear, J. 147
Crenshaw 130, 191, 192
Crenshaw, Mr. 193
Crenshaw, N.J.C. 135
Crittenden, Mr. 177
Crommp, W.A. 147
Cruikshanks, Mr. 14
Crumpler, A. 167
Cruz, Col. 13
Cummings, Alfred 75
Curry 130, 179, 191, 192
Curry, Mr. 187, 194, 195
Cushing, Caleb 28, 141
Cushing, Gen. 174
Cushing, General 165
Cushing, Mr. 165
Cuyler 84, 173

210

Cuyler, R. 37

D

Dallas, George M. 165
Dameron, Mr. 111
Daniel 31, 201
Daniel, A.T. 97
Daniel, John M. 125
Daniel, W.C. 65
Daniels, Dr. 74
Dansby, Richard A. 135
Dargan, Edward S. 4
Dargon, Judge 193
Davis 130
Davis, B.F. 106
Davis, B.F. & T.A. 89
Davis, Benjamin 57, 96
Davis, J.W. 191, 192
Davis, Jeff. 27
Davis, Lewis C. 115
Davis, Lewis R. 114
Davis, Mr. 177
Davis, N. 93
Davis, Nathan 8
Davis, Nathaniel 37
Davis, Samuel D. 48
Davis, Secretary 205
Davis, T.A. 57
Davis, W.P. 192
Davis, William P. 191
Davis, Zeb 37
Dawson, J.J. 179
de la Beche, Henry 83
de Montijo, Madame 36
de Silva, Francis 192
De Soto 39
De Wolf, Thos. 73
de Wolfe, Henry 197
de Zuluago, Thomas 105
DeBardelaban, F.P. 91
DeBardelaban, Francis F. 107
DeBardelaban, Henry 107
DeBardelaben, A.W. 167
DeBardelaben, F.F. 117, 203
DeBardelaben, F.S. 25
DeBardelaben, Henry 25, 117
DeBornie, John A.L. 193
DeBow, J.D.B. 16
DeBow, Mr. 42
DeBow, S.D.B. 15
DeJarnete, Jno P 57
DeJarnett, John P. 96
DeJarnett, W.P. 106
DeJarnett, Wm. P. 106
DeJarnette, I.T. 51
DeJarnette, James T. 109
DeJarnette, James T., Jr 57
DeJarnette, Jas. T. 57
DeJarnette, John P. 143
DeJarnette, Joseph P. 57

DeJarnette, Mary C. 205
DeJarnette, W.P. 106, 107
DeJarnette, Wm. 167
DeLeon, Mr. 102
Delhommeau, M. 131
Deloffree, Prof. 175
Dennis, Charles A. 96
Dennis, Henry 132
Dennis, James R. 132
Dennison, Alex R. 114
DICK 132
Dicken, J.B. 163
Dickens, Charles 75
Dickerson, C.C. 92, 106, 195
Dickerson, J.S. 48
Dickerson, L.H. 27
Dickerson, Mahlon 169
Dickinson 191, 192
Dickson, J.H. 195
Dickson, James 188
Dillon, F. 147
Dirden, S.C. 163
Dismukes, George W. 94
Ditto, J.S. 147
Divany, R. 167
Dix, John A. 124
Dix, Mr. 87, 141
Dixon 157
Dixon, Mr. 14, 177
Dobbin 32
Dobbin, J.C. 27
Dodds, W. 43
Donnell, Mrs. E.J. 184
Donovan, Jeremiah 124
Donovant, John 134
Dorsey, D.W. 95
Dorsey, Mr. 95
Doster, Absalom 96
Doster, Charles S.G. 203
Dougherty, Robert 5, 197
Douglas, Fred 124
Downs, P. 147
Drendon, W.B. 147
Drummond, B.J. 163
Drummond, Margaret A. 53, 63
Drummond, W.E. 29
Dunbar, W. 51
Duncan, John 142
Duncan, Lieut. 197
Duncan, Lucious 15
Duncan, Lucius C. 16
Dunn, Mr. 191
Dunn, Wm. D. 191
Durannus, Eli J. 109
Duran, Ben 48
Durden, Benj. 133, 146
Durden, Benjamin 141
Durden, C.B. 106
Durden, Charles W. 85, 206
Durden, Georgianna W. 85
Durden, Harriet D. 85
Durden, Jacob W. 206
Durden, Lawrence A. 85

Durden, Luisa 113
Durden, Robert E. 85
Duval 69
Duval, John 72

E

Earl of Clarendon 20
Earle, S.S. 147
Earnest 137
Earnest, Col. 148
Earnest, W.S. 147, 148, 149
Easterlin, B. 186
Easterlin, Mrs. 184
Easterlin, Mrs. F. 183
Easterling, B. 167
Echols, W.W. 93
Echols, Wm. 41
Eddy, A.D. 134
Edmonds, Judge 45, 46
Edwards, C.A. 106, 182
Edwards, Dr. 106
Edwards, G.A. 167
Edwards, W.H. 147
Eimit, T.A. 123
Eliza 207
Ellen 201
Ellesmere, Lord 83
Elmore, A. 106, 107
Elmore, A.S. 57
Elmore, Albert 58, 106
Elmore, Ann 167
Elmore, Anne 182, 183
Elmore, Gen. 142, 148, 150
Elmore, John A. 96, 167
Elmore, Laura 167
Elmore, Miss S. 185
Elmore, Mr. 177
Elmore, Mrs. A. 184
Elmore, R. 147, 149
Elmore, Rush 167
Elmore, Susan 167
Emanuel, Jonathan 1
Empress Eugenie 84
English, Joshua 3
Ericsson, Capt. 80
Ericsson, Mr. 79
Ernest 123
Ervine 191, 192
Everett, Edward 7, 138
Everett, Mr. 41
Everett, Secretary 23
Ewing, Pressly 205

F

F—y, Miss H. 17
Fair, E.Y. 167
Falconet, Francisco P. 112
Fannin 73
Fannin, Col. 70
Fannin, Colonel 70, 71
Faraior 130
Farrior 191, 192

Farris, C. 147
Farwell, Willard (?) 65
Faulkner 1
Faulkner, Samuel 114
Fay, E. 181, 184
Fay, Eleutheria 184
Fay, F. 167
Fay, Miss S.E.W. 183
Faye, Miss E. 184
Feagan, Peter 169
Felder, Edmond J. 89
Fernald, Charles 97
Field, Dudly 80
Field, John 36
Fielding, W.H. 92
Figh, J.P. 147, 148
Figh, John P. 133
Filisola, Gen 73
Filisola, Gen. 73
Filisola, General 73
Fillmore, Mr. 41
Fillmore, President 7, 37
Finley, M. 147
Fish, Mrs. 45, 46
Fisher, William 28
Fitts, James 147
Fitzpatric, Bishop 19
Fitzpatrick, B. 182
Fitzpatrick, Benj. 137, 146, 167, 191, 207
Fitzpatrick, Benjamin 5
Fitzpatrick, Elmore 167
Fitzpatrick, M. 146
Fitzpatrick, Mr. 191
Fitzpatrick, Mrs. A. 167
Fitzpatrick, Mrs. Ben 183, 184
Fitzpatrick, Mrs. H. 183
Fitzpatrick, Philip 96
Fitzpatrick, Phillip 96
Fitzpatrick, Wm. 23
Flagg, A.C. 199
Flanagan, Leroy 143
Fleming, Robert 189
Fleming, Samuel 189
Fleming, Wm. H. 93
Fletcher 191, 192
Fletcher, Philander 56
Fletchers 185
Floyd, G.W. 77
Floyd, George 3
Floyd, Joel 48, 77
Foote 193
Foote, Gov. 23, 205
Foote, Governor 83, 137
Foreman 191, 192
Forms, C. 91
Forno, Capt. 12
Foscue 130, 191, 192
Foscue, Mr. 177
Foster, 8
Foster, Jas. 207
Foster, Josia 175
Fountain, James 27
Fowler, Mrs. 207

Fowler, W.C. 21
Fox 130, 191, 192
Fox, Mrs. 45
Fralick, Adam 108
Fralick, Henry 77, 206
Fralick, Jacob H. 108
Fralick, John D. 206
Fralick, Mary 77
Francis, Jas E. 79
Franklin, Benjamin 2
Franklin, Sir John 2
Franks, W.A. 185
Frazier 191, 192
Frazier, Gen. 177
Frear, N.H. 27
Freely, James 188
Freeman, Thomas F. 72
French, L. Virginia 31
Frith, Thos. 167
Frith, Thos. P. 133
Frothingham, Dr. 87
Frothingham, T.R. 87
Frye, W.W. 171
Fuller, Mr. 18
Fulquez, Don Fedrico 112

G

Gadsden, Gen. 157
Gadson, Mr. 177
Galan, Gen. 7
Gales 153
Galt, A. 41
Gamble, K. 147
Gardiner, C.K. 153
Gardiner, Capt. 153
Gardiner, Dr. 45
Gardner, Benj. 92, 93
Gardner, Benjamin 92
Gardner, G. 179
Gardner, H. 106, 167
Gardner, J.T. 194
Garland, Gen. 105
Garland, General 198
Garland, L.C. 147, 148
Garland, Prof. 148, 149
Garner, John H. 79
Garret, Mr. 177
Garrett, 4
Garrison 7
Garrison, James R. 18
Garth 191, 192
Gasquet, W.E. 15
Gates, Frederic 3
Gavand, Father 48
Gay 191, 192
Gayle, Geo. W. 80
Gayle, Judge 83
Gazzam, C.W. 93
George III 33
George, Stewart 51
German, Gen. 165
Gholson, J.W. 106
Gholson, Judge 173
Gibbons, Lyman 5

Gibbs, Miss 200
Gibreath 191
Gibson 130, 191, 192
Gibson, A.M. 147, 149
Gibson, Mr. 149
Gibson, W.N. 147
Gilbreath 192
Gilbreath, Frank 147
Gillam 130, 191, 192
Gillespid, A.P. 147
Gillespie, Mr. 119
Gillespie, William 48
Gilmer, 27
Gilmer, G.R. 65
Gilmer, George R. 74
Gilmer, Gov. 65
Gingaris 24
Girard 67
Glackmeyer, Mr. 96
Glasscock, J.R. 147
Glasscock, M. 147
Glenn, Mrs. 185
Glenn, R.J. 167, 178, 179, 181, 184, 185, 186
Glenn, Robert 98
Glenn, Robert J. 43, 157, 178
Glover, B.F. 74
Gobbert, T.M. 147
Godman, S.A. 119
Goldschmidt, Jenny Lind 121
Goldsmith, Jenny Lind 155
Goldsmith, Madame 28
Goldthwaite, G. 4
Goldwaite, Geo. 133
Goldwhaithe, Goe. 167
Golsan, Charles 195
Golson, Jacob H. 56
Golson, John N. 62
Golson, W.G.M. 56
Gooden 192
Goodson, Elias B. 161
Goodson, J. 181
Goodson, James 179
Goodson, John W. 114
Goodwin, Dr. 182
Goodwyn, Harriet 167
Goodwyn, Mrs. H. 183
Gool, J. 186
Goolsby, T.B. 147
Gordon, J.M. 57, 106
Gordon, Mrs. J.M. 185
Gordy 191, 192
Gore, Mrs. C.A. 183
Goree, Milton 114
Gorgon, J.M. 62
Graham, J.G. 182
Graham, Mr. 177
Graham, N.S. 134, 147
Graham, R.H. 182
Graham, Robert H. 181
Graham, William 4, 166
Graham, Wm. 57, 178, 205
Grant, L.M. 163

Grant, W.A. 27
Granvgist, Mary C. 3
Graves, J.D. 167, 186
Graves, W. 147
Gray, Jesse 114
Gray, Mr. 39
Greagh 130
Greely, Mr. 154
Green, B.E. 147
Green, L.F. 147
Greene 191, 192
Greene, Mr. 149, 203
Greene, R.H. 147
Greer, Judge 67
Gregory, Jas. 147
Griffin, B.S. 167, 178, 185
Griffin, Col. 184
Griffin, W.M. 147
Griffis, Jacob 62
Griffis, John M. 62
Guby, 31
Gue, J. 167
Guthrie, 32
Guthrie, Jas. 27
Guthrie, Mr. 205
Guthrie, Secretary 169, 205
Guy, S.J. 163
Gwin, Dr. 111
Gwin, Senator 205

H

Hadnot 186
Hadnot, G. 179
Hadnot, G.W. 185
Hadnot, Guilford W. 68
Hadnot, Mrs. W.S. 167, 184
Hadnot, William S. 68
Hagan, J.A. 177
Hagood, Z. 147
Hails, G.W. 167
Hails, Geo. W. 179
Hale 19, 75
Hale, Mrs. 185
Hale, S.F. 93
Hale, Wm. T. 57, 195
Hall 130, 191, 192
Hall, Amanda 184
Hall, B.R. 167
Hall, Boling 62
Hall, Bolling 96, 105, 119, 123, 133, 142, 167, 179, 181, 182, 186
Hall, Dixon 95, 96, 150
Hall, Elizabeth 150
Hall, Francis C. 124
Hall, John 173
Hall, Jos H. 167
Hall, Jos. H. 166
Hall, Joseph H. 57
Hall, Louisa 167, 178
Hall, Louiza 182, 183, 185
Hall, Mary B. 167, 182, 183, 185, 186

Hall, Mr. 177, 187, 203
Hall, Mrs. D. 185
Hall, P.G. 106
Hall, T.D. 167, 182
Hall, W.B. 167, 185
Hall, W.T. 167
Hall, William 157
Hall, Wm. B. 182
Hallock, Fitz-Green 17
Hamilton, Gov. 45
Hamilton, Governor 46
Hamilton, Henry P. 158
Hamilton, J. 111, 119
Hamilton, John T. 106
Hampton, Green 15, 201
Hanby, D. 147
Hand, Capt. 67
Haney, Joel 3
Hanna, Noah 58
Hannah, M.H. 147
Hannegan, John 188
Hanserd 191, 192
Hansford, C.R. 23
Harbin, H.D. 147
Hardin, Ben 38
Hardy, John 57, 133, 134, 147, 150
Hargreaves, Mr. 177
Harriet Beecher Stowe 175
Harrington, W.B. 147
Harris 203
Harris, A.T. 203
Harris, Andrew S. 68, 132
Harris, Henry 150
Harris, J. 147
Harris, Louisa and Mary Ann 132
Harris, Maj. 65
Harris, Mary (H.?) 132
Harris, Miles G. 151
Harris, Mr. 55
Harris, S.W. 5, 65, 123
Harris, Samp W. 95
Harris, Sampson W. 57
Harrison 132, 203
Harrison, B.I. 147
Harrison, Gen. 101
Harrison, Robert R. 67
Hart, J.B. 114
Harwell, M. 135
Hatch, P.M. 113
Hatch, T.B.R. 113
Hatcher 130, 191, 192
Hatchet, W.T. 133
Hatchett, W.T. 147
Hatchett, Wm. T. 148
Hawkies, W. 147
Hawkins, M. 163
Haye 191
Hayes, J.S. 147
Hayne, Arthur 142
Hayne, Col. 142
Hays 192
Hays, Mrs. R. 163

212

Hearlth, J. 163
Heath, Caroline 48
Heidleman, Col. 33
Henderson, J.W. 207
Hendricks 191, 192
Hendricks, Mr. 193
Hendrix, David 147
Hendrix, J. 147
Hendrix, James 148
Hendrix, T.W. 147
Henry 24, 173, 191, 192, 194
Henry, Gustavus 79
Henry, J. 105
Henry, Martha M. 110
Henry, Mr. 188, 194
Heoely, P. 163
Herman, John G. 126
Herndon, Thomas 99
Hester, A.J. 110
Hester, William 96
Hewitt, G. 147
Hewitt, J.H. 147
Hewlett 191, 192
Hewlett, Mr. 193, 198
Hickey, John F. 155
Hicks, Frank 114
Higgins 203
Higgins, Mr. 203
Higley, H.L. 1
Hill 191, 192
Hill, Abner 93, 142, 157, 200, 201
Hill, H.R.W. 15
Hill, J. 147
Hill, Lewis B. 101
Hill, Thomas 157
Hilliard, H.W. 93
Hilliard, Henry W. 92
Hilliard, Mr. 93
Hilmes, Miss S.E. 163
Hines, Dr. 175
Ho(?), Wm. 17
Hobarts, John P. 110
Hobb, James 153
Hobbs, R. 134
Hobdy 191
Hobdy, Harrel 129
Hobly 192
Hodge, vice 36
Hoe 175
Hoffman, Luke 21
Hoffman, Ogden 163
Hogan, Wm. 98
Hogg, Thomas 85, 96
Holbrook, A.M. 15
Holcomb, C.P. 42
Holiday, 72
Holley, R.H.J. 191
Hollins, Mayor 137
Hollon, John W. 81
Holly 130
Holly, A. 191, 192
Holly, R.H.J. 192
Holmes, A.D. 92

Holmes, H.D. 57, 92, 182
Holmes, H.P. 106
Holmes, Henry 167
Holmes, Isaac E. 199
Holmes, O.W. 17
Holt, Laura 167, 185
Holt, M.A. 74
Holt, Mrs. D 185
Holt, Mrs. Daniel 183
Holton, William 3
Homes, H.D. 195
Hood, A.J. 147
Hooper, J.J. 5
Hopper, J.D. 92
Horn 191, 192
Horne 130
Horner, Dr. 88
Horton 69
Horton, Chapman 205
Horton, John F. 132, 203
Hoston, A. 163
House, J.P. 170
House, Jacob 174
House, Martha 174
Houser, 115
Houser, John A. 25, 107, 114, 117
Houser, Lewis 4
Houser, Louis 115
Houston, A.C. 92, 195
Houston, Geo. H. 5
Houston, Geo. S. 205
Houston, Martha J. 203
Houston, Sam 1
Houston, Samuel 13
Howard 1
Howard, C.C. 96
Howard, C.M. 106, 110, 134, 195
Howard, C.W. 124
Howard, Charles M. 92
Howard, Chas. M. 92
Howard, H.N. 18
Howard, J.H. 84
Howard, L. 92, 106, 109, 110, 167
Howard, Leonidas 120, 195
Howard, Leonidas B. 56, 57
Howard, Mark 115
Howard, Mrs. James 125
Howard, N.M. 57
Howell 11, 46, 95
Howell, Mrs. 184
Howell, Wm. C. 182
Hubbard 191, 192
Hubbard, Alfred 185
Hubbard, M. 147
Hubbard, Moses 147
Hubbard, Mr. 3, 98, 194
Hudson, J. 147
Hudson, W. 147
Huffstuller, H. 147
Huffstuller, L. 147
Huffstuller, W. 147

Hugo, Victor 97
Huie, J.H. 92
Humboldt 17
Humphrey, James 71
Humphreys 191
Humphries 130, 192
Hungford, Hon. 67
Hunt, J.J. 163
Hunt, Leigh 17
Hunter, Senator 48
Huntington, 5
Huntington, B.W. 146
Hurst, Warner 105
Hutchinson, A.R. 57
Hutchinson, Thomas W. 108
Hutchinson, Thos. W. 61, 103
Hutton, Aquilla D. 24

I

Inge 130, 191, 192
Ingraham, Duncan W. 154
Irby, W.S. 24
Irvine 191, 192
Irving, Washington 17
Irwin 130
Irwin, John 147
Ivey, N. 167

J

Jackson, A. 125
Jackson, Absalom 134
Jackson, Andrew 114
Jackson, C. 125
Jackson, C.M. 56, 57, 96, 182, 184
Jackson, Crawford M. 134
Jackson, Elizabeth 189
Jackson, Emily 167
Jackson, General 80, 150
Jackson, Jacob 56
Jackson, James 95, 96, 125, 158
Jackson, John 98
Jackson, Mrs. 125
Jackson, President 169
Jacob 8, 15
Jacobs, Meyer 48
Jacques, ntonio 105
James, G.P.R. 17
Jameson, Mrs. 96
Jamison, H.M. 37
Jarrete, Edward D. 89
Jarrette, Edward D. 89
Jarrott, E.P. 106
Jay 191, 192
Jeffrees, Nathaniel 68
Jemison 191, 192
Jemison, Mr. 198
Jemison, R., Jr. 93
Jemison, Robt., Jr. 130

Jenkins, J.D. 75
Jennifer, Mr. 45
Jernigan, Capt. 173
Jerrold, Douglas 17
John 179
John, Henry and Levi Sharp 83
Johns, Joseph R. 134
Johnson 72, 163, 173, 191, 192
Johnson, Adelia J. 48
Johnson, Andrew 79
Johnson, Cave 173
Johnson, Frank 45
Johnson, Gov. 23
Johnson, Governor 135
Johnson, J. 163
Johnson, J.A. 163
Johnson, James L. 114
Johnson, Joseph A. 21
Johnson, Joseph A. 98
Johnson, Mr. 194
Johnson, Robert S. 135
Johnson, W.C. 111
Jones, A. 147
Jones, Alpheus 101
Jones, Capt. 30
Jones, D.C. 57
Jones, E.P. 191, 192
Jones, H.C. 187, 191, 192, 198
Jones, Hugh 9, 59
Jones, J. 147
Jones, J.R. 109, 146
Jones, Jesse R. 56, 133, 134, 151
Jones, Jessee R. 92, 102
Jones, Lewis 114
Jones, Mr. 67
Jones, Nancy 3
Jones, R. 195
Jones, R.R. 27
Jones, Robert 3
Jones, Seaborn 84
Jones, Wm. 114, 195
Jordan 183, 186, 200
Jordan, F.W. 178
Jordan, Frederick W. 181
Josephine 11
Judge 130, 191, 192
Judge, Mr. 194
Judge, T.J. 148
Judge, Thos. J. 79, 147, 149
Julia 179

K

Kapp, F. 52
Katalaugh, G.(?) 41
Keener, Abram 178
Kelley, M. 147
Kelley, Moses 147
Kelly 191, 192
Kelly, Gen. 186

Kelly, Moses 130
Kelly, Mr. 177, 187
Kemp, William 9
Kemp, Wm. 59
Kendal 173
Kendal, Amos 173
Kendall, Mr. 113
Kennedy, J.S. 5
Kennedy, John 13
Kennedy, Miss 87
Key, Captain 36
Kilough, F. 163
Kimbal 130
Kimball 191, 193
Kimball, Mr. 192
King 69
King, A.B. 41
King, Alex 101
King, Captain 70
King, Dr. 154
King, Edmund 194
King, M.A. 88
King, Mr. 13, 19, 36, 48
King, Vice President 129
King, Vice-President 36
King, W.B. 147
King, W.R. 1, 19
King, William R. 55
King, Wm. R. 191
Kinnmore, John 72
Kinny, Wm. W. 163
Kip 12
Kirkbridge 102
Kirkland, Miss 184
Kirkland, Robert 28
Kittson, Mr. 24
Knap, Mr. 67
Knowles, Mr. 17
Knowles, Sheridan 17
Knox, C.N. 89
Knox, Eugenia E. 8, 15, 201
Knox, Harriet D. 85, 89
Knox, William L. 85
Knox, Wm.(?) 89
Kossta, Martin 130
Kossuth 14, 58, 84
Kossuth, M. 169
Krout, C. 4
Kyle, W.S. 93

L

Lamar 191, 192
Lamar, D. 72
Lamar, John 56, 109
Lamartine 17, 131
Lane, Gen. 124, 153
Lane, General 66
Lane, Gov. 105
Lane, H.C. 81
Lane, William Carr 171
Lane, Wm. Carr 2, 3, 79
Lang 166

Langford, J.M. 195
Lanier, C.G. 92, 195
Lanier, Mrs. 185
Lapsley, J.M. 147
Lapsley, J.W. 133, 147, 148, 149, 150
Larrainzar, Signor 157
LaRue, Judge 101
LaSere, E. 15, 16
Lassiter, John C. 143
Laughinghouse 192
Laughinhouse 130
Laughter, Henry C. 201
Laughter, Madora C. 201
Lavon 8
Law, Joseph 41
Lawler, J.A. 106, 107
Lawler, James A. 8, 15, 57, 62, 89, 106, 114, 132, 143, 176, 189, 190
Lawler, Jas. A. 151
Lawless, Captain 66
Lawless, James A. 89
Lawrence 191, 192
Lawrence, Abbot 17
Lawrence, Abbott 138, 165
Lawson, Andrew 195
Laycock, George 88, 140
Le Moine, Mr. 41
Le Vert, Octavio 116
Lea, Henry C. 62
Leach, S.J. 147
Leacock, D. 163
Lee 130, 191, 192
Lee, Col. 109
Leech 72
Leeds, C.J. 15
Legare, J.D. 134
Leidy, Joseph 87
Leigh, Grand Master 126
Leighardt 18
Leland, W.W. 199
Lenox, Walter 58
Leonard, John 52
Leonard, Mike 48
Lesesna, Joseph W. 4
Lewis 37, 200
Lewis, Dixon H. 56
Lewis, Susan 167, 183
Lewis, W.L. 147
Ligon, David G. 4
Limbrek, Wm. 195
Limbrick, Wm. 114
Lind, Jenny 28
Lindsay 194
Lindsay, Mr. 203
Lindsey 191, 192
Livingston, Henry J. 21
Livingston, John T. 21
Livingston, M. 69
Livingston, Rachel R. 21
Lloyd, Benjamin 57
L'Muller, Mr. 58
Lockwood, E. 80
Logan, R.L. 182

Long, Capt. 185
Long, E.A. 167, 182
Long, Evans A. 114
Long, J.O. 182
Long, James O. 178
Long, Jas. O. 166
Long, L. 125, 167, 185
Long, Nancy 167, 183, 184, 185
Longfellow, Henry W. 17
Longfellow, Stephen 17
Lord, Daniel 173
Louis Napoleon 32
Love, A.C. 92, 106
Love, A.T. 81, 113
Love, Arthur P. 56
Love, W.G. 106
Love, Wm. C. 92
Lowber, Capt. 29
Lowber, Captain 29
Loyd, Adaline 184
Lucas, Dr. 65
Luckett 11, 46, 95
Lucy 201
Lumpkin, Thuston 8
Luter, Elizabeth 3
Luter, Mathew 81
Luter, Matthew 3
Luter, Peter D. 3
Lyell, Charls 83
Lyman, H.R. 147
Lynch, Judge 42
Lynch, Mrs. 35, 102
Lynch, Wm. 191
Lyon, F.S. 134, 194, 198
Lyon, Frank S. 4
Lyon, Mr. 191, 198

M

Maberly, Mr. 153
Mabery, Mrs. S. 163
Mac Evoy, Prof. 31
Macauley 17
Macbeth, Joseph 154
Macon, S.E. 92
Macready 17
Macy, Miss 87
Madiai, Rosa 42
Magreder, E.L. 163
Maldinado 39
Mallet, Joseph 42
Malone 191, 192, 198
Malone, Mr. 187, 198
Manlove, J.D. 7
Manly, Patrick 173
Mann, Dudley 42
Mann, Horace 24
Manning, A.R. 93
Marcy, 116
Marcy, Gov. 87
Marcy, Mr. 51, 87
Marcy, Secretary 175, 192
Marcy, W.L. 7, 32

Marcy, Wm. L. 27
Marcy, Mr. 1
Marion, General 24
Maris, S.W. 167
Markie 48
Markoe, Mr. 66
Marks, T. 181
Marochetti, Baron 12
Marrset, Wm. D. 41
Marsh, M. 163
Marsh, Mr. 154
Marshall, Humphry 105
Marshall, Mr. 111
Marten, B.F. 163
Martin 130, 192
Martin, Abram 4, 99, 167
Martin, Henry Byam 32
Martin, John I. 48
Martin, Mr. 195
Martin, Wm. B. 130, 177
Marvel, Ik 17, 87, 102
Mary 201
Mason, Dr. 167
Mason, G.L.F. 57
Mason, George 3
Mason, George L.F. 57
Mason, J.P. 58
Mason, Mrs. Dr. 183
Mason, R.C. 147
Massey, M. 147
Massingale, John 200, 201
Massingale, Tabitha 200, 201
Matamoras 13
Mathany, O.W. 186
Mattison, W.W. 147, 148
Maxwell, Thomas 147
May, Catherin 3
May, Joe 143
May, Thomas P. 4
Mayo, Robert A. 36
Maywood, Miss 1
McBride 192
McBryde 130, 191
Mcbryde, John R. 57
McCaine, Mr. 41
McCall 130, 191, 192
McCanales, Col. 129
McCann, G. 38
McCerran, Capt. 197
McClanahan, J.M. 5
McClelen, Thomas M. 203
McClelland, R. 27
McClintock 102
McConaughoy, William 147
McCorkle, Mr. 111
McCrary 173
McCray, Mr. 39
McCulloch, Ben 35
McDonald, Charles J. 192
McDonnell, Patrick 114
McDuffer, Miss M. 163
McElroy, Thomas 150
McFarlane, Dr. 138

McGee, A.G. 93
McGehee, A.G. 93
McGehee, Abner 120
McGehee, Thomas 120
McIntyre, Mr. 186
McKeethen, Duncan 179
McKeethen, Mary 184
McKeetheren, Miss M. 163
McKeithen, A. 167
McKeithen, Alexander 14
McKeithen, D. 167
McKeithen, Duncan 114
McKeithen, Mary A. 207
McKeithre, A. 179
McKever, brother 172
McKibbon, John 3
McKiethen, Mrs. A. 183
McKnight, Col. 28
McLane, Robert M. 174
McLean, Judge 88, 138
McLemore 187, 191, 192
McLemore, Chas. 130
McLemore, Mr. 177
McLeod, Daniel 171
McMath, E. 147
McMillion, L.G. 147
McMillion, M.L. 147
McNeil, A.W. 57
McNeil, Ann L. 43
McNeil, Henry S. 56
McNeill, John 96
McQueen, Murdock 62
McRae 193
McRae, J.M. 147
McRae, John J. 97
McWhorter, Mrs. 183
McWhorter, S. 166
McWhorter, S.S. 106, 179
McWhorter, Sydney 57
McWhorton, A. A. 95
McWilliams, A.K. 109
McWilliams, J.W. 147
Meade, R.K. 125
Meager, Mr. 36
Meagher, Mr. 14
Meagher, Thos. F. 42
Medary, Sam'l 87
Meek 130, 191, 192
Meek, Mr. 191, 194
Meigs, Capt. 105
Mellville, Herman 17
Mercer, W.N. 15
Meredith, Justice 192
Meriwether, Charles 8, 15
Meriwether, David 79
Meriwether, Gov. 105
Merrett, John 114
Merrill, Major 124
Merritt, J. 182
Merritt, John 158
Merryman, John, Jr. 42
Metternich 17
Mickle, J.J. 4
Miles, B.F. 126, 141
Miles, H. 163

Miles, Wm. 98
Miller, 48
Miller, Captain 72
Miller, Dr. 101
Mills, A.E. 93
Mills, William 179
Mims, Elijah, Sr. 113
Mims, Mrs. S. 167, 183
Mims, Mrs. Shadrach 182
Mims, S. 3, 48, 142, 145, 163
Minor, Drury H. 72
Miss L P—e, 17
Mitchel, James 115
Mitchel, Margaret A. 207
Mitchell, Bolling 171
Mitchell, Donald G. 87, 102
Mitchell, Dr. 70
Mitchell, John 37, 169
Mitchell, John E. 96
Mitchell, Major 71
Mitchell, Margaret A. 200
Mitchell, Mr. 41
Mobly, G.B. 147
Moll, W. 124
Moncreif, Caleb 56, 134
Moncrief, C. 109
Moncrief, Caleb 92
Moncrief, Mrs. C. 183
Montez, Lola 12, 67, 125
Montgomery, G.W. 147
Montgomery, William 93, 94, 201
Montgomery, Wm. 134, 167, 200
Montgue, E.F. 186
Montigo, Eugenia 11
Montigo, Madame 8
Montijo, Countess 23
Moodie, J.D. 56
Moodie, John B. 146
Moon, Wm. L. 163
Moore, A.B. 148
Moore, Andrew 5
Moore, Andrew B. 147
Moore, J.T. 167
Moore, John 5
Moore, Judge 119, 123
Moore, Mr. 138
More 183, 186
More, Uncle 8
Morgan, E.S. 51, 167, 185
Morgan, F.E.L. 151
Morgan, J.C. 195
Morgan, J.P. 147
Morgan, Thos. P. 48
Morgan, W.A. 167, 181, 182
Morgan, William S. 96, 151
Morgan, Wm. S. 96
Morison, John A. 111
Morment, J.M. 147
Morrill, B.S. 199, 200
Morrill, Mr. 137

Morris 192
Morrison, A.J. 110
Morrison, J.C. 37
Morrison, M.F.G. 91
Morrissy 173
Morrow, Samuel 24
Morse, Professor 113
Morton, Richard 195
Mortu 179
Mosley, Mr. 8
Motley, R.-. 125
Motley, T.J. 57, 109, 110
Motley, William 57
Mowry 173
Mudd, W.S. 5, 147
Mudd, Wm. S. 134, 148, 149
Munro, Nathan 113
Murat, Madame Achille 137
Murdoch, Mr. 81
Murowslaski, General 174
Murph, 115
Murph, Jacob 56
Murph, Jacob A. 62, 189
Murphey 191, 192
Murphree, A. 147
Murray, Cyrus W. 19
Murray, John Ellis 165
Muse, D. 163
Musgroe, E.G. 148
Musgrove 191, 192
Musgrove, E.G. 147
Musgrove, F.A. 147
Musgrove, P.M. 147
Myers 181
Myers, C. 167
Myers, Claiborne 83
Myers, Clairborne 107
Myers, David Jr. 181
Myers, David R. 205
Myers, George 194
Myers, Mrs. C. 185
Myers, Mrs. Claborne 184
Myers, R. 167
Myers, R.C. 107
Myres, Mrs. C. 183
Myrick, Mrs. George 183

N

Nabers, D.B. 193
Napier 175
Napoleon 8, 11, 13
Napoleon III 36
Napoleon, Louis 32, 74
Napoleon the First 11
Nason, Mrs. J.W. 182
Neal, D.C. 114, 166, 178, 183
Neal, Mrs. Judge 182, 183, 184, 186
Neely, Dr. 119, 154, 155
Neely, P.P. 111, 154

Nels, Joseph 41
Nelms 191, 192
Nelson 130, 173, 179
Nelson, Mr. 65, 74
Nelson, Mrs. S.W. 183
Nelson, Thomas 57
Nenes, J. 147
Newell 191, 192
Newman 191, 192
Newton, David 125
Nichols, Major 105
Nichols, Mrs. 207
Nicholson, W.L. 177
Nickels, John 167
Nickles, John 183
Nicolls, Mr. 98
Nix 137
Nixon, Henry 3
Nixon, William 3
Nobles, Jno. W. 178
Noland, James 81
Noles 18
Norment, J.M. 147, 150
Norris, 84
Norris, M.E. 114
Norris, P. 182
Norris, Patrick 167
Norris, Rebecca 183
Northington, W.H. 21, 106
Northington, William H. 15, 57, 135, 201
Northington, Wm. H. 9, 15, 56, 106, 109, 110, 127, 134, 200, 201, 206
Norton, Betsy 41
Norton, Mr. 205
Nugent, Catharine 12
Nunn, T. 109
Nunn, Theodore 57
Nunn, Wm. 57

O

Oakes, J.H. 147
O'Bannon, J.D. 109, 127
O'Connell, Maurice 116
O'Connor, Mr. 169
Ogden, J.C. 3
Odom 192
O'Donahue, Wm. 123
Odum 130
Oliver, Eg 166
O'Neal, Judge 30
O'Neil, Jas. L. 174
O'Neil, P. 37
Oozby, J.T. 147
O'Reailly, Mr. 113
O'Reilly, Henry 36
Orleans, Duchess of 11
Ormsby, T.D. 33
Ornsby, Mary E. 184
Ornsby, T.D. 182
Ornsby, Wm. O. 61
Orr, James 3

215

Otey, J.W. 41
Otey, John W. 37
Owen 130, 191, 192, 194
Owen, B.C. 167, 182
Owen, L. 186
Owen, Lewis 27, 167
Owen, Robert 88
Owens, Alfred 87
Owens, B.C. 27

P

Pacha, Omar 173
Padelford, Edward 188
Paig, Captain 67
Paine 130
Palmer, P. 147
Palmer, V.B. 23
Paris, J. 106
Parish, James M. 113
Parker, Alfred 143, 189
Parker, L. 166
Parker, L.B. 57
Parker, R. 147
Parmer, Chas. H. 88
Parsons, L.F. 93
Patsey 200
Patten, Rev. Dr. 2
Patterson, Lucinda L.M. 58
Patton 187, 191, 192, 198
Patton, Gen. 134
Patton, Mr. 198
Pattou, Robert 84
Paulding, J.K. 17
Payne 191, 192
Payne, Levin 123
Peabody, Charles A. 22
Peabody, Chas. A. 22
Pearce, Mrs. S. 184
Pearce, Senator 83
Peeples, Wm. N. 85
Pegues, C.C. 147
Penick, Dr. 167
Perham, J.P. 147, 148
Perine, I. 92
Perry, John D. 40
Perry, Mr. 45
Perry, Mrs. 14
Perry, Parker 58
Peterson 129, 191, 192, 193
Peterson, Mr. 193
Petigru, Mr. 173
Petus 69
Pfister, Amand P. 4
Phelan, J.D. 4, 149
Phelan, Jno. D. 150
Phelan, John D. 147, 150
Phelan, Joseph H. 177
Philips, Hart 58
Philips, P. 80
Philips, W.S. 133
Philips, Wendell 7
Phillippe, Louis 11
Phillips 191, 192

Phillips, Amanda C. 21
Phillips, Col. 149
Phillips, W.S. 147
Phillis 130
Philpot, Gen. 148
Philpot, H.V. 147
Pickens, Andrew 18
Pickens, Ezkiel 5
Pickens, Joseph 18
Picket, Thos. L. 48
Pickett 191, 192
Pickett, A.J. 62, 166, 170
Pickett, Albert J. 7, 56
Pickett, Col. 115
Pickett, Mr. 39, 191, 195
Pickett, Sarah 167
Pickett, Wm. R. 95, 96
Pickitt, William R. 4
Pierce 1
Pierce, Gen. 1, 19, 27, 51
Pierce, General 13, 36, 58, 76
Pierce, Mr. 28, 142
Pierce, President 41, 76, 124, 165, 197
Pierce, R.S. 147
Pierpont 84
Pike, Easter 48
Pike, Geo. A. 113
Pike, George A. 113
Pike, Mary 12
Pillsbury, Parker 7
Pinckney, Wm. 55
Pitts, E.O. 3
Polk, Mr. 105
Polk, President 106
Pollard, Alcey F. 30
Pollard, Aley 142
Pollard, C.D. Jr 182
Pollard, C.J. 178
Pollard, C.S. 183
Pollard, Charles T. 135
Pollard, Chas. T. 133, 134, 167
Pollard, David 83
Pollard, M.B. 143
Pollard, W.P. 185
Pollard, Washington 179, 182
Pool, John 57
Pool, John H. 114
Pope, F. 167, 181
Pope, Francis 184
Pope, Frank 207
Pope, Isadore C. 207
Pope, L.B. 135
Pope, Matilda 20, 167
Pope, Mr. 186
Pope, Mrs. M. 185
Pope, Z. 142
Popwell, Jas. 114
Popwell, R. 179
Porter, Lot 158
Porter, M.T. 147
Portis 130, 191, 192

Potter, J.S. 20
Potter, Samuel R. 46
Potthoff, Charles 119
Powel, Mrs. A. 46
Powell 187, 191, 192, 193
Powell, Dr. 65
Powell, J.R. 130
Powell, James 167
Power, John 98
Powers, 17
Powers, H. 39
Powers, Hiram 38
Pratt, Daniel 35, 93, 133, 134, 135, 167, 178, 184
Pratt, M.E. 182
Pratt, Merril 101
Pratt, Mr. 141, 146
Pratt, Mrs. Daniel 167, 182, 183
Pratt, Senator 32
Prentice 17
Prescott 17
Presley, E. 181
Presley, Evans 167
Presley, Wm. 143
Presly, Evan 185
Pressly, Evans 57
Preston, Mr. 129
Prestridge, J.E. 147
Prewitt, Thomas L. 113
Price, J.L. 134
Price, Reese F. 35
Pringle, Mary F. 102
Pringle, William B. 102
Prouty, 2
Pulliam, J.H. 3
Pulszky, Mr. 58
Pursells, Messrs. 36
Purviance, James 161
Putman, Mr. 28

Q

Quarri 73
Queen 173
Quillen, Jasper J. 157
Quincy, John 111

R

Radstock, Lord 80
Rainer, T.G. 5
Ramsay, Dr. 74
Ramsey, B.B. 147
Ramsey, James 30
Randolph, John 153
Rankin, Mr. 31
Rast, Amos 189
Rast, Emma J. 189
Rast, Martha G. 189
Ray, Gabriel 59
Read, Miss 138
Ready, Aaron 3, 4, 99
Ready, Olivia M. 4

Rearis, T. 134
Reavis, Turner 146
Reddick, Mary F. 189
Reece, Joseph S. 181
Reed, W. 147
Reener, Elizabeth 183
Reese, Dr. 185
Reese, Emma 167
Reese, J.S. 48, 179, 181
Reese, Joseph S. 3, 57, 167, 179
Reese, Mrs. E. 183
Reese, Nat. 167
Reese, Sarah 184
Reid, Dr. 112
Reid, J.C. 56, 93
Reid, John C. 51, 56, 92, 109
Reives, Geo. 166
Rencher, Edward H. 3
Rexana 201
Reynolds 191, 192
Reynolds, Mr. 187
Reynolds, William 48
Rhodes 191, 192
Rice, Littleton 142
Rice, Luther S. 24
Rice, Miss S. 184
Rice, Thornton 24
Richards, John 84
Richards, Newton 15
Richardson, J.O. 80
Richardson, Marietta P. 167
Richbourg, W.F. 88
Rickard, John 33
Ricks, Jesse A. 114
Rieves, Martha F. 183
Rieves, Martha Francis 183
Riggs, Elisha 83
Riggs, Joel 4, 205
Riley 200
Riley, Gen. 106
Ringgold, Commander 97
Rivers, William C. 80
Rives, E.A. 167
Rives, Eliza 183
Rives, G. 178
Rives, Miss A.E. 184
Rives, Mr. 58
Rives, Mrs. E.A. 167
Rives, Mrs. W.H. 167
Rives, Wm. H. 167
Robb, James 15
Robb, Wilds 28
Roberts, Capt. 8
Robertson 130
Robertson, Lafayette 58
Robertson, Mr. 177
Robinson 191, 192
Robinson, 70
Robinson, Eli 3
Robinson, Jas B. 96
Robinson, John S. 52, 59
Robinson, L.G. 167, 182
Robinson, Ramond 167

Robinson, Raymond 52, 53, 59, 62, 63
Robinson, Tod 135
Robles, Gen. 197
Rocket, W.J. 147
Rockwell, O. 29
Rodgers, H. 83
Rodifer, Mr. 111
Rodney, J.M. 23
Rodney, Mr. 36
Rogers, Beng. A. 74
Rogers, Cader 62, 158
Rogers, E.S. 27
Rogers, George 114
Rogers, J.B. 182
Rogers, Joseph B. 114, 181
Rogers, Judge 173
Rogers, Mills 114, 167
Rogers, Professor 197
Rolette, 24
Rollison, Edna 146
Rose, Howell 95, 167
Rose, Mrs. 88
Ross, Howell 36
Ross, R. 195
Ross, Wiley 114
Roy, Joseph 3
Rudder, Wm. G. 135
Ruffin, F.G. 205
Runadel, James 48
Rusk, Gen. 117
Russell, John 20
Russell, Robert 56
Rust, Col. 123
Rutherford 130
Ryan, Mr. 98

S

Sadler, Mr. 174
Salton, Nancy 183
Sam 140
Sample, A. 172
Sample, Alex 62, 114
Sample, Margarette 172
Samples, A. 85, 143
Samples, Wm. 85
Sandford, A.M. 93
Sandford, Joseph 57
Sandiford, Jos. 167
Sands, Capt. 29
Sands, Mr. 20
Sanford 191, 192, 194
Sanford, Joseph 57
Sanford, Mr. 58
Sanford, T. 154
Sapp, B.H. 147
Savage, Jas. 147
Saxon, B.W. 106
Saxon, Benj. 166
Saxon, L.P. 134, 167
Saxon, Laura 184
Saxon, Lida P. 183
Sayre, Daniel 92, 93

Sayre, Mr. 93
Scarbro, J.A. 195
Scarcy 191
Sceitz, John 56
Schartz, Commander 131
Schaumburg 18
Schmidt, C. 36
Schouler, Col. 125
Scoggins, W.B. 184
Scott 191, 192
Scott, C. 163
Scott, Capt. 76
Scott, Maj. Gen. 32
Scott, Mr. 191, 194
Scott, Robert L. 58
Scott, Winfield 76
Scott, Wm. H. 157
Scoville, Mr. 177
Scruggs, H.F. 147, 148
Searcy 130, 192
Searcy, Mr. 193
Seaton 153
Seibells, J.J. 87
Seibels, Col. 73
Seward 17
Seward, Mr. 178
Sewot, J. 163
Seymour, Gov. 62
Seymour, Governor 173
Shackelford, E. 56, 109, 110
Shackelford, Edmond 92
Shackelford, Edmund 56
Shackelford, Gen. 56
Shackelford, Jack 95
Shackleford 69
Shackleford, E. 134
Sharkey, Judge 13
Sharp, Absolom 83
Sharp, George T. 18
Sharpe, George T. 41
Shasler, C.P. 48
Shaw, Benj. F. 18
Shaw, Mrs. 35, 102
Shaw, Robert G. 79
Shelley 130, 188, 191, 192
Shelton, C. 167
Shelton, Dr. 167
Shelton, P.S. 197
Shelton, S.R. 147
Shepard, Isaac F. 138
Sherer, E. 195
Sheridan, Richard Brinsley 17
Shields, Harriet 3
Shields, Mr. 32
Shorter, J. Gill 5
Shorter, Ruben C., Jr. 79
Shortridge, Geo. D. 5
Shufeldt, Capt. 32
Sibert, Lorenzo 80
Sierri, Joseph 48
Simmons, S.S. 96
Simmons, Sam'l S. 95
Simmons, Saml. S. 96

Simms, Martin M. 3
Simonds, John 38
Simpson 72
Skelton 191, 192
Skelton, Mr. 191
Skinner 124
Skugs, Richard 48
Slaton, Caroline E. 139
Slaton, Martha J. 139
Slaton, Nancy 139, 167
Slidell, Thomas 51
Sloo, Albert G. 112
Sloo, Mr. 19
Smedley, D.B. 88, 106, 133, 167
Smedley, John G. 3
Smith, A.Y. 106, 167, 185
Smith, Amos 61
Smith, D.N. 161
Smith, Daniel N. 56
Smith, Eugene A. 185, 186
Smith, George M. 48
Smith, Gerrit 76
Smith, Governor 70
Smith, H. 167
Smith, H.N. 105
Smith, H.S. 31, 48
Smith, J. McNiel 181, 185
Smith, J.M. 103, 183
Smith, Jas. M. 167
Smith, Jeremiah 49
Smith, John 14, 114
Smith, Joseph A. 207
Smith, Junius W. 83
Smith, Lopez. 157
Smith, M. 181
Smith, M.P. 106
Smith, Malcolm 89, 140, 158, 181
Smith, Malcom 56, 57, 88, 106, 107, 167, 186
Smith, Mrs. 48
Smith, Mrs. S.H. 184
Smith, Mrs. Amos 183
Smith, Mrs. M. 183
Smith, Mrs. Malcom 167
Smith, Mrs. S.P. 184
Smith, O.M. 147
Smith, Peyton B. 62
Smith, Pinckney 157
Smith, Porter 157
Smith, R.H. 93
Smith, S.P. 56, 157, 167, 181, 182, 184, 186
Smith, Samuel P. 55, 56
Smith, Sidney A. 93
Smith, T.C.H. 80
Smith, Thomas 158, 188
Smith, Thomas, Sr. 178
Smith, Thos., Sr. 56
Smith, W.D. 106
Smith, William 129
Smith, Wm. R. 5
Smoot, R. 147, 179
Smooth, Richard 178

Sneads, Henry 3
Snodgragss, Mrs. A. 184
Snow, Thomas H. 192
Snowden, Mr. 97
Soule, Mr. 87
Soule, P. 58
Soule, Senator 42
Spencer, F. 163
Spencer, J.C. 147
Spicer, James 80
Spigener, L. 51, 57, 113, 167
Spigener, Malachi 21
Spigner, L. 185
Spigner, M. 98
Spigner, R. 185
Spigners, Geo. 167
Spratlin, G.A.F. 68
Spratlin, M.C. 68
Spring, Arthur 35, 67, 102
Spring, Dr. 11
Srewder, R.F. 3
St. John 191, 192
Stallworth, J.A. 5
Stallworth, James A. 197
Stanton, Mr. 205
Steel, Mrs. J.W. 183
Steele, John 57, 62, 96, 167, 195
Steele, Mrs. John 167
Steele, O.D. 195
Steele, W.H. 1
Steiner, Assistant Surgeon 169
Stephens, A. 147
Stephens, James K. 188
Sterrett 191
Sterrett, Mr. 97
Sterritt 192
Sterritt, Mr. 194
Stevens, Governor 75
Stevens, Jack 48
Stewart, A.F. 186
Stewart, Aaron G. 189
Stewart, George A. 189
Stewart, Mary 189
Stewart, Thomas M. 98
Stidger, Judge 123
Stirling, Messrs. 41
Stockton, Commodore 7
Stoghin 32
Stoke, W.H. 147
Stone, Lucy 35, 88
Stoors, Seth P. 167
Storrs, J.S. 147, 150
Storrs, John S. 134, 148
Storrs, S.P. 134
Stors, Seth P. 95
Stoudemier, 115
Stoudemier, Edward 4
Stoudemier, H.J. 57
Stoudemier, Saml. 109
Stoudenmier, Lewis 21
Stoutamire, G. 163
Stovall, J.B. 135

Stowe, Harriett Beecher 161
Stowe, Mrs. 13, 75
Street, John 102
Street, T.W. 147
Strible, Agnes 124
Strible, Henry E. 124
Strible, Joseph M. 124
Stringfellow, H.M. 3
Stringham, Captain 130
Strobel, Professor 175
Strong, Mrs. 96
Strong, S.M. 79
Stuart, A.T. 205
Sturgeon, Ex-Senator 51
Sullens, Dr. 126
Sullivan 173
Sullivan, Dunklin 95
Sulton of Turkey 12
Summer, A.S. 74
Sumner 75
Sumner, Danl. 205
Sumner, John 147
Suram, James 113
Suttle, J.W. 5
Sutton, Bob 47
Swan, S. 167
Sweet, 111

T

Talbert 130, 191, 192
Talbert, Mr. 194
Talford 17
Tallmadge, N.P. 79
Tallman, Captain 177
Talmadge, Gov. 45, 46
Tancy, Chief Justice 75
Tarleton, Benj. F 93
Tarleton, Benj. F. 89
Tarleton, J.M. 87
Tarleton, Thomas J. 89, 93
Tarrant, S.A. 147
Tarrent, James 147
Tate, T.S. 93
Tatum 158
Tatum, Berry 77
Tatum, O. 106
Tatum, Or 166
Tatum, Organ 158
Taylor 27, 31, 116
Taylor, A.C. 59, 92, 106, 195
Taylor, Benjamin 120
Taylor, Col. 101
Taylor, E.A. 59
Taylor, General 75
Taylor, J.W. 147, 149
Taylor, John F. 59
Taylor, Jos. W. 148
Taylor, Miles 51
Taylor, Sallie 167, 183
Taylor, W.B. 101, 147
Taylor, William 66

Taylor, Wm. H. 3, 27
Taylor, Wm. L. 114
Teale 73
Teale, Colonel 73
Tefft, William 24
Temple, J.P. 121
Temple, Mr. 17
Tennyson, 17
Terrell 135
Terry, Eli 95, 96
Terry, John K. 49
Terzucanowski, Leonard P. 174
Thacker, Jemima 48
Thackery, Mr. 75
Thackery, W.M. 101
Thomas, F.W. 175
Thomas, John 48
Thomas, Judge 88
Thomas, Orville 121
Thomas, William 48
Thompson, Burket 206
Thompson, Clinton 206
Thompson, General 45
Thompson, J. 147
Thompson, Wm. N. 111, 123, 134
Thompson, Wm. N., Jr. 56
Thorington, Jack 93
Thornton 191, 192
Thornton, A.E. 28
Ticknor 69
Ticknor, Captain 70, 71
Ticknor, Harriett L. 151
Ticknor, Simon B. 151
Tidmore, H.M. 147
Tidwell, R. 147
Tienor, 17
Tilley, Wash. 27
Tinnin, William 129
Tinsley, Dr. 28
Todd 130, 191, 192
Tom 179
Toombs, Col. 74
Toombs, R. 84
Toombs, Robert 74
Toulmin, T.L 41
Toulmin, T.L. 154
Toumey, Prof. 65
Towns, Edw. 5
Townsend, James 176, 189
Townsend, Mary 184
Toxander, Robert B. 91
Trammell, Henry 98
Trask, Charles H. 3
Trimble, B. 133
Trousdale, Wm. 87
Troutman, Henry 76
Tucker, John R. 58
Tuckerman, H.T. 17
Turner, Reuben P. 98
Turner, Simon N. 58
Tuttle, C.W. 41
Twist, 98
Tyus 116

Tyus, L. 166
Tyus, Lewis 92, 93, 120
Tyus, Mr. 181

U

Ulrick, J.G. 163
Underwood, Benjamin 68
Underwood, James and Thomas 68
Underwood, John W. 165
Underwood, Thos. 195
Uraga 19
Urquiza 7
Urrea, Gen 70, 71
Urrea, General 71

V

Van Buren, Ex-President 195
Van Buren, ex-President 28
Van Buren, J. 22
Van Buren, Martin 80
Van Buren, Martin, Jr. 29
Van Buren, President 169
Van Hoose, Alfred E. 197
Varnell, Wm. N. 84
Varnum, Joseph B. 192
Vest 191, 192
Vest, Mr. 187
Vick, Colonel 65
Vick, H.W. 74
Vick, Miss P. 163
Vick, Penina 48
Victoria 17
Vidall, J.A. 98
Vilcent, Sarah 133
Vincent, J.H. 182
Vincent, Jos. 167
Vincent, Joseph H. 184
Vincient, J.H. 182
Violet 201
Vorrhies, C. 51
Vroom, Peter D. 87

W

Wagoner, W.J. 75
Wainwright 185
Waldrop, A.J. 147
Walker 130, 137, 191, 192
Walker, A. 15
Walker, A.P. 147, 150
Walker, Captain 154
Walker, Jas. 114
Walker, Judge 65
Walker, L. 48
Walker, L.P. 84, 191, 194
Walker, Mr. 46, 93, 177, 192, 199
Walker, Percy 191, 194
Walker, Peter J. 13

Walker, R.W. 191
Walker, Richard W. 92, 101
Walker, Robert J. 105, 199
Walker, T.A. 65
Walker, Thomas J. 5
Walker, W.A. 147
Walker, William 89, 178
Walker, Wm. 103, 167, 183, 185
Wallace, G. 195
Wallace, James B. 121
Wallace, Judge (D. or B.?) 129
Waller 135
Walsh, Thomas 58
Ward 130, 191, 192
Ward, Captain 69, 70
Ward, Colonel 69, 71, 73
Ward, Lieutenant Colonel 70
Ward, M. 147
Ward, Major 70
Ward, Obediah W. 13
Ward, Richard A. 137
Ward, Thomas 69
Ward, Thos. 73
Ward, William 69
Wardlaw, James 178
Wardsworth 69
Wardsworth, Captain 69
Ware, Col. 30
Ware, T.E. 30
Warren, Madam 31
Washington, George 61
Washington, Peter G. 35
Watkins 191, 192
Watrous, D.E. 147
Watrous, Daniel E. 149
Watts 187, 191, 192, 193
Watts, Mr. 191, 192
Watts, T.H. 116, 129
Watts, Thos. 119
Watts, Thos. H. 79, 123, 133, 134
Waugh, Mrs. Livinis 126
Weaver 191, 192
Weaver, John T. 203
Webb 130, 191, 192, 198
Webb, E. 45
Webb, J.D. 130
Webb, James 165
Webb, Mr. 198
Webster, Colonel 197
Webster, Daniel 83, 179
Webster, Fletcher 58
Webster, Mr. 157
Weedon, J. 147
Wellington 13
Wellington, Duke of 75
Wells, Kenon 114, 179
Westover 69
Whatley 130
Wheeler, Mary Ann 106
Whetstone, 115
Whetstone, A.H. 92

Whetstone, Ann L. 43
Whetstone, Arenia 189
Whetstone, Elizabeth 88
Whetstone, J.A. 74
Whetstone, J.D. 92, 185
Whetstone, Jacob 142
Whetstone, John A. 48, 126, 132
Whetstone, L.M. 109, 126
Whetstone, Lewis M. 57
Whetstone, P.H. 195
Whetstone, Wm. A. 43
Whetstone, Wm. W. 189
Whitaker 137
White, A. 147
White, Alexander 5
White, Maunsel 15
Whiting, Lieut. 197
Whitsett 130, 191
Whitsitt 192
Whitsitt, Mr. 194
Whitworth, Thomas D. 21
Wicker, Wm. 24
Wiggins, Martha 3
Wigglesworth, James W. 178
Wiglesworth, Wm. 166
Wikoff, Chevalier 42
Wilcox, Joseph 20
Wiley, J. McCaleb 92, 93
Wiley, Mr. 93
Wiley, Wm. 3, 114, 195
Wilkins 130, 191, 192
Wilkins, Margaret L. 48
Wilkinson 1
Wilkinson, J.B. 59, 106, 107
Wilkinson, Joseph B. 56, 57
Wilkinson, W. 72
Willcox, Geo P. 48
Williams, Aaron 48
Williams, David E. 3
Williams, Eleazer 28
Williams, George 42
Williams, John D. 87
Williams, Joseph M. 203, 207
Williams, Margaret A. 200
Williams, Mr. 76
Williams, W.P. 62
Willis, William 48
Wills 130, 191, 192
Willson, J.M. 48
Wilson 140, 151
Wilson, B.F. 79
Wilson, Col. 157
Wilson, D.F. 36
Wilson, Dr. 167
Wilson, Henry 153
Wilson, J.W. 195
Wilson, John 137
Wilson, Thos. A. 47
Wilson, W.D. 147
Wilson, W.L. 147

Winans, Harrison 7
Wingo 188
Winn 69
Winston 123, 137
Winston, Col. 79, 123
Winston, J.A. 65
Winston, John A. 65, 79, 105
Winston, Mr. 191
Winston, W.O. 5
Winter, J.G. 166
Winter, Mr. 91
Wise, Henry A. 135
Wisey, J.M. 93
Withers, Eliza H. 184
Withers, John W. 96
Withers, R.W. 74
Witlenan, John 179
Witter, Fanny 133
Witter, Maria 133
Wolfe, James C. 3
Woll, Adrian 8
Wood, Bennett 3
Wood, E. 147
Wood, J. 195
Wood, John 57, 96, 182
Wood, Martin 147
Wood, Wm. 48
Woodward 130, 187, 191, 192
Woodward, John J. 197
Woolsey, R.A. 194
Wortley, Emeline 116
Wren, Dr. 1
Wright, Edmund 51
Wyatt 69
Wyatt, Daniel H. 132
Wyatt, William C. 132
Wynne, James C. 70

Y

Yancey, Mr. 55
Yancey, W.L. 107
Yancey, William L. 95
Yancey, Wm. L. 167
Yeldell 130, 191, 192
Yelverton 191, 192, 194
Yelverton, Mr. 188
Young, Col. 65, 74
Young, Mrs. T. 185

Z

Zeigler, Catharine E. 206
Zeigler, E.J. 62
Zeigler, J. 167, 186
Zeigler, Joel 43, 178, 201
Zeigler, W. 167
Zeigler, William 43, 201
Zeigler, Wm. 185
Zentel, Martha 3
Ziegler, Paten 98

www.ingramcontent.com/pod-product-compliance
Lightning Source LLC
Chambersburg PA
CBHW071714160426
43195CB00012B/1676